JavaScript-mancy: Object-Oriented Programming

Mastering the Arcane Art of Summoning Objects in JavaScript for C# Developers

Jaime González García

This book is for sale at http://leanpub.com/javascript-mancy-object-oriented-programming

This version was published on 2017-09-22

ISBN 978-1976459238

This is a Leanpub book. Leanpub empowers authors and publishers with the Lean Publishing process. Lean Publishing is the act of publishing an in-progress ebook using lightweight tools and many iterations to get reader feedback, pivot until you have the right book and build traction once you do.

© 2016 - 2017 Jaime González García

Also By Jaime González García

JavaScript-mancy

JavaScript-mancy: Getting Started

To my beautiful wife Malin and my beloved son Teo

Contents

About The Author i
About the Technical Reviewers iii
Prelude iv
    A Note to the Illustrious Readers of JavaScript-mancy:
        Getting Started v
    A Story About Why I Wrote This Book vi
    Why Should You Care About JavaScript? vii
    What is the Goal of This Book? ix
    What is the Goal of The JavaScript-mancy Series? . . . ix
    Why JavaScript-mancy? x
    Is This Book For You? xi
    How is The Book Organized? xii
    How Are The JavaScript-mancy Series Organized? What
        is There in the Rest of the Books? xii
    Understanding the Code Samples in This Book xiv
    A Note About ECMAScript 5 (ES5) and ES6, ES7, ES8
        and ESnext within The Book xviii
    A Note Regarding the Use of `var`, `let` and `const` xix
    A Note About the Use of Generalizations in This Book . xx
    Do You Have Any Feedback? Found Any Error? xxi
    A Final Word From the Author xxi

Once Upon a Time.... xxii

CONTENTS

Tome II. JavaScriptmancy and OOP: The Path of The Summoner 1

Introduction to the Path of Summoning and Commanding
   Objects (aka OOP) 2
   Let me Tell You About OOP in JavaScript 5
   C# Classes in JavaScript 6
   OOP Beyond Classes 13
   Combining Classes with Object Composition 20
   The Path of the Object Summoner Step by Step 21
   Concluding 23

Summoning Fundamentals: Encapsulation and Information Hiding 25
   Let's get Started With The Basics of OOP! 27
   Encapsulation: Creating Objects in JavaScript 27
   Object Initializers 28
   Constructor Functions and the New Operator 31
   Data Hiding in JavaScript 39
   Object Initializers vs Constructor Functions 43
   Object Factories vs Constructor Functions 44
   Concluding 45
   Exercises 46

Summoning Fundamentals: Prototypical Inheritance . . . 54
   You Don't Repeat Yourself. Inheritance! 55
   Classical Inheritance vs Prototypical Inheritance 57
   JavaScript Prototypical Inheritance 59
   Object Prototypes 59
   Object Prototypes with Object.Create or OLOO 65
   Defining Prototypes with Constructor Functions 67
   Creating Longer Prototype Chains 69
   What About Concatenative Protypical Inheritance? . . . 71
   Object Initializers vs Object.create vs Constructor Functions 72

CONTENTS

    Concluding 72
    Exercises 74

Summoning Fundamentals: Polymorphism 85
    Polymorphism Means Many Forms 87
    Polymorphism in C# 87
    Polymorphism in JavaScript 92
    Concluding 95
    Exercises 97

White Tower Summoning: Mimicking C# Classical Inheritance in JavaScript 100
    Ever Heard of Classical Inheritance? 102
    Emulating a C# Class in JavaScript 103
    Constructor Function + Prototype = Class 108
    Mimicking Classical Inheritance in JavaScript 121
    Simplifying Classical Inheritance in ES5 128
    Concluding 130
    Exercises 132

White Tower Summoning Enhanced: The Marvels of ES6 Classes 139
    Create These Units Faster with ES6 Classes! 141
    From ES5 "Classes" to ES6 Classes 141
    Prototypical Inheritance via Extends 144
    Overriding Methods in ES6 Classes 146
    Static Members and Methods 148
    ES6 Classes and Information Hiding 151
    ES6 Classes Behind the Curtain 154
    Concluding 155
    Exercises 157

Black Tower Summoning: Objects Interweaving Objects with Mixins 162
    The Problem With Classes and Classical Inheritance... . 165

CONTENTS

Free Yourself From Classes With Object Composition
   and Mixins 168
   Limitations of Mixins as Objects 175
   Functional Mixins 177
   Combining Mixins with ES6 Classes 183
   Object.assign in Depth 185
   Object.assign Alternatives for ES5 JavaScript-mancers . 188
   Concluding 190
   Exercises 192

Black Tower Summoning: Safer Object Composition with
   Traits 202
   An Improvement Over Mixins 204
   Traits 204
   Traits with traits.js 207
   Composing Traits 209
   What Happens When You Miss Required Properties? . . 211
   Resolving Name Conflicts 212
   Traits and Data Privacy 218
   High Integrity Objects With Immutable Traits 221
   Traits vs Mixins 228
   Concluding 230
   Exercises 231

Black Tower Summoning: Next Level Object Composition
   With Stamps 241
   I Call Them Stamps 243
   What are Stamps? 244
   Stamps OOP Embraces JavaScript 249
   Stamps By Example 249
   Stamp Composition 259
   Stamp Fluent API 269
   Concluding: Stamps vs Mixins vs Traits 272
   Exercises 274

CONTENTS

Object Internals: The Secrets of Objects **288**
    A Nifty Trick... Object Internals 290
    All your Objects Are Belong to `Object` 291
    Defining Properties with Object.defineProperty 292
    Defining Multiple Properties with Object.defineProperties 297
    Beautiful Property Manipulation with ESnext Decorators 299
    Class And Method Decorators 308
    Create Objects With Object.create And Property Descriptors 315
    Metaprogramming 318
    Other Useful Object Methods 319
    Concluding 320
    Exercises 321

More Metaprogramming with Reflect, Proxies and Symbols 327
    How Good Are You at Reflection? 329
    ES6 Reflect 329
    Reflection? What is reflection? 329
    ES6 Proxies 339
    ES6 Symbols and Meta-programming 355
    Concluding 362
    Exercises 365

TypeScript **369**
    You Shall Only Use Types! 371
    JavaScript + Types = Awesome Dev Productivity 371
    Any JavaScript is Valid TypeScript 372
    So, What Are The Advantages and Disadvantages of TypeScript? 376
    Setting up a Simple TypeScript project 379
    Cool TypeScript Features 382
    Type Annotations In TypeScript 399
    Working with TypeScript in Real World Applications . . 420
    Concluding 424
    Exercises 427

CONTENTS

Tome II. Epilogue 439
Thank you! 441

References and Appendix 443

Appendix A. On the Art of Summoning Servants and Critters, Or Understanding The Basics of JavaScript Objects 444
    An Army of Objects 445
    Object Initializers (a.k.a. Object Literals) 446
    Creating Objects With Factories 453
    Data Privacy in JavaScript 454
    ES6 Improves Object Initializers 456
    ES6 Symbols and Data Privacy 459
    Concluding 462
    Exercises 464

Appendix B. Mysteries of the JavaScript Arcana 470
    A Couple of Tips About JavaScript Quirks and Gotchas 472
    A Quick Refresher of the JavaScript Arcana 101 473
    This, Your Most Dangerous Foe 474
    Global Scope by Default and Namespacing in JavaScript 485
    Type Coercion Madness 488
    Using JavaScript in Strict Mode 490
    Concluding 492
    Exercises 494

Appendix C. More Useful Function Patterns: Function Overloading 498
    Have you Heard About The Marvels Of Overloading? . 499
    The Problem with Function Overloading in JavaScript . 500
    How Do We Do Function Overloading Then? 501
    Function Overloading by Inspecting Arguments 502

Using an Options Object 503
Relying on ES6 Defaults 504
Taking Advantage of Polymorphic Functions 505
Concluding 508
Exercises 509

Appendix D. Setting Up Your Developing Environment For ES6 514
Using ES6 with Node.js 514
ES6 and Modern Browsers 515
Real-World ES6 Development Environments 516

Appendix E. Fantasy Glossary 517

References 520
Specifications 521
Books 521
White papers 521
Articles 522

About The Author

Jaime González García

Jaime González García (@Vintharas[1]) *Software Developer and UX guy, speaker, author & nerd*

Jaime is a full stack web developer and UX designer who thinks it's weird to write about himself in the third person. During the past few years of his career he has been slowly but surely specializing in front-end development and user experience, and somewhere and some time along the way he fell in love with JavaScript. He still enjoys developing in the full stack though, bringing ideas to life, building things from nothingness, beautiful things that are a pleasure and a delight to use.

Jaime works as a Technical Solutions Consultant at Google helping publishers be great. He spends part of his time as a Developer Relations for Angular and Google in the Nordics developer community. He speaks at conferences, writes articles, runs workshops and talks to developers and companies about how they can do cool things with Angular and JavaScript. He also arranges developer

---

[1] https://twitter.com/Vintharas

community events at the Google Office in Stockholm as a way to support and encourage the thriving local dev ecosystem and put it in contact with other Googlers.

In his spare time he builds his own products and blogs at barbarianmeetscoding.com (long story that one). He loves spending time with his beloved wife Malin and son Teo, drawing, writing, reading fantasy and sci-fi, and lifting heavy weights

About the Technical Reviewers

Artur Mizera

Artur Mizera (@arturmizera[2]) *Web developer*

Artur is a passionate software developer who has built various web applications for small as well as enterprise companies.

Sometimes he recollects the good, old times when jQuery was in beta, just about to be released as 1.0 and nobody even knew what the word SPA stood for... Everyday he tries to get better with modern front-end development and software craftsmanship.

Currently he works as Senior Applications Developer at Oracle. When he gets home he plays around with side projects, open source or gets outside and does some running.

---

[2]http://twitter.com/arturmizera

Prelude

It was during the second age
that the great founder of our order Branden Iech,

first stumbled upon the arcane REPL,
and learnt how to bend the fabric of existence to his very will,

then was that he discovered
there was a mechanism to alter the threads
being woven into The Pattern,

then that we started experiencing the magic of JavaScript

> \- Irec Oliett,
> The Origins of JavaScript-Mancy
> Guardian of Chronicles, 7th Age

Imagine... imagine you lived in a world were you could use JavaScript to change the universe around you, to tamper with the threads that compose reality and do anything that you can imagine. Well, welcome to the world of JavaScript-mancy, where wizards, also known as JavaScriptmancers, control the arcane winds of magic wielding JavaScript to and fro and command the very fabric of reality.

We, programmers, sadly do not live in such a world. But we do have a measure of magic [3] in us, **we have the skills and power to create things out of nothingness**. And even if we cannot throw fireballs or levitate (*yet*), we can definitely change/improve/enhance reality and the universe around us with our little creations. Ain't that freaking awesome?

Well, I hope this book inspires you to continue creating, and using this beautiful skill we share, this time, with JavaScript.

A Note to the Illustrious Readers of JavaScript-mancy: Getting Started

If you are a reader of *JavaScript-mancy: Getting Started* then let me start this book by thanking you. When I started writing the JavaScript-mancy series little did I know about the humongous quest I was embarking in. Two years later, I have written more than a thousand pages, loads of code examples, hundreds of exercises, spent an insane amount of time reviewing the drafts, reviewing the reviews, etc... But all of this work is meaningless without you, the reader. Thank you for trusting in me and in this series, I hope you enjoy this book more than you enjoyed the first one. Go forth JavaScript-mancer!

---

[3] "Any sufficiently advanced technology is indistinguishable from magic." Arthur C. Clarke. Love that quote :)

A Story About Why I Wrote This Book

I was sitting at the back of the room, with my back straight and fidgetting with my fingers on the table. I was both excited and nervous. It was the first time I had ventured myself to attend to one of the unfrequent meetings of my local .NET user group. *Excited* because it was beyond awesome to be in the presence of so many like-minded individuals, people who loved to code like me, people who were so passionate about software development that were willing to sacrifice their free time to meet and talk about programming. *Nervous* because, of course, I did not want to look nor sound stupid in such a distinguished group of people.

The meetup started discussing *TypeScript* the new superset of JavaScript that promised *Nirvana* for C# developers in this new world of super interactive web applications. TypeScript here, TypeScript there because writing JavaScript sucked… JavaScript was the worst… everybody in the room started sharing their old war stories about writing JavaScript, how bad it was in comparison to C#, and so on…

"Errr… the TypeScript compiler writes beautiful JavaScript" I adventured to say… the room fell silent. People looking astonishingly at each other, uncomprehending, unbelieving… Someone had dared use *beautiful* and *JavaScript* in the same sentence.

This was not the first, nor will be the last time I have encountered such a reaction and feelings towards JavaScript as predominant in the .NET community. JavaScript is not worthy of our consideration. JavaScript is a toy language. JavaScript is unreliable and behaves in weird and unexpected ways. JavaScript developers don't know how to program. JavaScript tooling is horrible…

And every single time I sat muted, thinking to myself, reflecting, racking my brains pondering… How to show and explain that JavaScript is actually awesome? How to share that it is a beautiful language? A rich language that is super fun to write? That's how this book came about.

And let me tell you one little secret. Just some few years ago I felt exactly the same way about JavaScript. And then, all of the sudden, I started using it, with the mind of a beginner, without prejudices, without disdain. It was hard at first, being so fluent in C# I couldn't wrap my head around how to achieve the same degree of fluency and expressiveness in JavaScript. Nonetheless I continued forward, and all of the sudden I came to love it.

The problem with JavaScript is that it looks too much like C#, enough to make you confident that you know JavaScript because you know C#. And just when you are all comfortable, trusting and unsuspecting JavaScript smacks you right in the face with a battle hammer, because, in many respects, JavaScript is not at all like C#. It just looks like it on the surface.

JavaScript is indeed a beautiful language, a little rough on the edges, but a beautiful language nonetheless. Trust me. You're in for a treat.

Why Should You Care About JavaScript?

You may be wondering why you need to know JavaScript if you already grok C#.

Well, first and foremost, *JavaScript is super fun to write*. Its lack of ceremony and super fast feedback cycles make it a fun language to program in and ideal for quick prototyping, quick testing of things, tinkering, building stuff and getting results fast. If you haven't been feeling it for programming lately, JavaScript will help you rediscover your passion and love for programming.

JavaScript is the language of the web, if you are doing any sort of web development, you need to understand how to write great JavaScript code and how JavaScript itself works. Even if you are writing a transpiled language like TypeScript or CoffeeScript, they both become JavaScript in the browser and thus knowing JavaScript will make you way more effective.

But *JavaScript is not limited to the web*, during the past few years JavaScript has taken the world by storm[4], you can write JavaScript to make websites, in the backend, to build mobile applications, games and even to control robots and IoT devices, which makes it a true cross-platform language.

JavaScript is a very approachable language, a forgiving one, easy to learn but hard to master. It is minimalistic in its contructs, beautiful, expressive and supports many programming paradigms. If you reflect about JavaScript features you'll see how it is built with simplicity in mind. Ideas such as type coercion (*are "44" and 44 so different after all?*) or being able to declare strings with either single or double quotes are great expressions of that principle.

JavaScript's openness and easy extensibility are the perfect foundations to make it a *fast-evolving language and ecosystem*. As the one language for the web, the language that browsers can understand, it has become the perfect medium for cross-pollination across all software development communities, where .NET developers ideas can meet and intermingle with others from the Ruby and Python communities. This makes knowledge, patterns and ideas spread accross boundaries like never before.

Since no one single entity really controls JavaScript[5], *the community has a great influence in how the language evolves*. With a thriving open source community, and openness and extensibility built within the language, it is the community and the browsers the ones that develop the language and the platform, and the standard bodies the ones that follow and stabilize the trends. When people

---

[4]http://githut.info/

[5]The ECMAScript standard in which JavaScript is based is evolved by the TC39 (Technical Committee 39) composed of several companies with strong interest in JavaScript (all major browser vendors) and distinguished members of the community. You can take a look at their GitHub page for a sneak-peek into how they work and what they are working in

find JavaScript lacking in some regard, they soon rush to fill in the gap with powerful libraries, tooling and techniques.

But don't just take my word for it. This is what the book is for, to show you.

What is the Goal of This Book?

This book is the second installment of the JavaScript-mancy series and its goal is to provide a great and smooth introduction to JavaScript Object-Oriented Programming to C# developers. Its goal is to teach you how you can bring and reuse all your C# knowledge into JavaScript and, at the same time, boost your OOP skills with new paradigms that take advantage of JavaScript dynamic nature.

What is the Goal of The JavaScript-mancy Series?

The goal of the JavaScript-mancy series is to make you fluent in JavaScript, able to express your ideas instantly and build awesome things with it. You'll not only learn the language itself but how to write idiomatic JavaScript. You'll learn both the most common patterns and idioms used in JavaScript today, and also all about the latest versions of JavaScript: ECMAScript 6 (also known ES6 and ES2015), ES7 (ES2016), ES2017 and beyond.

> You can use ECMAScript as a synonym for JavaScript. It is true that we often use ES (short for ECMAScript) and a version number to refer to a specific version of JavaScript and its related set of new features. Particularly when these features haven't yet been implemented by all major browsers vendors.

Prelude   x

> But for all intents and purposes ECMAScript is JavaScript. For instance, you will rarely hear explicit references to ES5.

But we will not stop there because what is a language by itself if you cannot build anything with it. I want to teach you everything you need to be successful and have fun writing JavaScript after you read this series. And that's why we will take one step further and take a glance at the JavaScript ecosystem, the JavaScript community, the rapid prototyping tools, the great tooling involved in building modern JavaScript applications, JavaScript testing and building an app in a modern JavaScript framework: Angular [6].

Why JavaScript-mancy?

Writing code is one of my favorite past times and so is reading fantasy books. For this project I wanted to mix these two passions of mine and try to make something awesome out of it.

In fantasy we usually have the idea of magic, usually very powerful, very obscure and only at the reach of a few dedicated individuals. There's also different schools or types of magic: pyromancy deals with fire magic, allomancy relates to magic triggered by metals, necromancy is all about death magic, raising armies of skeletons and zombies, immortality, etc.

I thought that drawing a parallel between magic and what we programmers do daily would be perfect. Because it is obscure to the untrained mind and requires a lot of work and study to get into, and because we have the power to create things out of nothing.

And therefore, **JavaScript-mancy, the arcane art of writing awesome JavaScript**.

---

[6] Previously known as Angular 2 and later re-branded to just Angular. The former version of Angular 1.x is now known as Angular.js

Is This Book For You?

I have written this book for you C# developer:

- you that hear about the awesome stuff that is happening in the realm of JavaScript and are curious about it. You who would like to be a part of it, a part of this fast evolving, open and thriving community.
- you that have written JavaScript before, perhaps even do it daily and have been frustrated by it, by not been able to express your ideas in JavaScript, by not being able to get a program do what you wanted it to do, or struggling to do so. After reading this book you'll be able to write JavaScript as naturally as you write C#.
- you that think JavaScript a toy language, a language not capable of doing real software development. You'll come to see an expressive and powerful multiparadigm language suitable for a multitude of scenarios and platforms.

This book is specifically for C# developers because it uses a lot of analogies from the .NET world, C# and static typed languages to teach JavaScript. As a C# developer myself, I understand where the pain points lie and where we struggle the most when trying to learn JavaScript and will use analogies as a bridge between languages. Once you get a basic understanding and fluency in JavaScript I'll expand into JavaScript specific patterns and constructs that are less common in C# and that will blow your mind.

That being said, a lot[7] of the content of the book is useful beyond C# and regardless of your software development background.

---
[7] Really, A LOT :)

How is The Book Organized?

The goal of this book is to provide a smooth ride in learning OOP to C# developers that start developing in JavaScript. Since we humans like familiarity and analogy is super conductive to learning, the first part of the book is focused on helping you learn how to bring your OOP knowledge from C# into JavaScript.

We'll start examining the pillars of object oriented programming: encapsulation, inheritance and polymorphism and how they apply to JavaScript and its prototypical inheritance model.

We will continue with how to emulate classes in JavaScript prior to ES6 which will set the stage perfectly to demonstrate the value of ES6 classes.

After that we will focus on alternative object-oriented paradigms that take advantage of the dynamic nature of JavaScript to achieve great flexibility and composablity in a fraction of the code.

Later we'll move onto object internals and the obscure art of meta-programming in JavaScript with the new Reflect API, proxies and symbols.

Finally, we'll complete our view of object-oriented programming in JavaScript with a deep dive into TypeScript, a superset of JavaScript that enhances your developer experience with new features and type annotations.

How Are The JavaScript-mancy Series Organized? What is There in the Rest of the Books?

The rest of the books are organized in 3 parts focused in the language, the ecosystem and building your first app in JavaScript.

After this introductory book **Part I. Mastering the Art of JavaScriptmancy** continues by examining **object oriented programming in JavaScript**, studying prototypical inheritance, how to mimic C# (classic) inheritance in JavaScript. We will also look beyond class OOP into mixins, multiple inheritance and stamps where JavaScript takes you into interesting OOP paradigms that we rarely see in the more conventional C#.

We will then dive into **functional programming in JavaScript** and take a journey through LINQ, applicative programming, immutability, generators, combinators and function composition.

Organizing your JavaScript applications will be the next topic with the module pattern, commonJS, AMD (Asynchronous module definition) and ES6 modules.

Finally we will take a look at **Asynchronous programming** in JavaScript with callbacks, promises and reactive programming.

Since adoption of ES6 will take some time to take hold, and you'll probably see a lot of ES5 code for the years to come, we will start every section of the book showing the most common solutions and patterns of writing JavaScript that we use nowadays with ES5. This will be the perfect starting point to understand and showcase the new ES6 features, the problems they try to solve and how they can greatly improve your JavaScript.

In **Part II. Welcome to The Realm Of JavaScript** we'll take a look at the JavaScript ecosystem, following a brief history of the language that will shed some light on why JavaScript is the way it is today, continuing with the node.js revolution and JavaScript as a true cross-platform, cross-domain language.

Part II will continue with **how to setup your JavaScript development environment** to maximize your productivity and minimize your frustration. We will cover modern JavaScript and front-end workflows, JavaScript unit testing, browser dev tools and even take a look a various text editors and IDEs.

We will wrap Part II with a look at the role of **transpiled languages**. Languages like TypeScript, CoffeeScript, even ECMAScript 6, and how they have impacted and will affect JavaScript development in the future.

Part III. Building Your First Modern JavaScript App With Angular 2 will wrap up the book with a practical look at building modern JavaScript applications. Angular 2 is a great framework for this purpose because it takes advantage of all modern web standards, ES6 and has a very compact design that makes writing Angular 2 apps feel like writing vanilla JavaScript. That is, you won't need to spend a lot of time learning convoluted framework concepts, and will focus instead in developing your JavaScript skills to build a real app killing two birds with one stone (Muahahaha!).

In regards to the size and length of each chapter, aside from the introduction, I have kept every chapter small. The idea being that you can learn little by little, acquire a bit of knowledge that you can apply in your daily work, and get a feel of progress and completion from the very start.

Understanding the Code Samples in This Book

How to Run the Code Samples in This Book

For simplicity, I recommend that you start running the code samples in the browser. That's the most straightforward way since you won't need to install anything in your computer. You can either type them as you go in the browser JavaScript console (F12 for Chrome if you are running windows or Opt-CMD-J in a Mac) or with

Prelude

prototyping tools like JsBin[8], jsFiddle[9], CodePen[10] or Plunker[11]. Any of these tools is excellent so you can pick your favorite.

If you don't feel like typing, all the examples are available in jsFiddle/jsBin JavaScriptmancy library: http://bit.ly/javascriptmancy-samples[12].

For testing ECMAScript 6 examples I recommend JsBin[13], jsFiddle[14] or the Babel REPL at https://babeljs.io/repl/[15]. Alternatively there's a very interesting Chrome plugin that you can use to run both ES5 and ES6 examples called ScratchJS[16].

If you like, you can download all the code samples from GitHub[17] and run them locally in your computer using node.js[18].

Also keep an eye out for **javascriptmancy.com**[19] where I'll add interactive exercises in a not too distant future.

A Note About Conventions Used in the Code Samples

The book has three types of code samples. Whenever you see a extract of code like the one below, where statements are preceded by a >, I expect you to type the examples in a REPL.

---

[8] http://jsbin.io
[9] https://jsfiddle.net/
[10] http://codepen.io
[11] http://plnkr.co/
[12] http://bit.ly/javascriptmancy-samples
[13] http://jsbin.io
[14] https://jsfiddle.net/
[15] https://babeljs.io/repl/
[16] https://bit.ly/javascriptmancy-scratchjs
[17] http://bit.ly/javascriptmancy-code-samples
[18] http://www.nodejs.org
[19] http://www.javascriptmancy.com

The REPL is Your Friend!

One of the great things about JavaScript is the REPL (Read-Eval-Print-Loop), that is a place where you can type JavaScript code and get the results immediately. A REPL lets you tinker with JavaScript, test whatever you can think of and get immediate feedback about the result. Awesome right?

A couple of good examples of REPLs are a browser's console (`F12` in Chrome/Windows) and node.js (take a look at the appendix to learn how to install node in your computer).

The code after `>` is what you need to type and the expression displayed right afterwards is the expected result:

```
> 2 + 2
// => 4
```

Some expressions that you often write in a REPL like a variable or a function declaration evaluate to `undefined`:

```
> var hp = 100;
// => undefined
```

Since I find that this just adds unnecessary noise to the examples I'll omit these `undefined` values and I'll just write the meaningful result. For instance:

```
> console.log('yippiiiiiii')
// => yippiiiiiii
// => undefined      <==== I will omit this
```

When I have a multiline statement, I will omit the `>` so you can more easily copy and paste it in a REPL or prototyping tool (*jsBin*, *CodePen*, etc). That way you won't need to remove the unnecessary `>` before running the sample:

Prelude

```js
let createWater = function (mana){
    return `${mana} liters of water`;
}
```

I expect the examples within a chapter to be run together, so sometimes examples may reference variables from previous examples within the same section. I will attempt to show smallish bits of code at a time for the sake of simplicity.

For more advanced examples the code will look like a program, there will be no > to be found and I'll add a filename for reference. You can either type the content of the files in your favorite editor or download the source directly from GitHub.

CrazyExampleOfDoom.js

```js
export class Doom {
  constructor(){
    /* Oh no! You read this...
    /
    /  I am sorry to tell you that in 3 days
    /  at midnight the most horrendous apparition
    /  will come out from your favorite dev machine
    /  and it'll be your demise
    /  that is...
    /  unless you give this book as a gift to
    /  other 3 developers, in that case you are
    /  blessed for ever and ever
    */
  }
}
```

A Note About the Exercises

In order to encourage you to experiment with the different things that you will learn in each chapter I wrap every single one of them with exercises.

It is important that you understand that there is almost no wrong solution. I invite you to let your imagination free and try to

Prelude

experiment and be playful with your new found knowledge to your heart's content. I do offer a solution for each exercise but more as a guidance and example that as the one right solution.

In some of the exercises you may see the following pattern:

```
// mooleen.weaves('some code here');
mooleen.weaves('teleport("out of the forest", mooleen, randalf)');
```

This is completely equivalent to:

```
// some code here
teleport("out of the forest", mooleen, randalf);
```

I just use a helper function weaves to make it look like *Moolen, the mighty wizard* is casting a spell (in this case teleport).

A Note About ECMAScript 5 (ES5) and ES6, ES7, ES8 and ESnext within The Book

Everything in programming has a reason for existing. That hairy piece of code that you wrote seven months ago, that feature that went into an application, that syntax or construct within a language, *all were or seemed like good ideas at the time.* ES6, ES7 and future versions of JavaScript all try to improve upon the version of JavaScript that we have today. And it helps to understand the pain points they are trying to solve, the context in which they appear and in which they are needed. That's why this book will show you ES5 in conjunction with ES6 and beyond. For it will be much easier to understand new features when you see them as a natural evolution of the needs and pain points of developers today.

How will this translate into the examples within the book? - you may be wondering. Well I'll start in the beginning of the book writing ES5 style code, and slowly but surely, as I go showing you ES6 features, we will transform our ES5 code into ES6. By the end of the book, you yourself will have experienced the journey and have mastered both ES5 and ES6.

Additionally, it is going to take some time for us to start using ES6 to the fullest, and there's surely a ton of web applications that will never be updated to using ES6 features so it will be definitely helpful to know ES5.

A Note Regarding the Use of `var`, `let` and `const`

Since this book covers both ES5, ES6 and beyond the examples will intermingle the use of the `var`, `let` and `const` keywords to declare variables. If you aren't familiar with what these keywords do here is a quick recap:

- `var`: use it to declare variables with function scope. Variables declared with `var` are susceptible to hoisting which can result in subtle bugs in your code.
- `let`: use it to declare variables with block scope. Variables declared with `let` are not hoisted. Thanks to this, `let` allows you to declare variables nearer to where they are used.
- `const`: like `let`, but in addition, it declares a one-time binding. That is, a variable declared with `const` can't be bound to any other value. Attempting to assign the value of a `const` variable to something else will result in an error.

The examples for ES5 patterns like mimicking classes before the advent of ES6 (and the new `let` and `const`) will use `var`. The examples for post ES6 features like ES6 classes and onwards will use `let` and `const`. Of these two we will prefer the latter that offers a safer alternative to `let`, and we will use `let` in those cases where we need or want to allow assigning a variable multiple times. That being said there may be occasions where I won't follow these rules when a particular example escapes mine and my reviewer's watchful eye.

If you want to learn more about JavaScript scoping rules and the `var`, `let` and `const` keywords then I recommend you to take a look at JavaScript-mancy: Getting Started[20] the first book of this series.

A Note About the Use of Generalizations in This Book

Some times in the course of the book I will make generalizations for the sake of simplicity and to provide a better and more continuous learning experience. I will make statements such as:

> *In JavaScript, unlike in C#, you can augment objects with new properties at any point in time*

If you are experienced in C# you may frown at this, cringe, raise your fist to the sky and shout: *Why!? oh Why would he say such a thing!? Does he not know C#!?*. But bear with me. I will write the above not unaware of the fact that C# has the `dynamic` keyword and the `ExpandoObject` class that offer that very functionality, but because the predominant use of C# involves the use of strong types and compile-time type checking. The affirmation above provides a much simpler and clearer explanation about JavaScript than writing:

> *In JavaScript, unlike in C# where you use classes and strong types in 99% of the situations and in a similar way to the use of dynamic and ExpandoObject, you can*

---

[20] https://www.javascriptmancy.com/

> *augment objects with new properties at any point in time*

So instead of focusing on being correct 100% of the time and diving into every little detail, I will try to favor simplicity and only go into detail when it is conductive to understanding JavaScript which is the focus of this book. Nonetheless, I will provide footnotes for anyone that is interested in exploring these topics further.

Do You Have Any Feedback? Found Any Error?

If you have any feedback or have found some error in this book that you would like to report, then don't hesitate to drop me an email at jaime@vintharas.com or reach me on twitter @vintharas[21].

A Final Word From the Author

The goal for this series of books is to be holistic. Holistic enough to give a good overview of the JavaScript language and ecosystem, yet contain enough detail to impart real knowledge about how JavaScript really works. That's a fine line to tread and sometimes I will probably cover too little or too much. If so don't hesitate to let me know. The beauty of a lean published book is that I have much more room to include improvements suggested by you.

There is a hidden goal as well, that is to make it as fun and enjoyable as possible. Therefore the fantasy theme of the whole book, the conversational style, the jokes and the weird sense of humor. Anyways, I have put my heart and soul into this book and hope you really enjoy it!

Jaime, 2017

---

[21] https://twitter.com/Vintharas

Once Upon a Time...

*Once upon a time, in a faraway land, there was a beautiful hidden island with captivating white sandy beaches, lush green hills and mighty white peaked mountains. The natives called it **Asturi** and, if not for an incredible and unexpected event, it would have remained hidden and forgotten for centuries.*

*Some say it was during his early morning walk, some say that it happened in the shower. Be that as it may, **Branden Iech**, at the time the local eccentric and today considered the greatest Philosopher of antiquity, stumbled upon something that would change the world forever.*

In talking to himself, as both his most beloved companions and his most bitter detractors would attest was a habit of his, he stumbled upon the magic words of JavaScript and the mysterious REPL.

In the years that followed he would teach the magic word and fund the order of JavaScriptmancers bringing a golden age to our civilization. Poor, naive philosopher. For such power wielded by mere humans was meant to be misused, to corrupt their fragile hearts and bring their and our downfall. It's been ten thousand years, ten thousand years of wars, pain and struggle.

It is said that, in the 12th day of the 12th month of the 12th age a hero will rise and bring balance to the world. That happens to be today.

12th Age, Guardian of Chronicles

This book has a story in it. It is a story of a fantasy[22] world where

---

[22] For those of you that are not fantasy nerds I have included a small glossary at the end of the book where you can check words that you find strange. You should be able to understand the book and examples without the glossary, but I think it'll be more fun if you do

some people can wield JavaScript to affect the world around them, to essentially program the world and bend it to their will. Cool right? The story follows the step of a heroine that comes to this hypothetical world to save it from evil, but of course, she needs to learn JavaScript first. **Care to join her in her quest to learn JavaScript and save the world?**

Tome II. JavaScriptmancy and OOP: The Path of The Summoner

Path of Summoning and Commanding Objects (Also Known as Object Oriented Programming)

Introduction to the Path of Summoning and Commanding Objects (aka OOP)

Many ways to build a Golem there are,

cast its blueprint in clay
then recite the instantiation chants,

or put together the parts
that'll made the whole alive,

or bring it forth at once
with no prior thought required.

Many ways to build a Golem there are,
in JavaScript.

> \- KeDo,
> Master Artificer,
> JavaScript-mancy poems

```
/*
Mooleen sits in a dark corner of a tavern sipping a jug of
the local brew.

She flinches. The local brew surely must have fire wyvern's
blood in it.

She silently observes the villagers around her.

They seem unhappy and nervous. As if they were expecting
something terrible was about to befall them any second.
*/

mooleen.says("A month has passed since we dispatched Great");
mooleen.says("You would think they would be happier");

rat.says("Well, people don't like change or surprises");
rat.says("They're expecting that someone worse will take control");
rat.says("Better the devil you know...");

/*
A maid stops by Mooleen's table confused
*/
maid.says("Are you feeling alright, sir? Speaking to yourself?");

rat.movesOutOfTheShadows();
maid.shrikes();

villager.shouts("A demon!!!");

rat.says("Great");
mooleen.says("That's just plain mean");

/*
The villagers quickly surround the dark corner with clubs, bottles
and whichever crude weapon they can muster.
*/
villager.shouts("Kill the demon!!");

mooleen.weaves("teleport('Caves of Infinity')");

/*
Mooleen and rat blink out of existence just as various pointy weapons
blink into existence precisely where they were sitting a second
earlier.
*/
```

Introduction to the Path of Summoning and Commanding Objects (aka OOP)

```
randalf.says("There you are!");
mooleen.says("here I am!");
rat.says("A demon!?");

randalf.exclaims("A demon? Where!!");
bandalf.says("Yes where!")
zandalf.looksWorriedAllAround();

mooleen.says("There's no demon");
randalf.asks("Are you sure?");

randalf.says("We need to be on our toes");
mooleen.asks("You too?");

randalf.says("Yes, it's been a month, they must be about to attack");
mooleen.says("They? Who!");

randalf.says("Could be anyone really... The Dark Brootherhood, " +
    "The Clan, The Silver Guild, The Red Hand... " +
    "They'll want to control Asturi");
randalf.says("You need to summon an army");

mooleen.says("An army?");
randalf.says("An army indeed, n' bigger than the one you had before"\
);

mooleen.says("Really? Cause that took a looooong time to summon");
randalf.says("Well, That's because you're a novice");

mooleen.says("That's encouraging");
randalf.says("Oh, don't you worry, " +
            "We'll take care of your ignorance");
mooleen.says("Ouch");

randalf.says("Let me tell you about OOP in JavaScript");
```

Let me Tell You About OOP in JavaScript

Welcome to *the Path of Summoning*[23] *and Commanding Objects*! In this part of this ancient manuscript you'll learn how you can work with objects in JavaScript, how to define them, create them and even how to interweave them. By the end of it you'll have mastered Object Oriented Programming in JavaScript and you'll be ready to command your vast armies of objects into eternal glory.

JavaScript OOP story is pretty special. When I started working seriously with JavaScript some years ago, one of my first concerns as a C# developer coming to JavaScript was to find out how to write a class. I had a lot of prowess in C# and I wanted to bring all my knowledge and abilities into the world of JavaScript, so my first approach was to try to map every C# concept into JavaScript. I saw classes, which are such a core construct in C# and which were such an important part of my programming style at the time, as my secret weapon to being proficient in JavaScript.

Well, for the life of me I couldn't find a good reference to this-is-how-you-write-a-class-in-JavaScript. It took me a long while to understand how to mimic classical inheritance. But it was time well spent because, along the way, I learnt a lot about JavaScript and about the many different ways in which it supports object-oriented programming. Moreover, this quest helped me look beyond classical inheritance into other OOP styles more akin to JavaScript where flexibility and expressiveness reign supreme over the strict and fixed taxonomies of classes.

In this part of the series I will attempt to bring you with me, hand in hand, through the same journey that I experienced. We will start with how to achieve classical inheritance in JavaScript, so you can

---

[23] In Fantasy, wizards of all sorts and kinds *summon* or *call forth* creatures to act as servants, or warriors, and follow the wizard's commands. As a JavaScript-mancer you'll be able to use Object Oriented Programming to summon your own objects into reality and do with them as you please.

get a basic level of proficiency by translating your C# skills into JavaScript. And then we will move beyond that into new patterns that truly leverage JavaScript as a language and which will blow your mind.

 Experiment JavaScriptmancer!!

You can experiment with all examples in this chapter directly within this jsBin[24] or downloading the source code from GitHub[25].

Let's have a taste of what is in store for you by getting a high level overview [26] of object-oriented programming in JavaScript. Don't worry if you feel you can't follow the examples. In the upcoming chapters we will dive deeper into each of the concepts and techniques used, and we will discuss them separately at a much slower pace.

C# Classes in JavaScript

A C# *class* is more or less equivalent to a JavaScript *constructor function* and *prototype* pair:

---

[24] http://bit.ly/javascriptmancy-oop-introduction
[25] https://github.com/vintharas/javascriptmancy-code-samples
[26] In this section I am going to make a lot of generalizations and simplifications in order to give a simple and clear introduction to OOP in JavaScript. I'll dive into each concept in greater detail and with an appropriate level of correctness in the rest of the chapters ahead.

Introduction to the Path of Summoning and Commanding Objects (aka OOP)

```javascript
// Here we have a Minion constructor function
function Minion(name, hp){
  // The constructor function usually defines
  // the data within a "class", the properties
  // contained within a constructor function
  // will be part of each object created with it
  this.name = name;
  this.hp = hp;
}

// The prototype usually defines the methods
// within a "class". It is shared across all
// Minion instances
Minion.prototype.toString = function(){
  return this.name;
};
```

The *constructor function* represents how an object should be constructed (or created) while the *prototype* represents bits of reusable behavior. In practice, the *constructor function* usually defines the data members within a *"class"* while the *prototype* defines its methods.

You can instantiate a new `Minion` object by using the `new` operator on the *constructor function*:

```javascript
var orc = new Minion('orc', 100);
console.log(orc);
// => [object Object] {
//   hp: 100,
//   name: "orc",
//   toString: function () {
//     return this.name;
//   }
// }

console.log(orc.toString())
// => orc

console.log('orc is a Minion: ' + (orc instanceof Minion));
// => true
```

Introduction to the Path of Summoning and Commanding Objects (aka OOP) 8

As a result of instantiating an orc we get a new Minion object with two properties hp and name. The Minion object also has a hidden property called [[prototype]] that points to its prototype which is an object that has a method toString. This *prototype* and its toString method are shared across all instances of the Minion class.

When you call orc.toString the JavaScript runtime checks whether or not the orc object has a toString method and if it can't find it, *like in this case*, it goes down the *prototype chain* until it does. The *prototype chain* is established by the object itself, its prototype, its prototype's prototype and so on. In this case, the *prototype chain* leads to the Minion.prototype object that has a toString method. This method will then be called and evaluated as this.name (whose value is orc in this example).

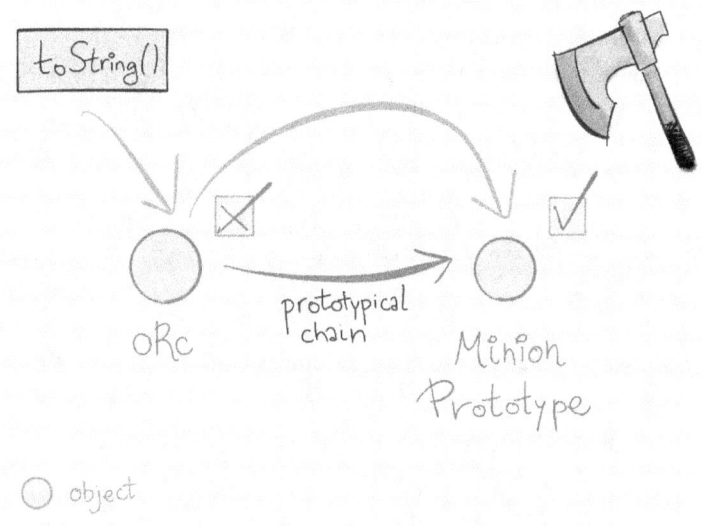

The prototypical chain

We can mimic classical inheritance by defining a new *"class"* Wizard and making it inherit from Minion:

```
1   // Behold! A Wizard!
2   function Wizard(name, element, hp, mana){
3       // the constructor function calls its parent constructor function
4       // using [Function.prototype.call] (or apply)
5       Minion.call(this, name, hp);
6       this.element = element;
7       this.mana = mana;
8   }
9
10  // the prototype of the Wizard is a Minion object
11  Wizard.prototype = Object.create(Minion.prototype);
12  Wizard.prototype.constructor = Wizard;
```

We achieve *classical inheritance* by:

1. Calling the `Minion` *constructor function* from the `Wizard` *constructor*.
2. Creating a new object that has Minion as its prototype (via `Object.create`) and assigning it to be the `Wizard` prototype. This is how you establish a prototypical chain between `Wizard` and `Minion`.

Wizard object => Wizard Prototype => Minion Prototype => Object Prototype

By following these two steps we achieve two things:

1. With the *constructor* delegation we ensure that a `Wizard` object has all the properties of a `Minion` object.
2. With the *prototype chain* we ensure that all the methods in the `Minion` prototype are available to a `Wizard` object.

We can also augment the `Wizard` *prototype* with new methods like this `castsSpell` method that allows the wizard to cast powerful spells:

```
// we can augment the prototype with a new method to
// cast mighty spells
Wizard.prototype.castsSpell = function(spell, target){
    console.log(this + ' casts ' + spell + ' on ' + target);
    this.mana -= spell.mana;
    spell(target);
};
```

Or even override or extend existing methods within its base *"class"* Minion:

```
// we can also override and extend methods
Wizard.prototype.toString = function(){
    return Minion.prototype.toString.apply(this, arguments) +
    ", the " + this.element +" Wizard";
};
```

Finally, we can verify that everything works as expected by instantiating our very own powerful wizard:

```
var gandalf = new Wizard(/* name */ "Gandalf",
                        /* element*/ "Grey",
                        /* hp */ 50,
                        /* mana */ 50);
```

The gandalf object is both an instance of Wizard and Minion which makes sense:

```
console.log('Gandalf is a Wizard: ' + (gandalf instanceof Wizard));
// => Gandalf is a Wizard: true
console.log('Gandalf is a Minion: ' + (gandalf instanceof Minion));
// => Gandalf is a Minion: true
```

The toString method works as defined in our overridden version:

```
console.log(gandalf.toString());
// => Gandalf, the Grey Wizard
```

And our great Grey wizard can cast potent spells:

```
// A lightning spell
var lightningSpell = function(target){
  console.log('A bolt of lightning electrifies ' + target + '(-10hp)\
');
  target.hp -= 10;
};
lightningSpell.mana = 5;
lightningSpell.toString = function(){ return 'lightning spell';};

gandalf.castsSpell(lightningSpell, orc);
// => Gandalf, the Grey Wizard casts lightning spell on orc
// => A bolt of lightning electrifies orc (-10hp)
```

As you can see from these previous examples, writing *"classes"* prior to *ES6* was no easy feat. It required a lot of moving parts and a lot of code. That's why *ES6* brings *classes* along which provide a much nicer syntax to what you've seen thus far. Instead of having to handle *constructor functions* and *prototypes* yourself, you get the new class keyword that nicely wraps both into a more coherent and developer friendly syntax:

```
// this is the equivalent of the Minion
class ClassyMinion{
  constructor(name, hp){
    this.name = name;
    this.hp = hp;
  }
  toString(){
    return this.name;
  }
}

const classyOrc = new ClassyMinion('classy orc', 50);
console.log(classyOrc);
```

```
// => [object Object] {
//   hp: 100,
//   name: "classy orc"
//}

console.log(classyOrc.toString());
// => classy orc

console.log('classy orc is a ClassyMinion: ' +
  (classyOrc instanceof ClassyMinion));
// => classy orc is a ClassyMinion: true
```

ES6 classes also provide the extend and super keywords which improve how classes can relate and interact with parent classes. extend lets you establish class inheritance in a readable, declarative fashion and super lets you access methods from parent classes:

```
// and this is the equivalent of the Wizard
class ClassyWizard extends ClassyMinion{
  constructor(name, element, hp, mana){
    // super lets you access the parent class methods
    // like the parent class constructor
    super(name, hp);
    this.element = element;
    this.mana = mana;
  }
  toString(){
    // or any other method
    return super.toString() + ", the " + this.element +" Wizard";
  }
  castsSpell(spell, target){
    console.log(this + ' casts ' + spell + ' on ' + target);
    this.mana -= spell.mana;
    spell(target);
  }
}
```

Again, we can verify that it works just like it did before by instantiating a *classy* wizard:

```
const classyGandalf = new Wizard(/* name */ "Classy Gandalf",
                                 /* element */ "Grey",
                                 /* hp */ 50,
                                 /* mana */ 50);
console.log('Classy Gandalf is a ClassyWizard: ' +
            (classyGandalf instanceof ClassyWizard));
// => Classy Gandalf is a ClassyWizard: true

console.log('Classy Gandalf is a ClassyMinion: ' +
            (classyGandalf instanceof ClassyMinion));
// => Classy Gandalf is a ClassyMinion: true

console.log(classyGandalf.toString());
// => Classy Gandalf, the Grey Wizard

classyGandalf.castsSpell(lightningSpell, classyOrc);
// => Classy Gandalf, the Grey Wizard casts lightning spell
//    on classy orc
// => A bolt of lightning electrifies classy orc(-10hp)
```

With ES6 classes we can achieve the same result than before with less code and better code at that. **It is important to highlight though that ES6 classes are just syntactic sugar**[27]. Under the hood, these ES6 classes that you have just seen are equivalent to *constructor function/prototype* pairs.

And that is how you mimic classical inheritance in JavaScript. Now let's look beyond.

OOP Beyond Classes

There are a lot of people in the JavaScript community who claim that the cause of JavaScript not having a nice way to mimic classical inheritance, not having classes, is that you were not meant to use them in the first place. You were meant to embrace *prototypical inheritance*, the natural way of working with inheritance in

---

[27] They are also safer to use: They aren't hoisted and JavaScript will alert you if you try to call a class constructor without the new operator.

JavaScript, instead of perverting it to make it behave sort of like *classical inheritance*.

In the world of *prototypical inheritance* you only have objects, and particularly objects that are based upon other objects which we call *prototypes*. Prototypes lend behaviors to other objects by means of delegation (via the *prototype chain*) or by the so called *concatenative inheritance* which consists in copying behaviors.

Let's illustrate the usefulness of this type of inheritance with an example. Imagine that, in addition to *wizards*, we also need to have some *thieves* for those occasions when we need to use a more gentle/shrew hand against our enemies.

A `ClassyThief` class could look something like this:

```
class ClassyThief extends ClassyMinion{
   constructor(name, hp){
      super(name, hp);
   }
   toString(){
      return super.toString() + ", the Thief";
   }
   steals(target, item){
      console.log(`${this} steals ${item} from ${target}`);
   }
}
```

And let's say that a couple of weeks from now, we realize that it would be nice to have yet another type of minion, one that can both cast spells and steal, and why not? Play some music. Something like a *Bard*. In *pseudo-code* we would describe it as follows:

```
1  // class Bard
2  // should be able to:
3  // - cast powerful spells
4  // - steals many items
5  // - play beautiful music
```

Well, we've put ourselves in a pickle here. *Classical inheritance tends to build rigid taxonomies of types where something is a* Wizard, *something is a* Thief *but it cannot be both.* How would we solve the issue of the Bard using classical inheritance in C#? Well...

- We could move both castsSpell and steals methods to a base class SpellCastingAndStealingMinion that all three types could inherit. The ClassyThief would throw an exception when casting spell and so would the ClassyWizard when stealing. Not a very good solution (goodbye Liskov principle [28])
- We could create a SpellCastingAndStealingMinion that duplicates the functionality in ClassyThief and ClassyWizard and make the Bard inherit from it. This solution would imply code duplication and thus additional maintenance.
- We could define interfaces for these behaviors ICanSteal, ICanCastSpells and make each class implement these interfaces. Nicer but we would need to provide an specific implementation in each separate class. No so much code reuse here.
- We could do as in the previous solution, but delegate the implementation of stealing and casting to another class that could be reused by wizards, thieves and bards. This would

---

[28] The Liskov substitution principle is one of the S.O.L.I.D. principles of object-oriented design. It states that derived classes must be substitutable for their base classes. This means that a derived class should behave as portrayed by its base class and not break the expectations created by its interface. In this particular example if you have a castsSpell and a steals method in the base class, and a derived class throws an exception when you call them you are violating this principle. That's because the derived class breaks the expectations established by the base class (i.e. that you should be able to use both methods).

achieve more code reuse but it'd require a lot of extra artificial plumbing to do the delegation.

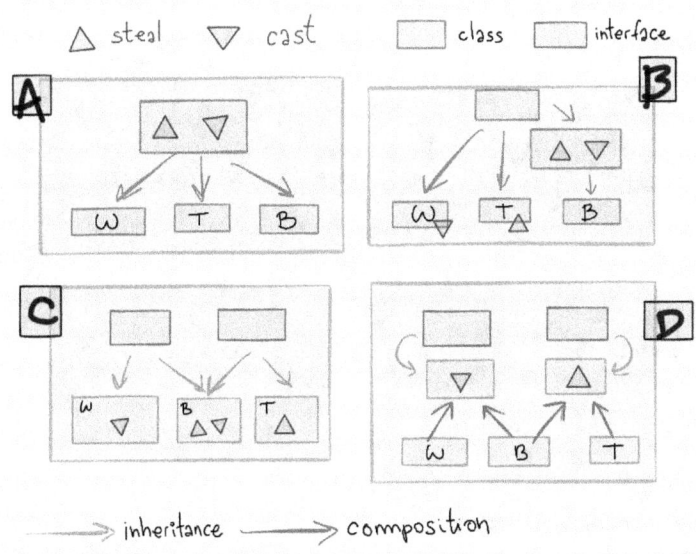

So none of these solutions are very attractive: They involve bad design, code duplication or both. *Can JavaScript help us achieve a better solution to this problem?* **Yes! It can!**

Imagine that we broke down all these behaviors and encapsulated them inside separate objects (canCastSpells, canSteal and canPlayMusic):

Introduction to the Path of Summoning and Commanding Objects (aka OOP) 17

```javascript
const canCastSpells = {
  castsSpell(spell, target){
    console.log(this + ' casts ' + spell + ' on ' + target);
    this.mana -= spell.mana;
    spell(target);
  }
};

const canSteal = {
  steals(target, item){
    console.log(`${this} steals ${item} from ${target}`);
  }
};

const canPlayMusic = {
  playsMusic(){
    console.log(`${this} grabs his ${this.instrument} ` +
                `and starts playing music`);
  }
};

// Bonus behavior to identify a character by name!
const canBeIdentifiedByName = {
  toString(){
    return this.name;
  }
};
```

Now that we have encapsulated each behavior in a separate object we can compose them together to provide the necessary functionality to a wizard, a thief and a bard:

Introduction to the Path of Summoning and Commanding Objects (aka OOP)

```javascript
// And now we can create our objects by composing
// these behaviors together
function TheWizard(element, mana, name, hp){
  const wizard = {element,
                  mana,
                  name,
                  hp};
  Object.assign(wizard,
                canBeIdentifiedByName,
                canCastSpells);
  return wizard;
}

function TheThief(name, hp){
  const thief = {name,
                 hp};
  Object.assign(thief,
                canBeIdentifiedByName,
                canSteal);
  return thief;
}

function TheBard(instrument, mana, name, hp){
  const bard = {instrument,
                mana,
                name,
                hp};
  Object.assign(bard,
                canBeIdentifiedByName,
                canSteal,
                canCastSpells,
                canSteal);
  return bard;
}
```

And in a very expressive way we can see how a `wizard` is someone than can cast spells, a `thief` is someone that can steal and a `bard` someone that not only can cast spells and steal but can also play music. By stepping out of the rigid limits of classical inheritance and static typing, we get to a place where we can easily reuse behaviors and compose new objects in a very flexible and extensible manner.

We can verify that indeed this approach works beautifully. The `Wizard` **casts powerful spells**:

```
const wizard = TheWizard('fire', 100, 'Randalf, the Red', 10);

wizard.castsSpell(lightningSpell, orc);
// => Randalf, the Red casts lightning spell on orc
// => A bolt of lightning electrifies orc(-10hp)
```

The `Thief` sneaks on you and **steals**:

```
const thief = TheThief('Locke Lamora', 100);

thief.steals('orc', /*item*/ 'gold coin');
// => Locke Lamora steals gold coin from orc
```

And the `Bard`, truly gifted `Bard`, **casts spells**, **steals** and **plays music**:

```
const bard = TheBard('lute', 100, 'Kvothe', 100);

bard.castsSpell(lightningSpell, orc);
// => Kvothe casts lightning spell on orc
// =>A bolt of lightning electrifies orc(-10hp)

bard.steals('orc', /*item*/ 'sandwich');
// => Kvothe steals sandwich from orc

bard.playsMusic();
// => Kvothe grabs his lute and starts playing music
```

The `Object.assign` in the examples is an *ES6* method that lets you extend an object with other objects. This is effectively the *concatenative prototypical inheritance* we mentioned previously.

> We usually call these objects *mixins*. A *mixin* in JavaScript is just an object that you compose with other objects to provide them with additional behavior or state. In the simplest example of *mixins* you just have a single object extending another object, but there're also functional *mixins*, where you use functions instead. We will cover all these *mixin* patterns in detail later in the book with a deep dive into Object.assign and possible alternatives in ES5.

This object composition technique constitutes a very interesting and flexible approach to object-oriented programming that isn't available in C#. But in JavaScript we can use it even with *ES6 classes*!

Combining Classes with Object Composition

Do you remember that *ES6 classes* are just syntactic sugar over the existing *prototypical inheritance model*? They may look like *classical inheritance* but they are not. This means that the following mix of *ES6 classes* and *object composition* would work:

```
class ClassyBard extends ClassyMinion{
  constructor(instrument, mana, name, hp){
    super(name, hp);
    this.instrument = instrument;
    this.mana = mana;
  }
}

Object.assign(ClassyBard.prototype,
        canSteal,
        canCastSpells,
        canPlayMusic);
```

In this example we extend the ClassyBard prototype with new functionality that will be shared by all future instances of ClassyBard. If we instantiate a new *bard* we can verify that it can **steal**, **cast spells** and **play music**:

```
const anotherBard = new ClassyBard('guitar', 100, 'Jimmy Hendrix', 1\
00);

anotherBard.steals('orc', /*item*/ 'silver coin');
// => Jimmy Hendrix steals silver coin from orc

anotherBard.castsSpell(lightningSpell, orc);
// => Jimmy Hendrix casts lightning spell on orc
// => A bolt of lightning electrifies orc(-10hp)

anotherBard.playsMusic();
// => Jimmy Hendrix grabs his lute and starts playing music
```

This is an example of *delegation-based prototypical inheritance* in which methods such as steals, castsSpell and playsMusic are delegated to a single *prototype* object (instead of being appended to each object individually).

So far you've seen classical inheritance mimicked in JavaScript, *ES6 classes* and object composition via mixin objects, but there's much more to learn and in greater detail! Take a sneak peak at what you'll learn in each of the upcoming chapters and get excited!

The Path of the Object Summoner Step by Step

In **Summoning Fundamentals: an Introduction to Object Oriented Programming in JavaScript** you'll start by understanding the basic constructs needed to define and instantiate objects in JavaScript. In this chapter, *constructor functions* and the new operator will join what you've discovered thus far about *object initializers*. You'll review how to achieve **information hiding**, you'll learn the basics of JavaScript's **prototypical inheritance** model and how you can use it to reuse code/behaviors and improve your memory footprint. You'll complete the foundations of JavaScript OOP by understanding how JavaScript achieves **polymorphism**.

In **White Tower Summoning or Emulating Classical Inheritance in JavaScript** you'll use *constructor functions* in conjunction with *prototypes* to create the equivalent of C# classes in JavaScript. You'll then push the boundaries of JavaScript inheritance model further and emulate C# classical inheritance building inheritance chains with method extension and overriding just like in C#.

In **White Tower Summoning Enhanced: the Marvels of ES6 Classes** you'll learn about the new *ES6 Class* syntax and how it provides a much better *class* development experience over what it was possible prior to *ES6*.

In **Black Tower Summoning: Objects Interweaving Objects with Mixins** we'll go beyond classical inheritance into the arcane realm of *object composition* with mixins. You'll learn about the extreme extensibility of object-oriented programming based on object composition. How you can define small pieces of reusable behavior and properties that combined together can create powerful objects (effectively achieving multiple inheritance).

In **Black Tower Summoning: Safer Object Composition with Traits** you'll learn about an object composition alternative to mixins called traits. Traits are as reusable and composable as mixins but are even more flexible and safe as they let you define required properties and resolve conflicts.

In **Black Tower Summoning Enhanced: Next Level Object Composition With Stamps** you'll find out about a new way to work with objects in JavaScript called *Stamps* that brings object composability to the next level.

You'll then dive into the depths of **Object Internals and meta-programming** in JavaScript. You'll discover the mysteries of the low level JavaScript `Object` APIs, the new ESnext decorators, ES6 proxies, ES6 `Reflection` APIs and symbols.

Finally, we will complete the path of the Summoner by taking a look at **TypeScript**. TypeScript offers the nearest experience to C# that you can find on the web. It is a superset of JavaScript that enhances your developer experience with new features and type annotations. These type annotations bring static typing to JavaScript but they are flexible enough not to sacrifice JavaScript's dynamic nature.

Concluding

JavaScript is a very versatile language that supports a lot of programming paradigms and different styles of Object-Oriented Programming. In the next chapters you'll see how you can combine a small number of primitive constructs and techniques to achieve a variety of OOP styles.

JavaScript, like in any other part of the language, gives you a lot of freedom when working with objects, and sometimes you'll feel like there are so many options and things you can do that you won't know what's the right path. Because of that, I'll try to provide you with as much guidance as I can and highlight the strengths and weaknesses of each of the options available.

Get ready to learn some JavaScript OOP!

```
randalf.says("See? There's a lot of stuff for you to learn");
mooleen.says("Is any of that going to help me get home?");

randalf.says("Most definitely.");
randalf.says("I have scourged our library and found nothing " +
    "about this 'earth' you speak of. And now that I think about " +
    "it, what a weird name for a kingdom...");
randalf.says("Anyway, the only other option is the golden " +
    "library of Orrile...");

mooleen.says("Awesome! Then just show me the way");
```

```
randalf.says("... in Tates, guarded by The Deadly Seven... ");
mooleen.says("I can take care of them");

randalf.says("... and the vast host of armies " +
             "of the most powerful sorcerer alive");
mooleen.says("I see");
rat.says("downer");

mooleen.says("You were saying something about OOP techniques?...");
```

Summoning Fundamentals: Encapsulation and Information Hiding

Encapsulation means drawing a boundary.
There's something in the inside,
there's something in the outside.

Information Hiding means hiding details,
avoiding unintended coupling,

the first is a capability,
the second a design decision

> \- Dacun Whirnnmar
> Keeper of the Sacred Index

```
randalf.says(`Follow me! ` +
             `We're gonna need some space for your practice`);
randalf.says(`One does not simply go and summon an army ` +
             `in a library`);

/*
 * Mooleen follows Randalf into the depths of the caves.
 * Down and down they travel through the darkest corners
 * deep in the earth until a tiny speck of reddish
 * light illuminates the path ahead.
 */

randalf.stopsSuddenly();
mooleen.runsInto(randalf);

/*
 * Mooleen almost succeeds in killing both herself and Randalf by
 * deadly fall continued by diving into a river of molten lava.
 */

randalf.says('That nearly solved all of our problems');

rat.says(`The fate of the world would've fallen on my shoulders`);
rat.says(`Rat, the hero of ages... like the way it sounds`);

mooleen.says('You should probably signal ' +
             '*"Deadly fall to molten lava ahead"*');

randalf.says(`Good idea! But I'm afraid it'd lose its charm`);
randalf.asks(`See that immense plateau in the middle?`);

mooleen.responds(`The one surrounded by rivers ` +
                 `of incandescent lava?`);
randalf.says('Yes...');

mooleen.asks(`The one with no apparent way to get onto?`)
randalf.says('Exactly, if nothing gets in, nothing gets out');

mooleen.says('Nothing like what?');
randalf.says('Nothing deadly that wicked mind of yours ' +
             'decides to bring forth into existence');

mooleen.says('Oh come on... those were just drawings!!');

randalf.says(`Let's get Started With the Basics of OOP!`);
```

Let's get Started With The Basics of OOP!

Time to start raising your own army of objects! In these introductory chapters you'll learn the fundamentals of object-oriented programming in JavaScript. In each chapter we'll traverse each one of the classical pillars of OOP: *encapsulation, inheritance* and *polymorphism*.

We'll start by taking a look at the principle of *encapsulation* and how to create objects through both *object initializers* and *constructor functions*. You'll also refresh the techniques that you have at your disposal to achieve *information hiding*. We will wrap the chapter with a comparison between *object initializers, factories* and *constructor functions* in a attempt to understand their strengths and weaknesses.

In the coming chapters you'll learn about JavaScript's *prototypical inheritance* and *polymorphism*, and understand how both differ from what we are accustomed to in C#.

Encapsulation: Creating Objects in JavaScript

The principle of encapsulation consists in putting data and the functions that operate it together into a single component. In some definitions it includes the principle of *information hiding* (or *data hiding*), that is, the ability to hide implementation details from consumers by defining a clear boundary or interface that is safe to use from a consumer perspective.

Information hiding allows the author to change hidden implementation details without breaking the contract established by the public interface of a component. Thus both author and consumer can continue developing without getting in the way of each other:

The author can tweak its implementation and the consumer can rest assured that the author won't break her code.

In this chapter, we will separate *encapsulation* from *data hiding* because JavaScript uses different approaches to solve each one of these problems.

Let's start with **encapsulation**. JavaScript provides different strategies for achieving *encapsulation*:

- object initializers
- constructor functions
- ES6 classes

We will now take a look at the first two, and we will devote a whole chapter to *ES6 classes* later in the book.

Object Initializers

 Experiment JavaScriptmancer!!
You can experiment with all examples in this chapter directly within this jsBin[29] or downloading the source code from GitHub[30].

In **JavaScript-mancy: Getting Started** (the first book of the series) you learned the intricacies of using *object initializers* (also known as *object literals*).

---

[29] http://bit.ly/javascriptmancy-oop-fundamentals-encapsulation
[30] https://github.com/vintharas/javascriptmancy-code-samples

Didn't Read JavaScript-mancy: Getting Started?

Don't you worry, I got you covered. I have added the whole chapter of object initializers including the ES2015 features in the first appendix of this book. So if you haven't read it jump to the end of the book for a refresher of the basics of objects in JavaScript followed by a chapter of the quirky behavior of this.

Regardless, this section gives you a quick reminder of how to use *object initializers*.

Using object initializers to create new objects is dead easy:

```
// creating a simple object
let object = {};
console.log(object);
// => [object Object] { ... }
```

And so is defining any number of properties and methods within your objects:

```
// you can create objects with any number
// of properties and methods
let minion = {
  hp: 10,
  name: 'minion',
  toString(){ return this.name;}
};

console.log(minion);
// => [object Object] {
//   hp: 10,
//   name: "minion",
//   toString: function toString() {
```

```
14  //    return this.name;
15  // }
16  // }
```

You can even augment objects after they have been created:

```
1  minion.armor = 'chain mail';
2  console.log(minion.armor);
3  // => chain mail
```

And use **factory functions** to aid object creation:

```
1  // we can use factories to ease object creation
2  function createMinion(name, hp=10){
3    return {
4      hp: hp,
5      name: name,
6      toString: function(){ return this.name;}
7    };
8  }
```

Relying on the new ES6 short-hand syntax, we can rewrite our factory functions in a more concise manner:

```
1  // we can use factories to ease object creation
2  function createMinion(name, hp=10){
3    return {
4      hp,
5      name,
6      toString(){ return this.name;}
7    };
8  }
```

After you are sasistified with your factory function you can just call it to create a new object and use it as you please:

Summoning Fundamentals: Encapsulation and Information Hiding

```
let orc = createMinion(/* name */ 'orc', /* hp */ 100);

console.log(orc);
// => [object Object] {
//   hp: 100,
//   name: "orc",
//   etc...
// }
```

In addition to *object initializers*, there's another way to create objects in JavaScript that will feel more familiar to a C# developer: **constructor functions** and the new operator.

Constructor Functions and the New Operator

In the previous section we saw how to create an object using an *object initializer*:

```
let object = {};
```

We can achieve the same result by applying the new operator to a constructor function. An equivalent statement to the one above using this approach would look like this:

```
let anotherObject = new Object();

console.log(anotherObject);
// => [object Object] { ... }
```

While the Object function let's you create empty objects, you can apply the new operator on any function in JavaScript to instantiate new objects of your own devise.

Functions that are called with the new operator are known as **constructor functions**:

```
function Minion(name='minion', hp=10){
  this.hp = hp;
  this.name = name;
  this.toString = () => this.name;
};

let anotherMinion = new Minion();
console.log(anotherMinion);
// => [object Object] {
//   hp: 10,
//   name: "minion",
//   toString: () => this.name
// }
```

The first thing to highlight in this example is that, while in C# we use the `new` operator on classes to instantiate new objects, in JavaScript we use it on *constructor functions*. The *constructor function* is, in a way, acting as a **custom type** and a **class definition** since it defines the properties and methods of the object that will be created when we invoke it.

We can bring this point home using the `instaceof` operator. `instanceof` lets you verify whether an object has a given type[31]. Using the `anotherMinion` from the previous example we can quickly verify that it is indeed of type `Minion`:

```
console.log(`anotherMinion is a Minion: ` +
            `${anotherMinion instanceof Minion}`);
// => anotherMinion is a Minion: true

console.log(`anotherMinion is an Object: ` +
            `${anotherMinion instanceof Object}`);
// => anotherMinion is an Object: true
```

Now take a moment to examine the `Minion` *constructor function* and compare it with the *factory function* from the previous section. You will notice that they are a little bit different. In the *factory function*

---

[31] It works both for custom and built-in types. So ya know.

we create an object via an *object initializer* and then return it. In this example, however, there is no object being created nor returned as far as we can see. *What is going on here? How does an object get created then?*

It all comes down to the new operator. When you use the new operator on a function there are several things happening in the background that are hidden from our sight:

1. First an **empty object is created and set as this for the function being executed**. That is, the this keyword refers to a new object that has just been created.
2. If the constructor function has a *prototype* the new object is given that prototype (more about prototypes in the next chapter).
3. After that, the function body is invoked. In the example above, we augment the object with some properties: hp, name and toString.
4. **Finally the value of this is returned**. This is done implicitly without us needing to do anything. And, as you can see from our examples above, the object is created successfully.

But what happens if we return something explicitly from a *constructor function*? Well, it depends on what you return. Let's say that we try to return a primitive type like a string:

Summoning Fundamentals: Encapsulation and Information Hiding

```javascript
// if you try to return a primitive it is ignored
function MinionOrBanana(name='minion', hp=10){
  this.hp = hp;
  this.name = name;
  return 'banana';
}

let isItAMinionOrIsItABanana = new MinionOrBanana();
console.log(isItAMinionOrIsItABanana)
// => [object Object] {
//   hp: 10,
//   name: "minion"
// }
```

In this example above we can see how if we try to return a string explicitly the JavaScript runtime will completely ignore it an return the constructed object (this). This is also applicable to all primitive types.

What happens if we return an object?

```javascript
// if you try to return an object it is returned
// instead of the `this` object
function MinionOrBanana(name='minion', hp=10){
  this.hp = hp;
  this.name = name;
  return {name: 'banana'};
}

let isItAMinionOrIsItABanana = new MinionOrBanana();
console.log(isItAMinionOrIsItABanana)
// => [object Object] {
//   name: "banana"
// }
```

If you try to return an object explicitly (like the {name: 'banana'} above) this object will be returned and your original object (the one injected as this to the *constructor function*) will be ignored.

JavaScript Arcana: Returning Explicitly from Constructor Functions

Returning expressions explicitly from *constructor functions* behaves in mysterious and hidden ways. If you return a primitive type such as a `string` or a `number` it will be ignored. If you return an object it will be returned from the *constructor function* and the original object (the one injected as `this` in the function) will be lost in the fringes between space and time. In general, if you want your constructor functions to behave in a way akin to constructors in classical inheritance, prefer not to return anything from them.

You may have noticed that I called the *constructor function* `Minion` using uppercase instead of following the common JavaScript naming convention of using camel case (`minion`). *Why is that?*. Using uppercase to name *constructor functions* is a popular convention in the JavaScript community as a means to differentiate them from other functions. This convention is a way to tell the consumers of an API that they should use the `new` operator when calling these functions instead of just calling them outright. But *why do we need to differentiate them? Aren't all of them functions anyway?*

Well, consider what happens if we call a *constructor function* without the `new` operator:

```
let yetAnotherMinion = Minion();
console.log(yetAnotherMinion);
// => undefined
```

Hmm, no object is being returned... But why? Can you remember what happened with `this` when a function is called without a context? Yes! That's right! Whenever we call a function without a context the value of `this` is set to the `Window` object (unless you are in `strict` mode in which case it will be `undefined`). What is *happening here then?* By calling a *constructor function* without the new operator the function is evaluated in the context of the `Window` object and instead of creating a new object, we have just extended the `Window` object with two new properties `hp` and `name`. Ouch!

```
console.log(window.hp);
// => 10
console.log(window.name);
// => 'minion'
```

If we had made the same mistake in *strict mode* we would've immediately received an error that would've alerted us much faster that something was terribly wrong:

```
let yetAnotherMinion = Minion();
// => TypeError: Cannot set property 'hp' of undefined
// wat
```

JavaScript Arcana: Calling a Constructor Function Without The New Operator

When you call a *constructor function* without the new operator you run the risk of evaluating it in the context of the `Window` object or undefined in the case of *strict mode*.

So this is the reason why we usually use the uppercase notation when writing *constructor fuctions*. We want to avoid unsuspecting developers from forgetting the new operator and causing weird side-effects or errors in their programs.

But conventions are not a very reliable thing, are they? Wouldn't it be better to have a foolproof way to protect our constructor functions so that even if we forget to use the new operator they'll still work?

Summoning Fundamentals: Encapsulation and Information Hiding　　37

We humans are prone to errors. Whenever you find your colleagues or yourself making mistakes consider how you can prevent these from happening by providing a **path of least resistance to the right solution**. This can be done by automating repetitive tasks, setting up tools to highlight problems early in the development process, etc...

In this particular case we can make our *constructor functions* more sturdy by following this pattern:

```
function MinionSafe(name='minion', hp=10){
  'use strict';
  if (!this) return new MinionSafe(name, hp);

  this.name = name;
  this.hp = hp;
}
```

And now it doesn't matter how we call the *constructor function*. Call it with new:

```
console.log('using new operator: ', new MinionSafe());
// => [object Object] {
//   hp: 10,
//   name: "minion"
// }
```

Call it without:

```
console.log('using function call: ', MinionSafe());
// => [object Object] {
//   hp: 10,
//   name: "minion"
// }
```

And it will work as expected. Great! But can we improve it? Wouldn't it be nice if we didn't have to write the guard clause for every single constructor function we create?

Functional programming to the rescue! We can define a `safeConstructor` function that represents an abstraction of the guard clause and which can be composed with any constructor function of our choosing:

```javascript
function safeConstructor(constructorFn) {
  return function() {
    return new constructorFn(...arguments); // ES6
    // return new (constructorFn.bind.apply(null, arguments); // ES5
  }
}
```

The `safeConstructor` function takes a *constructor* as argument (`constructorFn`) and returns a new function that ensures that the `new` operator is always called regardless of the circumstances. You can think of this new function as an improved or augmented *constructor*.

From now on we can reuse this function to guard any of the *constructor functions* in our application:

```javascript
// function Minion(name='minion', hp=10){
//    etc...
// }
let SafeMinion = safeConstructor(Minion);
```

By composing `safeConstructor` with the `Minion` *constructor function* we obtain a new function `SafeMinion` that will work even if we forget to use the `new` operator:

```javascript
console.log(`using function: ${SafeMinion('orc', 110)}`);
// => using function: [object Object] etc...
console.log(`using new operator: ${new SafeMinion('pirate', 50)}`);
// => "using new operator: [object Object] etc..."
```

Enjoyed the Functional Programming Bit?

Functional programming is awesome! Once you dip your feet in the forbidden fountain of functional programming and get a feel for it you won't be able to stop. If you've enjoyed what you've seen thus far, then prepare for the next book in the series that will guide you through the mystical path of the functional programeer.

 ES6 Classes Protects Thy Constructors

A cool thing about ES6 classes is that they improve the developer ergonomics of writing class-like code in JavaScript. If you use ES6 classes, the JavaScript runtime will throw an error if you forget to use the new operator to call a constructor function. Yey!

Data Hiding in JavaScript

In **JavaScript-mancy: Getting Started** you learned two patterns to achieve data hiding in JavaScript: *closures* and *ES6 symbols*. Of these two, only *closures* provide real data privacy whilst *ES6 symbols* make accessing "private" data less convenient.

 Can't Quite Remember How Data Hiding Works?

It's OK! Take a look at the appendix towards the end of the book for a refresher of the basics of objects and data hiding in JavaScript.

Since *constructor functions* are just functions, you can take advantage of both *closures* and *ES6 symbols* to create private properties and methods. Using *closures* is as easy as declaring variables in your *function constructor* body and referencing them from the methods that you want to expose:

```
// just like with factory methods you can implement data privacy
// using closures with constructor functions
function WalkingMinion(name='minion', hp=10){
   let position = {x: 0, y: 0};

   this.hp = hp;
   this.name = name;
   this.toString = () => this.name;

   // this function is a closure
   // that encloses the position variable
   this.walksTo = (x,y) => {
      console.log(`${this} walks from (${position.x}, ${position.y}) \
                   to (${x}, ${y})`);
      position.x = x;
      position.y = y;
   };

};
```

In this example we have a `WalkingMinion` *constructor function* that we can use to create many teeny tiny walking minions. Within it, we declare a variable `position` that represents the minion position in a two-dimensional space and a `walksTo` method that allows the minion to move around in this space. The `walksTo` method is a closure because it encloses the value of the `position` variable.

If you take a close look at the *constructor function* you'll realize that the `position` variable is not a property of the object being created. That is, we never augment the `this` object with the `position` property. As a result, the minions that we create using this function will, for all intents and purposes, have a private property `position`

Summoning Fundamentals: Encapsulation and Information Hiding

and limit any consumer interaction with it to using the `walksTo` method. **The beauty of encapsulation lets us call this method to command each minion to walk without revealing the actual implementation of the positioning system** (which in this case is just an object with x and y properties).

Indeed if we instantiate a `walkingMinion` using the above constructor we can see how there's no way to access the `position` property:

```
let walkingMinion = new WalkingMinion();
console.log(walkingMinion.position);
// => undefined
```

The `position` property is not really part of the object itself but it's effectively part of its **internal state** as the variable has been enclosed or captured by the `walksTo` function. This means that the `walksTo` method can read or update the state of the `position` property as demonstrated below:

```
walkingMinion.walksTo(2, 2)
// => minion walks from (0, 0) to (2, 2)
walkingMinion.walksTo(3,3)
// => minion walks from (2, 2) to (3, 3)
```

In addition to achieving data hiding with *closures* you can use *ES6 symbols*:

```
function FlyingMinion(name='minion', hp=10){
  let position = Symbol('position');

  this.hp = hp;
  this.name = name;
  this.toString = () => this.name;

  this[position] = {x: 0, y: 0};
  this.fliesTo = (x,y) => {
    console.log(`${this} flies like the wind from (${this[position].\
x}, ` +
                `${this[position].y}) to (${x}, ${y})`);
    this[position].x = x;
    this[position].y = y;
  };
};
```

And attain a similar behavior to that we saw with *closures*. That is, there's no apparent way to access the `position` property from outside the `FlyingMinion` object:

```
// again you cannot access the position property (almost)
let flyingMinion = new FlyingMinion();
console.log(flyingMinion.position);
// => undefined
```

But we can do it through its interface via the `fliesTo` method:

```
flyingMinion.fliesTo(1,1);
// => minion flies like the wind from (0, 0) to (1, 1)
flyingMinion.fliesTo(3,3);
// => minion flies like the wind from (1, 1) to (3, 3)
```

Notice that even though *ES6 symbols* give the appearance of privacy, they don't offer true privacy. You can always use the methods `Object.getOwnPropertySymbols` or `Reflect.ownKeys` to retrieve the symbols from an object and thus its *"private"* properties. Because of this, **prefer using closures over symbols**, you get true data hiding with less code.

Object Initializers vs Constructor Functions

Object initializers	Constructor functions
Easy to write, convenient and readable	Little bit more complicated. They look like normal functions but you need to implement them in a different way since the new operator will inject a new object as context of the function (this)
One-off creation of objects	You can reuse them to create many objects
They only support information hiding via ES6 symbols	They support information hiding via ES6 symbols and closures
Very simple syntax to define getters (read-only properties) and setters	The only way to define getters and setters is using low level Object methods like Object.defineProperty
You don't create subtypes and can't use instanceof, but it is much better to rely on polymorphism than checking types	Allows the creation of custom types and enables the use of instanceof
	Calling a constructor function without the new operator can cause bugs and unwanted side-effects if you don't take measures to allow it

Object Factories vs Constructor Functions

When you combine *object initializers* with factories you get all the benefits from both *object initializers* and *constructor functions* with none of the weaknesses of *constructor functions*:

Object Initializers + Factories	Constructor functions
Easy to write, convenient and readable. Factory functions really behave like any other function, no need to worry about `this`.	Little bit more complicated. They look like normal functions but you need to implement them in a different way since the `new` operator will inject a new object as context of the function (`this`).
You can reuse them to create many objects.	You can reuse them to create many objects.
They support information hiding via *ES6 symbols* and closures.	They support information hiding via *ES6 symbols* and closures.
Very simple syntax to define getters (read-only properties) and setters.	The only way to define getters and setters is using low level Object methods like Object.defineProperty.
You don't create subtypes and can't use `instanceof`, but it is much better to rely on polymorphism than checking types.	Allows the creation of custom types and enables the use of `instanceof`.
Factory functions work just like any other function. No need to use `new` and thus no need to remember to use it or guard from forgetting it. They are very easy to compose with other functions.	Calling a constructor function without the `new` operator can cause bugs and unwanted side-effects if you don't take measures to allow it.

Concluding

In this chapter you learned about the first piece of JavaScript Object Oriented Programming, **encapsulation**, and how you can achieve it using *object initializers*, *factory functions* and *constructor functions*.

Object initializers resemble C# *object literals*. They are very straightforward to use and very readable, but you can only create one-off objects with them and they only allow for *information hiding* through ES6 symbols (which is just slightly better than convention-based *information hiding*).

You can enhance your *object initializers* by wrapping them in *factory functions*. Factory functions give you the ability to create many objects of the same type and true *information hiding* via closures.

Finally, you can use *constructor functions* as a method of encapsulation. A *constructor function* lets you define custom types with properties and methods of your own choosing. We achieve that by augmenting the object (this) that is passed to the function when it is called with the new operator. Because constructors are functions, they support *information hiding* with both ES6 symbols and closures. At the same time, they behave slightly differently than normal functions because they expect to be called with the new operator and have a this object to augment. This means that if they are called as regular functions they may cause bugs and have unexpected side-effects. We can guard against this weakness by implementing a guard for when a constructor is called directly without the new operator.

In the next chapter you'll discover the next piece of JavaScript Object Oriented Programming: **prototypical inheritance**.

```
/*
    Mooleen weaves a spell that summons a malformed
    sheep with two heads and six legs of diverse lengths
*/

randalf.looksPained();
randalf.says('Great job! You almost got that sheep right!');
rat.says('Super job indeed master!');

mooleen.says('Thank you!');
mooleen.says(`It's actually a sheep 2.0`);
mooleen.says(`A better, improved sheep`);
mooleen.says(`Double the brains, double the speed`);

/*
 * The sheep v2.0 speedily jumps over the plateau chasm
 * into the lava below
 */
sheepV20.says('beeeeeeeeh');

mooleen.says('ehm');
mooleen.says(`let's keep practicing`);
```

Exercises

 ### Experiment JavaScriptmancer!

You can experiment with these exercises and some possible solutions in this jsFiddle[32] or downloading the source code from GitHub[33].

---

[32] http://bit.ly/javascriptmancy-oop-fundamentals-encapsulation-exercises
[33] https://github.com/vintharas/javascriptmancy-code-samples

Summoning Fundamentals: Encapsulation and Information Hiding

 Create a New Sheep 3.0!!

Mooleen is about to try out a new version of the Sheep! Help her by creating the weirdest sheep you can imagine **using an object initializer**. Free your creativity! At the very least it should satisfy the following code snippet:

```
sheep.describe();
// => You look at what you think is a sheep
sheep.baa();
// => 'Baaaaaaaaa'
// => The sheep makes a wailing sound vaguely resembling bleating
//    that gives you goose bumps
sheep.goesTo(1, 1);
// => The sheep slowly moves to position (1,1)
```

Solution

```
mooleen.says(`Ok... let me see... what about this version?`);

var leglessSheep = {
  position: {x:0, y:0},
  toString: function(){
    return `You look at what you think is a sheep. ` +
      `It's hard to be sure though was it's a legless ` +
      `lump on the ground`;
  },
  describe: function(){ return console.log(this.toString());
  },
  baa: function(){
    console.log(`'Baaaaaaaaa'
The sheep makes a wailing sound vaguely resembling bleating
that gives you goose bumps
    `);
  },
  goesTo: function(x,y){
    this.position.x = x;
    this.position.y = y;
    console.log(`The sheep slowly crawls to position (${x},${y})`);
  },
```

```
23    };
24
25    mooleen.says('Voila!');
26
27    leglessSheep.describe();
28    // => You look at what you think is a sheep. It's hard to be sure
29    //     though was it's a legless lump on the ground
30    leglessSheep.baa();
31    // => 'Baaaaaaaaa'
32    //     The sheep makes a wailing sound vaguely resembling bleating
33    //     that gives you goose bumps
34    leglessSheep.goesTo(1,1);
35    //=> The sheep slowly crawls to position (1,1)
36
37    randalf.says(`That's the saddest sheep I've ever seen`);
38    mooleen.says(`It's incredibly light and suited for stealth missions`\
39    );
40    rat.says('Look at that crawl! Majestic!');
```

And Remember! With ES2015 You Can Use Shorthand Syntax!

You could rewrite the sheep above like this:

```
1    let leglessSheep = {
2      legs: 0,
3      position: {x:0, y:0},
4      // collapsed implementation which would remain the same
5      toString(){ ... },
6      describe(){ ... }
7      baa(){ ... },
8      goesTo(x, y){ ... },
9    };
```

Good try! But Can you Do Better!?

Now try again using a factory function. You can call it createSheep and it should return a new version of a sheep with an arbitrary number of legs and position:

```
1   var sheep = createSheep(/* legs */ 5, /* x */ 1, /* y */ 2);
```

It should satisfy the same interface as the sheep in the previous exercise.

Solution

```
1   function createSheep(legs, x, y){
2     return {
3       position: {x:x, y:y},
4       legs: legs,
5       toString: function(){
6         return `You look at what you think is a sheep. It has ${legs} \
7   legs`;
8       },
9       describe: function(){ return console.log(this.toString());},
10      baa: function(){
11        console.log(`'Baaaaaaaaa'
12  The sheep makes a wailing sound vaguely resembling bleating
13  that gives you goose bumps
14        `);
15      },
16      goesTo: function(x,y){
17        this.position.x = x;
18        this.position.y = y;
19        console.log(`The sheep slowly goes to position (${x},${y})`);
20      },
21    };
22  }
23
24  var newAbominationSheep = createSheep(50, 2, 2);
25  newAbominationSheep.describe();
26  // => You look at what you think is a sheep. It has 50 legs
27
28  randalf.says('Ok what is the purpose of a sheep having 50 legs?');
29  mooleen.says('Reliability, have you heard about ' +
```

```
30              ' the concept of fault tolerance?');
31   mooleen.says('Even wounded, this sheep will be able ' +
32                'to keep going and crush our enemies');
33   rat.says('Boooya!');
```

And Remember! With ES2015 You Can Use Shorthand Syntax Also In Properties!

You could rewrite the sheep above like this:

```
 1   function createSheep(legs, x, y){
 2     return {
 3       // short-hand syntax for properties
 4       position: {x, y},
 5       legs,
 6       // short-hand syntax for methods
 7       toString(){ ... },
 8       describe(){ ... },
 9       baa(){ ... },
10       goesTo(x,y){ ... }
11     };
12   }
```

Three Sheeps' a Charm!

Ok. And now one last time, use a *constructor function* to create a new custom type that represents a sheep.

```
 1   var sheep = new Sheep(/* legs */ 5, /* x */ 1, /* y */ 2);
```

It should satisfy the same interface as the sheep in the previous exercises.

Solution

```javascript
function Sheep(legs, x, y){
  this.legs = legs;
  this.position = {x:x, y:y};
  this.toString = function(){
    return `You look at a beautiful sheep! It has ${this.legs} legs`;
  };
  this.describe = function(){
    return console.log(this.toString());
  };
  this.baa = function(){
    console.log(`'Baaaaaaaaa'
The sheep makes a beautiful musical sound reminiscent
of spring and wildberries.
`);
  };
  this.goesTo = function(x,y){
    this.position.x = x;
    this.position.y = y;
    console.log(`The sheep promptly goes to position (${x},${y})`);
  };
}

var theUltimateSheep = new Sheep(4, 0, 0);
theUltimateSheep.describe();
// => You look at a beautiful sheep! It has 4 legs
theUltimateSheep.baa();
// => 'Baaaaaaaaa'
//    The sheep makes a beautiful musical sound reminiscent
//    of spring and wildberries.

mooleen.says("I think I'm starting to get the gist of it");
randalf.says("Excellent...");
rat.says("Superb!");
randalf.says("... but...");
rat.says("but!?");

randalf.says("You have all the sheep internals exposed");
randalf.says("Take a look at this");
theUltimateSheep.legs = 0;

randalf.says("Your sheep has no legs now");
randalf.says("And I can even make it explode");
theUltimateSheep.position = undefined;
try {
```

```
      theUltimateSheep.goesTo(1,1);
   } catch(e){
      console.log("sheep explodes to teeny tiny pieces");
   }
   randalf.says('Oh yeah, that happened');
   randalf.says('You have to be careful and disallow for' +
                  'malicious or ignorant javascriptmancer from ' +
                  'breaking your creations');
```

 Protect Thy Sheep!!

Use whichever data hiding technique you want to protect your sheep from malicious or ignorant tampering.

Solution

```
function SuperSheep(legs, x, y){
   var legs = legs,
       position = {x: x, y: y};

   this.toString = function(){
      // this is a closure that encloses the leg variable
      return `You look at a beautiful sheep! It has ${legs} legs`;
   };
   this.describe = function(){
      return console.log(this.toString());
   };
   this.baa = function(){
      console.log(`'Baaaaaaaaa'
The sheep makes a beautiful musical sound reminiscent
of spring and wildberries.
      `);
   };
   this.goesTo = function(x,y){
      // this is a closure that encloses the position variable
      position.x = x;
      position.y = y;
```

Summoning Fundamentals: Encapsulation and Information Hiding

```
22          console.log(`The sheep promptly goes to position (${x},${y})`);
23      };
24  }
25
26  var superSheep = new SuperSheep(4, 0, 0);
27
28  mooleen.says('What about this one?');
29  randalf.says('Hmm let me see...');
30
31  superSheep.legs = 100;
32  superSheep.describe();
33  // => You look at a beautiful sheep! It has 4 legs
34  randalf.says('Good job...');
35
36  superSheep.position = undefined;
37  superSheep.goesTo(1,1);
38  // => The sheep promptly goes to position (1,1)
39  randalf.says('Good. Solid. Job');
40
41  mooleen.says('haha hell yeah');
42  rat.applaudes();
```

Summoning Fundamentals: Prototypical Inheritance

Don't Repeat Yourself

> - Tunh Ynad
> Guildmaster School of Pragmatics,
> Principles

```
 1  /*
 2   * The world. We dive into it through a sea of clouds,
 3   * a majestic endless mountain range,
 4   * a white peaked mountain, down into the rock, into the
 5   * entrails of the earth. Magma, the world's own blood and
 6   * life essence surrounds you, magma and... Sheep?!
 7   */
 8
 9  randalf.says("And that's the 999 sheep... Excellent!
10              You've clearly mastered the principle
11              of encapsulation");
12  randalf.says("Now let's say that you want to expand
13               your army to minions other than sheep");
14
15  rat.says('Something mighty like a badger');
16  mooleen.says('... A badger?');
17  rat.says('Yeah, a badger, they can be awfully mean');
18
19  randalf.says("Well the more creatures you command,
20     the more similarities you'll find between them.
21     And since you have a limited amount of breaths left
22     on this rock, you'll want to save them for what's
23     truly important");
24
25  mooleen.says('like eating chocolate...');
26  rat.says('...or going to a spa');
27  randalf.says('... or pondering about the life,
28               the universe and everything...')
29
30  mooleen.says('So, how do you that?')
31
32  randalf.says("You Don't repeat yourself.
33               Inheritance!");
```

You Don't Repeat Yourself. Inheritance!

In the last chapter you learned how you can achieve *encapsulation* in JavaScript by using **object initializers, factory functions** and **constructor functions**. Object initializers should be pretty familiar to you because C# has object literals, factory functions are comparable to C# factory methods and constructor functions are not so different from a class constructor. Things started getting a little bit strange when you discovered how to achieve data hiding through **closures** and **ES6 symbols** both concepts pretty foreign to C# [34]. The next step towards OOP badassery is **inheritance** and beware because things are about to become even weirder.

In C#, you can achieve inheritance by deriving from a concrete class, an abstract class or by implementing an interface. Either way, **inheritance is a mechanism of code reuse and polymorphism**. On one hand you use inheritance any time you want to share a piece of behavior across several classes to avoid code duplication. On the other, you use it to achieve flexible and extensible object oriented designs where a specific interface [35] is replaced at runtime by a concrete implementation.

Inheritance in JavaScript differs greatly from what you are accustomed to in C# and that's mainly due to two reasons:

*First, JavaScript doesn't depend on inheritance to implement polymorphism. It is a dynamic language after all, and gets by with duck typing[36]. This means that, in JavaScript, inheritance is mainly a technique for code reuse[37]. * Second, and even more important, JavaScript supports another flavor of inheritance very different from traditional or class-based inheritance: **Prototypical Inheritance.**

Prototypical Inheritance you say?

Yes! JavaScript exhibits a special kind of inheritance where the blueprint for an object is actually - *drumroll* - another object. This role of acting like a blueprint is traditionally played by the almighty class in C# and other statically typed languages. In languages

---

[34] Although closures do exist in C# they are not used as a mechanism of data hiding... if you do use them for that purpose, respect, you're a trendsetter...

[35] In this case I use interface in a loose sense to denote interfaces, abstract classes or even concrete classes that are a generalized version of more specific classes.

[36] We'll look into more into duck typing and polymorphism in the next chapter.

[37] And, in some cases, even as a means of memory optimization.

with prototypical inheritance like JavaScript, it is performed by the humble object. Within the context of prototypical inheritance everything is about objects being modeled after other objects which are henceforth called **prototypes**. In this universe of objects, any single object can be based on a prototype, inherit all its properties and methods, and then have its own specific properties and methods on top. There's no need for classes.

So, if you only need objects, **how does JavaScript prototypical inheritance stack against C# classical inheritance?**

Classical Inheritance vs Prototypical Inheritance

At a high level, this is how C# classical inheritance compares to JavaScript prototypical inheritance:

C# Classical Inheritance	JavaScript - Prototypical Inheritance
Focuses on classes	Focuses on objects
Classes cannot be modified at runtime: You define a class with a series of methods and properties and you cannot add new methods or properties, nor modify the existing ones at runtime.	Prototypes are more flexible and extensible than classes. They can be immutable but you also have the option to extend them or modify them at runtime. When you do so, you affect all objects that inherit that prototype.
You have classes, abstract classes, interfaces, objects, override, virtual, sealed, etc.	You have mainly objects. Depending on your preferences you may have classes, constructor functions, factories, etc. But overall it is a simpler model that requires less elements and rules.

C# Classical Inheritance	JavaScript - Prototypical Inheritance
C# classes promote rigid taxonomies. This requires a lot of additional code and artifice to come to good designs.	JavaScript prototypical inheritance is more flexible. Composing objects is very straightforward.
C# doesn't support multiple inheritance	JavaScript lets you compose an object with as many prototypes as you want achieving something similar to multiple inheritance.
C# has great support for information hiding	JavaScript does information hiding via closures and symbols.

Where C# focuses on classes and creating taxonomies, JavaScript focuses on objects and can achieve a class-free inheritance that is more flexible and extensible than its C# counterpart. Where C# classes are immutable at runtime, JavaScript prototypes can be augmented or modified at any point in time. Where C# provides a lot of keywords and constructs that let you be very thorough and explicit about how someone can interact with a class of your creation, JavaScript does away with these concepts in favor of a simpler inheritance model. And where C# provides a pretty clear and opinionated path on how to do inheritance, JavaScript gives you so much freedom that it can be daunting at times.

Now that we've seen the differences between the inheritance models in C# and JavaScript, let's dive into prototypical inheritance and find out what it means in terms of actual code.

What About ES6 Classes?

If you have had the opportunity to look at ES6 classes you may be wondering: *This looks like class-based inheritance, doesn't it?* Well the syntax is a little bit deceptive because although ES6 classes really look like C# classes the reality is very different: **ES6 Classes are just syntactic sugar over the existing prototypical inheritance model.**

We will dive deeper into ES6 classes later in the book and you'll also be able to learn the equivalent of a ES6 class in plain class-less JavaScript code.

JavaScript Prototypical Inheritance

We can distinguish between two types of *prototypical inheritance*:

The first one and most common is **delegation-based inheritance**. In delegation-based inheritance object and prototype establish what is known as a **prototypical chain** or **prototype chain** where property or method calls are dispatched or delegated from the object to the prototype.

The second is **concatenative inheritance**. With this brand of inheritance an object is merged with a prototype and thus gains its properties and methods. The merging of object and prototype consists in copying or concatenating the properties of the prototype into the object.

But, **what are object prototypes?**

Object Prototypes

Any object can be a prototype. What makes an object a prototype is just another object that *specifies* it as its prototype. It is as simple as that.

The way that you specify that an object is a prototype depends on the method you use to create new objects:

- Object initializers
- Object.create
- Constructor functions

Let's review each of these methods in turn:

Object Prototypes with Object Initializers

 Experiment JavaScriptmancer!!
You can experiment with all examples in this chapter directly within this jsBin[38] or downloading the source code from GitHub[39].

When you use *object initializers* you can define a *prototype* via the __proto__ property. If you set this property in an object O to another object P, P effectively becomes a *prototype*.

For instance, if we have the `minion` from previous examples:

```
let minion = {
  hp: 10,
  name: 'minion',
  toString(){
    return this.name;
  }
};
```

---

[38] http://bit.ly/javascriptmancy-oop-fundamentals-inheritance
[39] https://github.com/vintharas/javascriptmancy-code-samples

And then we devise a new spell to summon a giantScorpion. We can set minion as a prototype of giantScorpion by using its __proto__ property (*available from ES6* [40]):

```
let giantScorpion = {
  // here we set the minion as prototype
  '__proto__': minion,
  name: 'scorpion',
  stings() {
    console.log(`${this} pierces your shoulder with its venomous sti\
ng`);
  }
}
```

And TaDa! Now minion is the prototype of giantScorpion, that is, there is a *prototypical inheritance* relationship between them. If we try to access properties that only exist in minion via giantScorpion we will be able to see the *prototypical chain* in action:

```
// access a prototype property via prototype chain
console.log(`giant scorpion has ${giantScorpion.hp} hit points`);
// => giant scorpion has 10 hit points
```

Indeed we can see how giantScorpion, which doesn't have an hp property itself, is accessing the hp property of its prototype. And *what happens with the name property that is shared by both?*

---

[40]The __proto__ property has been available in some browsers prior to ES6 but it wasn't part of the ECMA standard until ES6. Because it not being part of any standard and thus not having a specific defined behavior it was very unreliable to use. With ES6 you can use it with your object initializers as it makes the prototype chain very apparent and easy to understand. __proto__ only works on browsers, if you are working with node you can use Object.create and follow a very similar flow.

```
// if a property is shared between an object and its prototype
// there's no need to traverse the prototype chain
// the nearest property wins
giantScorpion.stings();
// => scorpion pierces your shoulder with its venomous sting
```

In this example above, we call the `stings` method that, in turn, calls the `toString` method which returns `this.name`. Because the name variable exists in the `giantScorpion` object, there's no need to traverse the *prototypical chain*. As a result, the property `giantScorpion.name` is used to generate the string representation of `giantScorpion` and we get `"scorpion pierces your shoulder..."` (instead of `"minion pierces your shoulder..."`).

From here on you have two options in regards to how to use your prototype: You can use one prototype instance per object instance or share a prototype across many objects. While there's nothing stopping you from having one prototype per object, the real benefits of inheritance in terms of code reuse come from sharing the same prototype across several objects:

```
let smallScorpion = {
  // here we set the minion as prototype
  '__proto__': minion,
  name: 'small scorpion',
  stings() {
    console.log(`${this} pierces your shoulder with its tiny venomou\
s sting`);
  }
};

let giantSpider = {
  // here we set the minion as prototype
  '__proto__': minion,
  name: 'giant spider',
  launchWeb() {
    console.log(`${this} launches a sticky web and immobilizes you`)\
;
  }
};
```

In these examples, the properties and methods in the `minion` prototype are contained within a single object. These properties are shared between the `giantScorpion`, `smallScorpion` and `giantSpider` objects by virtue of the prototypical chain. Whereas if we ignored inheritance we would need to define and allocate them in each specific derived object with the additional memory footprint.

You may be wondering, *wait, the `minion` object had a property `hp`, doesn't that mean that all derived objects are coupled? That if I change `hp` in one object it will affect all others?*

Well spotted! When you use the same prototype with several objects you want to avoid storing state in your prototype. While having properties with primitive values such as numbers or strings won't couple your objects, having properties with arrays or objects will definitely couple them. This can be better illustrated with an example.

First, if you try to set the value of a property located in your prototype you'll just create a new property in the derived object. This newly created property will shadow that of the *prototype*. This is why properties with primitive values in *prototypes* act sort of as *initial or default values*:

```
console.log(`Small scorpion has ${smallScorpion.hp} hp`);
// => Small scorpion has 10 hp
smallScorpion.hp = 22;

console.log(`Small scorpion has ${smallScorpion.hp} hp`);
// => Small scorpion has 22 hp

console.log(`Giant Spider *still* has ${giantSpider.hp}`);
// => Giant spider still has 10 hp
```

If you however try to interact with prototype properties holding objects or arrays, all objects that share that prototype will be affected.

Imagine that you have a `minion` prototype with a `stomach` property represented by an array where your evil minion will digest its victims. Since all derived objects share `minion` as prototype all of them will hold the same reference to the `stomach` property. As a result, if `giantScorpion` eats an `elf` all of the sudden the `giantSpider` (and the `smallScorpion`) will show the same side-effect:

```javascript
// Imagine that a minion had a stomach
// what a wonderful thing stomachs are
minion.stomach = [];

// if a giant scorpion eats an elf
giantScorpion.stomach.push('elf')
// we can verify that yeah, it has eaten an elf
console.log(`giant scorpion stomach: ${giantScorpion.stomach}`);
// => giant scorpion stomach: elf

// but so has the spider
console.log(`giant spider stomach: ${giantSpider.stomach}`);
// => giant spider stomach: elf
// Waaaat!?
```

So the most common practice when you share a prototype across many objects is to only place methods in the prototype, and keep the state in the object itself.

By the by, did you notice something special in the previous example? We added a `stomach` property to `minion` and magically all objects with that prototype got access to that property.

A very interesting characteristic of prototypical inheritance is that it allows you to **augment all objects that share a prototype at runtime by augmenting the prototype itself**. This means that if we add a new method `eats` to `minion`:

Summoning Fundamentals: Prototypical Inheritance

```javascript
// A cool thing is that if you augment a prototype
// you automatically augment all its derived objects
minion.eats = function(food){
  console.log(`${this} eats ${food} and gains ${food.hp} health`);
  this.hp += food.hp;
};
```

All objects that have `minion` as prototype will automatically gain that method by virtue of the *prototype chain*:

```javascript
giantScorpion.eats({name: 'hamburger', hp: 10, toString(){return thi\
s.name}});
// => scorpion eats hamburger and gains 10 health

smallScorpion.eats({name: 'ice cream', hp: 1, toString(){return this\
.name}});
// => scorpion eats ice cream and gains 11 health

giantSpider.eats({name: 'goblin', hp: 100, toString(){return this.na\
me}});
// => giant spider eats hamburger and gains 100 health
```

Awesome right?

Object Prototypes with Object.Create or OLOO

`__proto__` is in an Annex of the ECMA standard and only works in browsers. If you don't feel comfortable with this, or you are working with JavaScript in another environment like *node.js* then you can use *ES5* `Object.create`.

`Object.create` lets you create a new object that will have as prototype another object of your choice. It works like a factory function for creating objects with a given *prototype*.

For instance, if we adapt this example from the previous section:

Summoning Fundamentals: Prototypical Inheritance

```
let giantScorpion = {
  // here we set the minion as prototype
  '__proto__': minion,
  name: 'scorpion',
  stings() {
    console.log(`${this} pierces your shoulder with its venomous sti\
ng`);
  }
}
```

To use `Object.create` instead of `__proto__` it would look like this:

```
// 1) create new object with minion as prototype
let newGiantScorpion = Object.create(minion);

// 2) augment object with desired properties
newGiantScorpion.name = 'scorpion';
newGiantScorpion.stings = function(){
    console.log(`${this} pierces your shoulder with its venomous sti\
ng`);
};
```

Just like in the case of the `__proto__` property, the result of this snippet of code is a new object `newGiantScorpion` that has two properties (`name` and `stings`) and the `minion` object as prototype.

You can achieve a more compact syntax if you use *ES6* `Object.assign`:

```
// 1) create new object with minion as prototype
let newGiantScorpion = Object.create(minion);

// 2) augment object with desired properties
Object.assign(newGiantScorpion,
    /* new giant scorpion properties */
    {
    name: 'scorpion',
    stings(){
        console.log(`${this} pierces your shoulder with its venomous sti\
ng`);
    }
};
```

Object.assign copies the properties from one (or several) objects into a target object of your choice (in this case newGiantScorpion).

Defining Prototypes with Constructor Functions

Defining prototypes with *constructor functions* works in a slightly different way than what we've seen thus far. Let's illustrate these differences with an example.

Imagine that we have a TeleportingMinion that can teletransport itself wherever it desires and is represented by a constructor function:

```
function TeleportingMinion(){
  let position = {x: 0, y: 0};

  this.teleportsTo = function(x, y){
    console.log(`${this} teleports from ` +
            `(${position.x}, ${position.y}) to (${x}, ${y})`);
    position.x = x;
    position.y = y;
  };

  this.healthReport = function(){
    console.log(`${this} has ${this.hp} health. It looks healthy.`);
  };
}
```

In this case, instead of using the __proto__ property, we assign the prototype minion to the prototype property of the constructor function:

```
// Remember, the minion object looked like this:
// let minion = {
//   hp: 10,
//   name: 'minion',
//   toString(){ return this.name;}
// };

TeleportingMinion.prototype = minion;
TeleportingMinion.prototype.constructor = TeleportingMinion;
```

From this point forward, every object that we create with this *constructor function* will have the `minion` object as prototype:

```
let oneCrazyTeleportingMinion = new TeleportingMinion();
oneCrazyTeleportingMinion.healthReport();
// => minion has 10 health. It looks healthy.

let anotherCrazyTeleportingMinion = new TeleportingMinion();
anotherCrazyTeleportingMinion.healthReport();
// => minion has 10 health. It looks healthy.
```

As you can appreciate in the example above, the `healthReport` method of these teleporting minions accesses the `hp` property of the original `minion` object through the prototypical chain.

You Can Also Use a New Object As Prototype

A common practice when setting the prototype of a constructor is to use a completely new object:

```
TeleportingMinion.prototype = Object.create(minion);
```

That is, instead of using `minion` directly, we create a new object that has `minion` as prototype. This object will now become the prototype of any new `TeleportingMinion` that we create in the future.

> But why follow this approach? What do we gain? The advantage of this technique is that we still have the `minion` object in our prototypical chain (so we can inherit all its methods) and, additionally, we gain the ability to augment the TeleportingMinion prototype without affecting the original `minion` prototype or any of its descendants.
>
> If we want to add a new behavior to all teleporting minions that normal minions shouldn't have, we only need to augment the teleporting minion prototype. If we want to add a new behavior to all minions regardless of their teleporting nature we can augment the original `minion` prototype as usual.

Creating Longer Prototype Chains

You should know that you are not limited to a one level deep *prototype chain* with just an object and a *prototype*. You can create big inheritance structures just like in C#.

Let's say that we want to create a `wizard`. We can make it inherit from the `TeleportingMinion` using the `__proto__` property:

```
let wizard = {
  '__proto__': new TeleportingMinion(),
  name: 'Evil wizard',
  castsFireballSpell(target){
    console.log(`${this} casts fireball spell `+
                `and obliterates ${target}`);
  }
};
```

Effectively establishing a *prototype chain* that looks like this:

```
wizard => teleportingMinion => minion
```

Where our new object `wizard` now inherits the behavior of both a `teleportingMinion` and a `minion` as you can appreciate in this example below:

```
// The wizard can cast fireballs
wizard.castsFireballSpell('sandwich');
// => Evil wizard casts fireball spell and obliterates sandwich
// damn that was my last sandwich

// It can teleport
wizard.teleportsTo(1,2);
// => Evil wizard teleports from (0, 0) to (1, 2)

// And it has hit points
wizard.healthReport();
// => Evil wizard has 10 health. It looks healthy.
```

And we can do the same with *constructor functions* like with this `Druid`:

```
function Druid(){
  this.name = 'Druid of the Forest';
  this.changesSkinIntoA = function(skin){
    console.log(`${this} changes his skin into a ${skin}`);
  }
}
```

Since this time we have a *construction function* in our hands, instead of using the __proto__ property we use `Druid.prototype`:

```
Druid.prototype = new TeleportingMinion();
Druid.prototype.constructor = Druid;
```

And create a *prototype chain* like this:

Summoning Fundamentals: Prototypical Inheritance

```
1  Druid => teleportingMinion => minion
```

Now any `druid` object that we instantiate using the `Druid` constructor function will inherit all its mighty abilities from `teleportingMinion` and `minion`:

```
1   let druid = new Druid();
2
3   // the druid can change skin
4   druid.changesSkinIntoA('wolf');
5   // => Druid of the Forest changes his skin into a wolf
6
7   // it can teleport
8   druid.teleportsTo(2,2);
9   // => Druid of the Forest teleports from (0, 0) to (2, 2)
10
11  // and has hit points
12  druid.healthReport();
13  // => Druid of the Forest has 10 health. It looks healthy.
```

What About Concatenative Protypical Inheritance?

In this first dive into OOP we are going to follow the most natural path for a C# developer coming to JavaScript. We have begun at the beginning: with prototypical inheritance. We'll continue by mimicking *classical inheritance* and from there we'll jump to *ES6 classes*. The flavor of prototypical inheritance that enables having a similar inheritance flow to that of classes is the delegation-based inheritance and that's why we have focused on it first.

We will come back to *concatenative inheritance* and object composition after we've reviewed *ES6 classes*. Stay tuned!

Let's wrap this chapter by comparing prototypical inheritance with object initializers, `Object.create` and constructor functions.

Object Initializers vs Object.create vs Constructor Functions

Object initializers __proto__	Object.create OLOO	Contructor Functions
Very simple and readable way to setup prototypical inheritance.	Simple way to setup prototypical inheritance. Less terse than initializers. You can use `Object.assign` to make it more terse.	Less straightforward as you set the prototype on the constructor function and not an object.
Need to set it every time you create an object unless you use a factory function.	Need to set it every time you create an object unless you use a factory function.	Set it once on the constructor function and is reused for all instances created afterwards.
It is only reliable in ES6 and on web browsers.	Available from ES5 (all modern browsers and other JS environments)	Supported in any environment.
Simple syntax for defining getters and setters.	Can only define getters and setters via `defineProperty`.	Can only define getters and setters via `defineProperty`.

Concluding

Let's summarize what you've learned so far about *prototypical inheritance*. JavaScript doesn't have the concept of *traditional class-based inheritance* since it doesn't have real classes. Instead

JavaScript *inheritance* revolves around objects, just simple objects. You can use any object as a *prototype* and create new objects that are based on this prototype and inherit properties and methods from it.

In order to establish an *inheritance relationship* between an object and a *prototype* you can either use the __proto__ property within an *object initializer*, `Object.create` or the `prototype` property within a *constructor function*. The two first methods, which completely prescind of functions, are also called *OLOO* (Objects Linked to Other Objects). They provide a simpler approach to *prototypical inheritance* as there's one less element you need to think about (the *constructor function*). You can have an *inheritance tree* with many levels of depth where an object has a *prototype* which in turn has a *prototype*, and so on.

Whenever you try to access a property or method of an object that has a prototype the JavaScript runtime will try to find that property or method within the object itself, if it can't find it, it will continue down the *prototypical chain* until it finds it. This is known as *delegation-based inheritance* and is the most common flavor of *prototypical inheritance* in JavaScript. If you use the same prototype object for several objects in this delegating fashion you should avoid storing state in the *prototype* since it may couple all your *"derived"* objects.

There's also another flavor of prototypical inheritance called *concatenative inheritance*. It consists on copying properties from a prototype to an object and leads to object composition. We will take a look at it later within the book.

```
1  randalf.says("And those were the basics of prototypes");
2
3  mooleen.says('Great! ');
4      "Now I should be able to encapsulate common behaviors" +
5      "inside prototypes and reuse them across your minions");
6
```

```
7   randalf.says("Exactly!");
8   randalf.says("Let's expand your mighty armies with cows" +
9                "and goats");
10  rat.says("And badgers!");
```

Exercises

 Experiment JavaScriptmancer!

You can experiment with these exercises and some possible solutions in this jsBin[41] or downloading the source code from GitHub[42].

---

[41] http://bit.ly/javascriptmancy-oop-fundamentals-inheritance-exercises
[42] https://github.com/vintharas/javascriptmancy-code-samples

A Cow and __proto__

Remember the sheep from the previous chapter?

```
1  var sheep = {
2    position: {x:0, y:0},
3    legs: 0,
4    toString: function(){
5      return "You look at what you think is a sheep. It's " +
6        "hard to be sure though was it's a legless lump on the ground";
7    },
8    describe: function(){ return console.log(this.toString());},
9    baa: function(){
10     console.log(`'Baaaaaaaaa'
11 The sheep makes a wailing sound vaguely resembling bleating
12 that gives you goose bumps
13     `);
14   },
15   goesTo: function(x,y){
16     this.position.x = x;
17     this.position.y = y;
18     console.log(`The sheep slowly crawls to position (${x},${y})`);
19   },
20 };
```

Create a new minion cow, extract the common behaviors between sheep and cow inside a prototype minion and take advantage of prototypical inheritance to reuse these behaviors in sheep and cow.

Tip: Use the __proto__ property inside an object initializer.

Solution

```
1  // the minion prototype
2  // encapsulates the common behaviors
3  // of describing a minion and moving
4  var minion = {
5    describe: function(){
6      console.log(this.toString());
7    },
```

Summoning Fundamentals: Prototypical Inheritance

```javascript
  goesTo: function(x,y){
    this.position.x = x;
    this.position.y = y;
    console.log(`The ${this.name} slowly crawls to `+
        ` position (${x},${y})`);
  }
};

var sheep = {
  "__proto__": minion,
  name: "sheep",
  position: {x:0, y:0},
  legs: 0,
  toString: function(){
    return "You look at what you think is a sheep. "+
       "It's hard to be sure though was it's a legless "+
       "lump on the ground";
  },
  baa: function(){
    console.log(`'Baaaaaaaaa'
The sheep makes a wailing sound vaguely resembling `+
A. `bleating that gives you goose bumps`);
  }
};

var cow = {
  "__proto__": minion,
  name: "cow",
  position: {x:0, y:0},
  legs: 0,
  toString: function(){
    return "You look at what you think is a cow. " +
       "It's hard to be sure though was it's a big " +
       "legless lump on the ground";
  },
  moo: function(){
    console.log(`'Moooooooo'
The cow makes a torturing sound vaguely resembling mooing.`);
  }
};

sheep.describe();
// => You look at what you think is a sheep.
// It's hard to be sure though was it's a legless
// lump on the group
sheep.goesTo(1,1);
// => The sheep slowly crawls to position (1,1)
```

```
56  cow.describe();
57  // => You look at what you think is a cow.
58  // It's hard to be sure though was it's a big
59  // legless lump on the ground
60  cow.goesTo(2,2);
61  // => The cow slowly crawls to position (2,2)
62
63  randalf.says('Take a look at that!');
64  mooleen.says('Yes haha see how I reuse those two ' +
65               'behaviors in the sheep and the cow');
66  rat.says('Marvellous!');
```

A Goat and Object.create

Now let's review the sheep factory function from the previous chapter.

```
function createSheep(legs, x, y){
  return {
  position: {x:x, y:y},
  legs: legs,
  toString: function(){
    return `You look at what you think is a sheep. ` +
        `It has ${legs} legs`;
  },
  describe: function(){ return console.log(this.toString());},
  baa: function(){
    console.log(`'Baaaaaaaaa'
The sheep makes a wailing sound vaguely resembling bleating
that gives you goose bumps
    `);
  },
  goesTo: function(x,y){
    this.position.x = x;
    this.position.y = y;
    console.log(`The sheep slowly goes to position (${x},${y})`);
  },
  };
}
```

Create a new factory function `createGoat` and take advantage of prototypical inheritance to reuse the behaviors defined by the `minion` prototype in both sheep and goats.

Tip: Take advantage of `Object.create` inside the factory function.

Solution

```
function createSheep(legs, x, y){
  var sheep = Object.create(minion);
  
```

Summoning Fundamentals: Prototypical Inheritance

```
    return Object.assign(sheep, {
      name: 'sheep',
      position: {x:x, y:y},
      legs: legs,
      toString: function(){
        return `You look at what you think is a ${this.name}.`+
               ` It has ${legs} legs`;
      },
      baa: function(){
        console.log(`'Baaaaaaaaa'
The ${this.name} makes a wailing sound vaguely resembling bleating
that gives you goose bumps
        `);
    }});
}

function createGoat(legs, x, y){
  var goat = Object.create(minion);

  return Object.assign(goat, {
    name: 'goat',
    position: {x:x, y:y},
    legs: legs,
    toString: function(){
      return `You look at what you think is a ${this.name}.`+
             ` It has ${legs} legs`;
    },
    scream: function(){
      console.log(`'Waaaaaaa'
The ${this.name} makes a wailing sound resembling`+
` a person being tortured.
      `);
  }});
}

var newSheep = createSheep(4, 0, 0);
newSheep.describe();
// => You look at what you think is a sheep. It has 4 legs
newSheep.goesTo(1,1);
// => The sheep slowly crawls to position (1,1)

var goat = createGoat(4, 2, 2);
goat.describe();
// => You look at what you think is a goat. It has 4 legs
goat.goesTo(1, 1);
// => The goat slowly crawls to position (1,1)
```

```
62    randalf.says('Great! See how Object.create works ' +
63               'perfectly and how `describe` and `goesTo` ' +
64               'are delegated to the prototype?');
65    mooleen.says('Yes!');
```

 ## The Mighty Badger

Ok and now it's time for the mighty and mean badger. Remember this constructor function from the previous chapter?

```
1   function Sheep(legs, x, y){
2     this.legs = legs;
3     this.position = {x:x, y:y};
4     this.toString = function(){
5       return `You look at a beautiful sheep!`+
6              ` It has ${this.legs} legs`;
7     };
8     this.describe = function(){
9       return console.log(this.toString());
10    };
11    this.baa = function(){
12      console.log(`'Baaaaaaaaa'
13  The sheep makes a beautiful musical sound reminiscent
14  of spring and wildberries.
15      `);
16    };
17    this.goesTo = function(x,y){
18      this.position.x = x;
19      this.position.y = y;
20      console.log(`The sheep promptly goes to position (${x},${y})`);
21    };
22  }
```

Rewrite this function and create a new constructor function Badger that takes advantage of prototypical inheritance to reuse the behaviors defined by the minion prototype.

Hint: Remember constructorFunction.prototype.

Solution

```javascript
function Sheep(legs, x, y){
    this.name = "sheep";
    this.legs = legs;
    this.position = {x:x, y:y};
    this.toString = function(){
        return `You look at a beautiful sheep!`+
            `It has ${this.legs} legs`;
    };
    this.baa = function(){
        console.log(`'Baaaaaaaaa'
The sheep makes a beautiful musical sound reminiscent
of spring and wildberries.
        `);
    };
}
Sheep.prototype = Object.create(minion);
Sheep.prototype.constructor = Sheep;

function Badger(legs, x, y){
    this.name = "badger";
    this.legs = legs;
    this.position = {x:x, y:y};
    this.toString = function(){
        return `You look at a mighty mean badger!`+
            `It has ${this.legs} legs`;
    };
    this.growl = function(){
        console.log(`'Grrrrrrr'
The badger growls fiercely.
        `);
    };
}
Badger.prototype = Object.create(minion);
Badger.prototype.constructor = Badger;

var beautySheep = new Sheep(4, 2, 2);
beautySheep.describe();
// => You look at a beautiful sheep! It has 4 legs
beautySheep.goesTo(1, 1);
// => The sheep slowly crawls to position (1,1)

var badger = new Badger(4, 1, 1);
badger.describe();
// => You look at a mighty mean badger! It has 4 legs
```

```
45  badger.goesTo(2, 2);
46  // => The badger slowly crawls to position (2,2)
47
48  randalf.says('Good job! You have mastered it!');
49  mooleen.says('Thanks!');
50  rat.says('Wait... Why is the mighty badger crawling?');
```

 ## Wait! Why is my badger crawling??

The badger from the previous example doesn't move at the speed it befits a mighty badger. Take advantage of the prototypical chain to add a goesTo method that is only used with badgers. The result should be like this:

```
1  var yetAnotherBadger = new Badger(4, 0, 0);
2  yetAnotherBadger.goesTo(4, 4);
3  // => swift like the wind the mighy badger goes to (4,4)
```

No sheep should be affected by this change:

```
1  beautySheep.goesTo(2, 2);
2  // => The sheep slowly crawls to position (2,2)
```

Solution

```
1  Badger.prototype.goesTo = function(x,y){
2    this.position.x = x;
3    this.position.y = y;
4    console.log(`Swift like the wind the mighy badger `+
5                ` goes to (${x},${y})`);
6  }
7
8  var yetAnotherBadger = new Badger(4, 0, 0);
```

```
 9  yetAnotherBadger.goesTo(4, 4);
10  // => Swift like the wind the mighy badger goes to (4,4)
11
12  beautySheep.goesTo(2, 2);
13  // => The sheep slowly crawls to position (2,2)
14
15  mooleen.says("And that's it!");
16  randalf.says('Exactly, now that you have implemented ' +
17     'a new method in the badger prototype this method gets ' +
18     'called instead of the one within the minion prototype');
19
20  mooleen.says('Yep the chain goes ' +
21     'badger object => badger prototype => minion prototype');
22
23  randalf.says('Btw, did you notice that now all badgers are swift?');
24  rat.says('Yes! Even the ones created before augmenting the prototype\
25  !');
```

You may be wondering. Ey! Now we needed to re-implement the whole method! Shouldn't we be able to reuse at least part of the functionality of the method in the `minion` prototype?? And the answer is **yes!!**. We'll take a look into how to achieve that within a couple of chapters. Stay put!

 Did You Notice That All Badgers Are Swift?

An interesting property of the prototypical chain is that when you augment a prototype all objects that share it automatically get access to the new behavior. Take a look at the original badger:

```
1  badger.goesTo(1, 1)
2  // => Swift like the wind the mighy badger goes to (4,4)
```

Take advantage of this property to gift all your minions with the ability to fly. Hell yeah! Volaaareee!

Solution

```javascript
badger.goesTo(1,1);
// => Swift like the wind the mighy badger goes to (4,4)

mooleen.says(`Wo... it's true!`);
mooleen.says(`Hmm this gives me an idea... `+
             `that'll make this army unstoppable`);

minion.fly = function(x, y){
  this.position.x = x;
  this.position.y = y;
  console.log(`The ${this.name} takes off suddenly `+
    `and flights soaring like an eagle until it `+
    `gets to position (${x},${y})`);
};

sheep.fly(1,1);
// => The sheep takes off suddenly and flights
// soaring like an eagle until it gets to position (1,1)
goat.fly(1, 1);
// => The goat takes off ...
badger.fly(2, 2);
// => The badger takes off ...

mooleen.says('Amazing!');
rat.says('Superb!');
randalf.says('Indeed it is!');

/*
The entrails of the earth, up into the rock, onto the top
of a white peaked mountain, and a majestic endless mountain range.
Up into a sea of clouds, the world... and a freaking goat breaching
into the stratosphere...
*/
```

Summoning Fundamentals: Polymorphism

If it flights like a dragon,
breathes fire like a dragon,
eats peasants like a dragon,
then, my friend,
that is a dragon.

> - KinnLar Sane,
> Dragon Hunter, 8th Age

Summoning Fundamentals: Polymorphism

```
/*
 * Mooleen, Randalf and rat, 900 cows, 728 sheep and 200 goats stand
 * on the top of a cliff. This sounds like the beginning of a joke,
 * yet it is true as water is clear and the sky is blue. Although
 * in this part of the world, there's no water but sweat, and no sky
 * just blackness.
 */

randalf.says("All right, you're starting to become pretty good" +
             "at the summoning arts");
mooleen.says("Thank you!");

randalf.says("The next step is to understand one very " +
    "interesting property of the REPL. Many of us have " +
    "pondered about this for centuries yet haven't " +
    "discovered the reason, the fact of the matter is that " +
    "you don't really need to tell the REPL what things are " +
    "for things to just work");
mooleen.says("Alright?");

randalf.laughs();
randalf.says("I know! I'm not making a lot of sense, right? " +
    "Well, imagine that you want to make these creatures that " +
    "you have summoned attack each other.");
mooleen.says("Yeah?");

randalf.says("You don't need to teach a cow how to attack " +
    "a sheep and a goat. You just tell them how to attack " +
    "and everything just works");
mooleen.says("Really? That sounds very convenient");

randalf.says("Indeed it is. We haven't found a very good name " +
    "for it yet. We just call it polymorphism. " +
    "'Poly' for the javascriptmancer that discovered it " +
    "and 'morphism' for an ancient word that means shape");

rat.coughsSlightly();
randalf.looks("little bewildered");
rat.coughsVeryStrongly();

rat.says("Sorry for breaking your mood dear Randalf but I can't stan\
d the bullshit. Polymorphism means 'many forms'");
randalf.says("Oh yeah, that was it");
mooleen.says("Really? Poly the JavaScriptmancer?");
```

Polymorphism Means Many Forms

> *Polymorphism* allows a function to be written to take an object of a type `Minion`, but also work correctly if passed an object that belongs to a type `Troll` that is a subtype of `Minion`.

Polymorphism is a mechanism we often find in static and strongly typed languages. In these languages, we take advantage of polymorphism to reuse algorithms or computation with different types that have a common ancestor. These types will either derive from a shared base class or implement the same interface.

Let's refresh how you can take advantage of polymorphism in C#.

Polymorphism in C#

Imagine that you are building an army to rule the known world. You have a diverse host of minions in this army of the undead (undead are cheaper to maintain: skeletons need no food, and ghouls are not very picky about what they choose to eat).

Behold! A Skeleton!

```
public class Skeleton{
    public int Health {get;set;}
    private Position position;

    public Skeleton(){
        Health = 50;
        position = new Position();
    }

    public void MovesTo(int x, int y){
        position.X = x;
```

```
            position.Y = y;
        }
}
```

A skeleton that can only move is not a very useful weapon. You'll need to give it the ability to attack your enemies:

```
public class Skeleton{
        public int Health {get;set;}
        private int damage;
        private Position position;

        public Skeleton(){
                Health = 50;
                damage = 10;
                position = new Position();
        }

        public void MovesTo(int x, int y){
                position.X = x;
                position.Y = y;
        }

    public void Attacks(Skeleton enemySkeleton){
        enemySkeleton.Health -= damage;
    }
}
```

Ok. Now you have a skeleton that can attack other skeletons! Yippi! Let's imagine that your most bitter enemy has a vast army of goblins:

```
public class Goblin{
    public int Hp {get;set;}

    public void MovesTo(int x, int y){
        position.X = x;
        position.Y = y;
    }
}
```

A `Goblin` is not a `Skeleton` and therefore your skeletons, as deadly as they are, will have a hard time beating that army. So you decide to be one step ahead of your enemy and teach your skeletons how to deal with goblins. You add a new `Attacks` method just for goblins:

```
public void Attacks(Skeleton enemySkeleton){
    enemySkeleton.Health -= damage;
}

public void Attacks(Goblin goblin){
    goblin.Health -= damage;
}
```

And then you find out that not only does he have goblins, but also orcs, trolls, wargs and wyrms. Ok, easy enough, you just add multiple `Attacks` methods and make sure that you have all bases covered:

```
public void Attacks(Skeleton enemySkeleton){
    enemySkeleton.Health -= damage;
}

public void Attacks(Goblin goblin){
    goblin.Health -= damage;
}

public void Attacks(Orc orc){
    orc.Health -= damage;
}
```

```
public void Attacks(Troll troll){
    troll.Health -= damage;
}

public void Attacks(Warg warg){
    warg.Health -= damage;
}

public void Attacks(Wyrm wyrm){
    wyrm.Health -= damage;
}
```

You'll agree with me that this whole thing got out of hand reaaaally fast. This is one scenario in which *polymorphism* could come in handy. We can take advantage of *polymorphism* by defining a common base class for all these creatures. This class Monster would encapsulate the contract needed for *being attacked* which, based on the examples that we've seen thus far, consists in the Health property:

```
public class Monster{
    public int Health {get;set;}
}

public class Skeleton : Monster {}
public class Goblin : Monster {}
public class Orc : Monster {}
public class Troll: Monster {}
// etc
```

Now we can redefine the Attacks method in terms of that new type:

```
public void Attacks(Monster monster){
    monster.Health -= damage;
}
```

Of course, we would also like our minions to be able to attack defensive structures like towers, or walls, or even fences which are most definitely not monsters. So after reflecting about it, perhaps it would be more appropriate to use an interface `IAttackable` instead of the `Monster` base class.

This new interface would represent the contract of something very generic that can be attacked:

```
public interface IAttackable {
    int Health {get;set;}
}
public class Monster : IAttackable{
    public int Health {get;set;}
}
public class Skeleton : Monster {}
public class Goblin : Monster {}
// etc
public class Tower: IAttackable {}
public class Fence: IAttackable {}
// etc
```

We redefine the `Attacks` method to be even more abstract and applicable to any type that implements the `IAttackable` interface: be it a creature, a tower or a mailbox.

```
public void Attacks(IAttackable target){
    target.Health -= damage;
}
```

Let's summarize what we've achieved thus far. We rewrote the `Attacks` method to take advantage of *polymorphism* so that our `Skeleton` could attack anything that implements the `IAttackable` interface. From being able to attack Skeletons alone, we went to attacking many types of monsters implemented with many many functions, and finally we reduced it into a single function thanks to *polymorphism*.

Notice that the benefits of our new solution don't come only from the fact that we have a single function instead of many. The biggest advantage from our new design is the **increased extensibility**. Thanks to *polymorphism* the new Attacks function will work with new creatures, defensive structures, and virtually anything that hasn't even been thought of yet. As long as that *anything* implements the contract defined by the IAttackable interface everything will work just fine. We've succeeded in future-proofing our domain model for this specific use case. Congrats!

Polymorphism in JavaScript

Experiment JavaScriptmancer!!

You can experiment with all examples in this chapter directly within this jsBin[43] or downloading the source code from GitHub[44].

Polymorphism in JavaScript is much simpler than in C#. As a dynamically typed language, JavaScript exhibits what is known as *duck typing*[45]. With duck typing an object's semantics are based on the object's own methods and properties and not on the inheritance chain or interface implementations (like in C#). This means that, in JavaScript, we don't really care about inheritance. As long as an object has the interface required by a function everything will just work. Magic!

Let's see JavaScript's *duck typing* in action using the same example from the previous section. Everything started with a skeleton:

---

[43] http://bit.ly/javascriptmancy-oop-fundamentals-polymorphism
[44] https://github.com/vintharas/javascriptmancy-code-samples
[45] http://en.wikipedia.org/wiki/Duck_typing

Summoning Fundamentals: Polymorphism

```javascript
let skeleton = {
  health: 50,
  damage: 10,
  position: {x: 0, y: 0},

  toString() {
    return 'Skeleton';
  },

  movesTo(x, y){
    this.position.x = x;
    this.position.y = y;
  },

  attacks(monster){
    monster.health -= this.damage;
    console.log(`${this} attacks ${monster} fiercely!`);
  }
}
```

When we define the `attacks` method as illustrated above, the only thing JavaScript cares about in what regards to `monster` is that it has a `health` property:

```javascript
// An orc, a goblin and a tower...
let orc = {
  name: 'orc',
  health: 100,
  toString(){return this.name;}
};
let goblin = {
  health: 10,
  toString(){return 'goblin';}
};
let tower = {
  health: 1000,
  toString(){ return 'fortified tower';}
};

skeleton.attacks(orc);
// => Skeleton attacks orc fiercely!
```

```
skeleton.attacks(goblin);
// => Skeleton attacks goblin fiercely!
skeleton.attacks(tower);
// => Skeleton attacks tower fiercely!
```

JavaScript doesn't care about the type of creature or thing that you pass into the function. It only cares about the object exposing a matching interface, which in this case is the `health` property.

We can push this point even further by doing something crazy. In the example below we augment the function `skeleton.attacks` itself with a `health` property, and now the `skeleton` can attack it!

```
skeleton.attacks.health = 50;
skeleton.attacks(skeleton.attacks);
// => Skeleton attacks function attacks(monster) { ...
// OMG that was sooo meta

console.log(skeleton.attacks.health);
// => 40
```

So as long as an object has a `health` property, it will behave as something that can be attacked as defined by the `attacks` method regardless of inheritance. And thus the popular saying regarding *duck typing*...

> If it walks like a duck, swims like a duck and quacks like a duck, I call it a duck.

If it has a `health` property, then it is something that can be attacked. This is the reason why I've claimed that inheritance is not a means of *polymorphism* in JavaScript like it is in C#.

Let's see a summary of the differences between C# *polymorphism* and JavaScript *duck tiping*:

C# Polymorphism	JavaScript Duck Typing
Deriving from a base class or implementing an interface is going to determine whether or not you can use *polymorphism* with a particular type.	In JavaScript it all comes down to having the expected properties or methods when an object is evaluated.
In C# you establish an explicit expectation about which type can be used within a function in the function's signature.	In JavaScript the expectation is determined by how an object is used within a function implementation.
In order to take advantage of polymorphism you need to be very intentional about it since it requires a specific architecture in your application. In practice, it means that you'll need to create additional classes or interfaces.	JavaScript duck typing gives you the most granular level of polymorphism with no additional investment. You don't need to create additional classes or equivalents.
The intent of the author of the code is very clear since polymorphism only works if the right structures are in place. The extensibility points are very explicit in C#	In JavaScript any point is extensible.

Concluding

In this chapter we did a short review of the concept of *polymorphism* in C# and how you can use it as a mechanism of code reuse and as a means of creating extensible applications.

Next you learned how *polymorphism* works in JavaScript with the concept of *duck typing*, the idea that **an object is not defined by what it is but by what it can do.** Thus if something walks like a duck, swims like a duck and quacks like a duck then you treat it as a duck.

We wrapped the chapter with a brief comparison between C# *polymorphism* and JavaScript *duck typing* and how the latter can achieve everything C# can, with far less code and a simpler design.

```
/*
 * Asturi hadn't seen a battle as terrible as this one in ages.
 * Many dead. Many more fatherless and motherless sons that would
 * live to grief their loved ones. The scene of the conflict,
 * terrible, devastating to look at. Corpses lay here and there,
 * blood everywhere, the horrible spoils of war no one remembers
 * to talk about in the stories. No glory to be gained this day.
 *
 * No party had won, all of them had lost, the cow armies had decimat\
ed
 * their bitter enemies, the goat and sheep alliance and vice versa.
 * No one ever knew livestock could be so bloodthirsty.
 */

mooleen.says("And that got out of hand very quickly");
randalf.says("Yeah, that teaches you to beware of the arts of magic"\
);

mooleen.asks("Where is rat?");
randalf.says("I don't know, last time I saw it, it was " +
    "trying to hold a charge of cows on the left flank");
mooleen.says("Oh yeah I remember that, you looked very " +
    "funny running away before that angry cow berserker");

/*
 * Picture a middle aged man, in long robes, lifting his skirts
 * to show two spindly and very white legs finished in pink
 * slippers, running for his live followed by an angry looking cow.
 */

randalf.says("haha Yeah that was fun. " +
    "I should've worn my traveling attires");

rat.shouts("aaaaaaaaaah Freeeedoooooom");
/*
 * A tiny piece of red fur appears from out of nowhere
 * charging at the two wizards. Then it stops.
 */
rat.says("Oh... it's you");
```

Exercises

 Experiment JavaScriptmancer!
You can experiment with these exercises and some possible solutions in this jsBin[46] or downloading the source code from GitHub[47].

---

[46] http://bit.ly/javascriptmancy-oop-fundamentals-polymorphism-exercises
[47] https://github.com/vintharas/javascriptmancy-code-samples

The Secrets of Polymorphic Functions

Imagine that you have a legion of undead cows, sheep and goats. Brrrr! Horrible! I'm getting goosebumps only thinking about it... Create a single polymorphic function to exorcise all these evil undead creatures given that they look as follows:

```javascript
var undeadCow = {
  position: {x: 0, y:0},
  legs: 1,
  toString: function(){ return 'undeadCow'; }
  describe: function(){
    return "A terrible sight unfolds before you. " +
      " A half eaten, half rotten cow, half standing, " +
      "half crawling looks at you with sightless eerie eyes";
  },
  charge: function (target){
    console.log('UndeadCow charges ' + target + ' with cold rage');
    target.hp -= 50;
  },
  soulPoints: 100
};

var undeadSheep = {
  position: {x: 2, y:10},
  legs: 4,
  wings: 2,
  toString: function() { return 'undeadSheep'; },
  describe: function(){ return "blablabla"; },
  bite: function(target){
    console.log('UndeadSheep bites ' + target + ' meanly');
    target.hp -= 60;
  },
  soulPoints: 70
};

var undeadGoat = {
  position: {x: 0, y:0},
  legs: 1,
  toString: function() { return 'undeadGoat'; },
  describe: function(){ return "blablabla"; },
  soulPoints: 80,
  jumpAttack: function(target){
    console.log('UndeadGoat jumps on ' + target +
      ' with its full weight');
    target.hp -= 70;
  }
};
```

The function should reduce the soulPoints of all the diverse undead host to 0

Solution

```javascript
function exorcise(undead){
  undead.soulPoints = 0;
  console.log(`You exorcise ${undead} freeing its soul from the dark\
 plane.`);
}

mooleen.weaves('exorcise(undeadCow)');
// => You exorcise undeadCow freeing its soul from the dark plane.

mooleen.weaves('exorcise(undeadSheep)');
// => You exorcise undeadSheep freeing its soul from the dark plane.

mooleen.weaves('exorcise(undeadGoat)');
// => You exorcise undeadGoat freeing its soul from the dark plane.

mooleen.says('yep, it was that easy');
```

White Tower Summoning: Mimicking C# Classical Inheritance in JavaScript

Life is like a stream,
you can never touch the same water twice.
The water that has flowed will never flow again.
So enjoy every second of life.

Life is not a stream
but now you know more about life.

>   - Kinvalso Immax
> JavaScript-mancer 2nd Age,
> The Principles of Teaching

```
someone.shouts("The ships have arrived!!");
/*
  A voice in the distance
*/

mooleen.asks("Did you hear anything?");
randalf.says("Nope");
rat.says("Sorry, that was me");

mooleen.says('Not that. I think I heard a voice');
bandalf.shouts("The ships have arrived!!!")

randalf.says("Oh he must be confused to think " +
    "that the *sheep are alive*");

/* Bandalf arrives beside the group panting heavily */
bandalf.says("The ships...");
bandalf.says("The ships have arrived");

mooleen.says('The ships?');

randalf.says("Yeah, no javascriptmancer would allow a " +
    "rival near his or her territory. We can only teleport " +
    "to places we've already been to, you see?");
mooleen.says("I see, a rival could then attack you by surprise" +
    "whenever and wherever he pleased");

rat.says("Precisely!");
randalf.says("Come on we need to stop them " +
    "before they take a foothold on the island");

/*
  Randalf, Rat, Bandalf and Mooleen teleport
  on top of a hill overseeing the vast ocean.
  Nearing the island they see...
  a teeny tiny rowboat with a red clad figure atop.
*/

mooleen.says("I don't know what I was expecting...
    but that wasn't it");
rat.says("Very anti-climatic");

randalf.says("Would you build an armada if you could
    just teleport a whole army?");
```

```
randalf.says("Quickly! They'll be here in no time" +
"There's one last thing I need to teach you. " +
"Have you ever heard of classical inheritance?");
```

Ever Heard of Classical Inheritance?

In this chapter we are going to take a deep-dive into how you can emulate *classical inheritance* in JavaScript arriving to the nearest equivalent of what you can do with C#. We will focus on the alternatives we had prior to *ES6 classes* so that you can work with *classes* even if you are stuck in *ES5*. And even better, so that you can understand the underlying implementation of *ES6 classes* which are just syntactic sugar over JavaScript's *prototypical inheritance* model.

We will start by emulating a single C# *class* in JavaScript and attempt to find equivalents to C# constructs like access modifiers, static classes and method overloading. We will then continue by expanding our knowledge from a single class to many, in order to arrive to something similar to C# *classical inheritance*. A technique that will allow you to work in JavaScript just like you usually do in C#, building your domain models using *class* taxonomies and working with instances of *classes*.

Can I Just Jump Over to the ES6 Class Chapter Directly?

In this chapter we are going to focus completely in learning how you can implement *classes* and *classical inheritance* in JavaScript without using *ES6 classes*. This is important because it will teach you how to do a *class* equivalent in *ES5*, what lies behind *ES6 classes* and how *ES6 classes* relate to the rest of JavaScript.

If you are working on a project where you only use *ECMAScript 6* then you can jump to the next chapter, learn everything about classes and then come back if you are curious of how *classes* work under the hood.

Emulating a C# Class in JavaScript

In order to create the equivalent of a *class* in JavaScript you need to combine a *constructor function* with a *prototype*. Let's do a quick review of each of these constructs and see how combining them results in something similar to a C# class.

In this chapter I am going to be using the word *class* a lot and I am going to be referring to a *constructor function* and *prototype* pair, the equivalent to C# *classes* in JavaScript prior to *ES6*. I won't refer to *ES6 classes* unless I say *ES6 classes*.

Constructor Functions

 Experiment JavaScriptmancer!!
You can experiment with all examples in this chapter directly within this jsBin[48] or downloading the source code from GitHub[49].

---
[48] http://bit.ly/javascriptmancy-oop-classical-inheritance
[49] https://github.com/vintharas/javascriptmancy-code-samples

Constructor functions allow us to create objects that share the same properties. They work as a recipe for object creation and represent a custom type:

```
function Barbarian(name){
  this.name = name;
  this["character class"] = "barbarian";
  this.hp = 200;
  this.weapons = [];

  this.talks = function(){
    console.log("I am " + this.name + " !!!");
  };

  this.equipsWeapon = function(weapon){
    weapon.equipped = true;
    this.weapons.push(weapon);
  };

  this.toString = function(){
    return this.name;
  };
}
```

Notice how the *constructor*, not only initializes an object with a set of values like in C#, but also determines which properties an object is going to have. This means that a **constructor function works effectively as both a constructor and a class definition** [50].

After having defined a *constructor function*, you can create a new object using the new keyword just like in C#:

```
let conan = new Barbarian("Conan, the Barbarian");
```

This new instance is of type `Barbarian` as revealed by the instanceof operator:

---

[50] The constructor will be responsible for at least part of that class definition. The rest of the class definition will be specified by the prototype as we'll soon see. In the absence of a prototype the constructor will represent the complete class definition.

```javascript
console.log(`Conan is a Barbarian: ${conan instanceof Barbarian}`);
// => Conan is a Barbarian: true

console.log(`Conan is an Object: ${conan instanceof Object}`);
// => Conan is an Object: true
```

And all its properties are publicly available:

```javascript
conan.talks();
// => I am Conan, the Barbarian!!!

console.log(conan.name);
// => Conan, The Barbarian"

conan.equipsWeapon({
  name: "two-handed sword",
  type: "sword",
  damage: "2d20+10",
  material: "cimmerian steel",
  status: "well maintained"
});

console.log(`Conan has these weapons: ${conan.weapons}`);
// => Conan has these weapons: two-handed sword
```

Prototypical Inheritance

In previous chapters we saw how inheritance in JavaScript is slightly different than in C#. For one, there are no *classes*. Furthermore, inheritance doesn't play as big a part in polymorphism since JavaScript is a dynamically typed language that relies on *duck typing*.

JavaScript is all about objects, and achieves inheritance not via *class inheritance* but via **prototypical inheritance**, that is, objects that inherit from other objects called **prototypes**.

Prototypes

Every *constructor function* (and every function) in JavaScript has a `prototype` property. This property holds an object that will act as a *prototype* - will provide shared properties - for all objects created by calling the *constructor function* with the `new` keyword.

```
1  // every function has a prototype property
2  console.log(`Barbarian.prototype: ${Barbarian.prototype}`);
3  // => Barbarian.prototype: [object Object]
```

And the `prototype` object also has a `constructor` property that points back to the *constructor* function:

```
1  // and the prototype has a constructor property
2  // that points back to the function
3  console.log(`Barbarian.prototype.constructor:
4    ${Barbarian.prototype.constructor}`);
5  // => Barbarian.prototype.constructor:
6  //   function Barbarian(name) {...}
```

We can easily verify how all objects instantiated using that *constructor function* will inherit properties and methods from the prototype object. If we take the *prototype* from the previous example, extend it with a simple `saysHi` function:

```
1  Barbarian.prototype.saysHi = function() {
2    console.log("Hi! I am " + this.name);
3  }
```

And then we instantiate two rough barbarians:

```
1  var krull = new Barbarian("krull");
2  var conan = new Barbarian("Conan");
```

We can appreciate how both objects `krull` and `conan` expose the `saysHi` method even though it wasn't part of the `Barbarian` *constructor function* (which only had the `talks`, `equipsWeapon` and `toString` methods):

```
krull.saysHi();
// => Hi! I am krull

conan.saysHi();
// => Hi! I am Conan
```

This is possible due to the *prototype chain* existing between instance (`krull`) and *prototype* (`Barbarian.prototype`) which allows the instance to delegate method calls to the *prototype*.

A common idiom to avoid the need to write:

```
ConstructorFunction.prototype.property = ...;
```

each time you want to augment the prototype is to assign the *prototype* to a new object:

```
// like this:
var barbarianPrototype = {
    constructor: Barbarian
    saysHi: function(){console.log("Hi! I am " + this.name);}
}
Barbarian.prototype = barbarianPrototype;

// or simply:
Barbarian.prototype = {
    constructor: Barbarian
    saysHi: function(){console.log("Hi! I am " + this.name);}
}
```

This pattern saves you from typing more code and also provides a more consistent and unified view of the properties that belong to the prototype.

Now that we have reviewed both *constructor functions* and *prototypes* let's see how putting them together brings us nearer to C# *inheritance model*.

Constructor Function + Prototype = Class

The nearest equivalent to a C# *class* in JavaScript is a *constructor function* and a *prototype* pair:

- **The constructor function defines a custom type with a series of properties.** It will determine which specific properties an instance of that custom type is going to have. **Typically it will contain the members of a class.**
- **The prototype provides a series of methods that are shared across all instances of a given type. Typically it will contain the methods of a class.** It is also the bridge between classes and the means to achieve *class* inheritance by connecting them together through a *prototype chain*.

Putting *constructor* and *prototype* together we can define a `Classy-Barbarian` *class* similar to our first `Barbarian` as follows:

```
// The constructor function:
//   - defines the ClassyBarbarian type
//   - defines the properties a ClassyBarbarian
//     instance is going to have
//
function ClassyBarbarian(name){
  this.name = name;
  this["character class"] = "barbarian";
  this.hp = 200;
  this.weapons = [];
}

// The prototype:
//   - defines the methods shared across
//     all ClassyBarbarian instances
//
ClassyBarbarian.prototype = {
  constructor: ClassyBarbarian,
```

```
19    talks: function(){
20      console.log("I am " + this.name + " !!!");
21    },
22    equipsWeapon: function(weapon){
23      weapon.equipped = true;
24      this.weapons.push(weapon);
25      console.log(`${this.name} grabs a ` +
26                  `${weapon.name} from the cavern floor`);
27    },
28    toString: function(){
29      return this.name;
30    },
31    saysHi: function (){
32      console.log("Hi! I am " + this.name);
33    }
34  };
```

We can use this new class just like we would use a *class* in C#. We instantiate it with the *new* operator:

```
1  var logen = new ClassyBarbarian('Logen Ninefingers');
```

And interact with it as we please:

```
1   logen.saysHi();
2   // => Hi! I am Logen Ninefingers
3
4   logen.talks();
5   // => I am Logen Ninefingers !!!
6
7   logen.equipsWeapon({name:'very large axe'});
8   // => Logen Ningefingers grabs a very large
9   //    axe from the cavern floor
10
11  console.log(logen.weapons.map(w => w.name));
12  // => ["very large axe"]
```

What is the difference between this and our previous example with the *constructor function*? Both work exactly the same from a consumer perspective but the *constructor* and *prototype* pair improves our original example in two ways:

1. All methods within the prototype are shared amongst all instances of `ClassyBarbarian`. This reduces the memory footprint of your application.
2. This technique opens the way to more advanced features that take advantage of prototypical inheritance and which we'll see throughout this chapter.

Access Modifiers

Unfortunately, we don't have the concept of built-in access modifiers in JavaScript[51]: *public*, *protected* and *private* do not exist. Every property that you add to an object is public and accessible by anyone that has access to that object.

That being said there are two patterns that you can use to achieve something similar to private variables and methods and the benefits of *information hiding*. You've learned about them in previous chapters:

- **Closures**: You can use them to capture the value of variables from outer scopes (in this case the methods of a class are closures that capture variables defined within a *constructor function*). These variables are not part of the object itself, they are just captured by the object methods, and therefore are not directly accessible through the object API.
- **ES6 Symbols**: When you use *symbols* to index properties and methods in your objects, because a symbol is unique, you can only access these properties or methods if you have access to the symbol. When using a *symbol* the object has a property

---

[51] You'll be happy to know that there's an early ECMA-262 proposal that aims to bring private members to classes. Yippi! Also, in the last chapter of the book you'll discover how one of the killer features of TypeScript are access mofidiers.

indexed by that *symbol* that is public, but even if you have access to the object, because you don't have a reference to the symbol, you cannot access the property. [52]

Let's see how we can use each of these approaches with our JavaScript *classes* and the implications of either choice.

Classes and Information Hiding with Closures

In order to use *closures* to achieve data privacy you need to have a function that encloses a variable. This poses a small problem if we want to follow the *constructor function* for state plus *prototype* for behavior pattern. That's because the *prototype* methods are defined outside of the *constructor* function and therefore cannot enclose any of the variables defined within it.

As a result, if we want to use *closures* to manage *data privacy* we need to move our methods from the *prototype* into the *constructor function*. Imagine that we no longer want to expose the weapons property of our barbarian class:

```
// constructor function
function PrivateBarbarian(name){
  // private members
  var weapons = [],
      hp = 200;

  // public members
  this.name = name;
  this["character class"] = "private barbarian";
  this.equipsWeapon = function(weapon){
    weapon.equipped = true;
    // this function encloses the weapons variable
    weapons.push(weapon);
    console.log(`${this.name} grabs a ${weapon.name}
```

---

[52] Remember that you can get access to all symbols used within an object via Object.getOwnPropertySymbols() or Reflect.ownKeys() and therefore *symbols* don't offer true privacy like *closures* do.

```
          from the cavern floor`);
   };
   this.toString = function(){
     if (weapons.length > 0)
       return `${this.name} looks angry and
               wields a ${weapons.find(w => w.equipped).name}`;
     else
       return `${this.name} looks peaceful`;
   }
 }

 // the prototype:
 PrivateBarbarian.prototype = {
     constructor: PrivateBarbarian,
     talks: function(){
         console.log("I am " + this.name + " !!!");
     },
     saysHi: function (){
         console.log("Hi! I am " + this.name);
     }
 };
```

In this snippet of code we've done the following changes:

- We have modified the *constructor function* so that the weapons variable is no longer a property of a Barbarian instance but a simple variable inside the function itself.
- We have moved the equipsWeapon function from the *prototype* to the *constructor function* and updated its body so that it encloses the weapons variable.

As a result, if we create a new PrivateBarbarian instance, it will not expose any weapons property to the outside world:

```
1  var privateBarbarian = new PrivateBarbarian('krox');
2
3  console.log(`Barbarian weapons: ${privateBarbarian.weapons}`);
4  // => Barbarian weapons: undefined
5  // we cannot access the weapons of the barbarian because
6  // they are not part of the object
```

The variable weapons will still exist and act *as if* it was a private member of the object. Indeed you can easily verify that the equipsWeapon, which encloses this variable, still works:

```
1  privateBarbarian.equipsWeapon({name: 'Two-handed Hammer'});
2  // => krox grabs a Two-handed Hammer from the cavern floor
3
4  console.log(privateBarbarian.toString());
5  // => krox looks angry and wields a Two-handed Hammer
```

In the same way that you have private members you can have private methods. Imagine that we had some formatting functions for our barbarian that we don't want to expose to the public. We can make them private by following the same pattern that we used before:

 Keep your APIs Small!

APIs should be kept small to minimize cognitive load and ease of learning and use. When possible try to keep your APIs surface small and hide the methods that are not meant to be used by a consumer. This will make your code more intentional and guide the consumer of your classes towards the right way to use them.

```
function PrivateBarbarian(name){
  // unchanged code from previous example

  this.toString = function(){
    if (weapons.length > 0) return formatWeaponizedBarbarian();
    else return formatPeacefulBarbarian();
  }

  // "private" method
  function formatWeaponizedBarbarian(){
    return `${name} looks angry and wields
        a ${weapons.find(w => w.equipped).name}`;
  }

  // "private" method
  function formatPeacefulBarbarian(){
    return `${name} looks peaceful`;
  }
}
```

The `formatWeaponizedBarbarian` and `formatPeacefulBarbarian` functions are now private and enclosed by the `toString` method that is part of the barbarian public interface.

In summary, if you want to use *closures* to manage *data privacy* with *classes* you are going to need to define your methods inside the *constructor function* and not the *prototype*. This has one additional caveat that may not be immediately apparent: Each single instance of a class will have its own method property, and therefore these won't be shared by all instances via the *prototype*. As a result, using closures as your *information hiding* strategy will force you to incur in a bigger memory footprint than the alternative.

Classes and Information Hiding With ES6 Symbols

Using *ES6 symbols* allows you to achieve *data privacy* and keep your methods in the *prototype*. The trick is to keep your symbols private as well.

In order to do that we are going to define a very simple *module*. JavaScript *modules* let you wrap pieces of related functionality and expose them to the rest of your application as you choose, so they work perfectly to keep our symbols private. We'll create a simple characters module to store our characters using this pattern:

```
// A simple module
(function(characters){
    characters.SymbolicBarbarian = SymbolicBarbarian;

    // etc...
}(window.characters = window.characters || {}))

// outside world only has access to whatever we expose
// via the characters object
```

Where we use a function - a new variable scope - to represent the module itself. We pass a characters object to the *module* function that will augment it with functionality that can later be used by the rest of the application.

JavaScript Modules

In this example we use the module pattern to create a simple module implementation via an IIFE, an immediately invoked function expression. An IIFE is just a function that you execute immediately. By virtue of being a function it creates a new scope where any variable that you define remains contained and therefore unaccessible to the outside world.

This used to be the most common pattern followed by developers to write modules in JavaScript before the advent of more complex systems like CommonJS, AMD, UMD and **ES6 modules**. ES6 modules attempt to provide a native module implementation for JavaScript so that we, developers, don't need to roll out our own custom implementation. We'll take a deep dive into modules later within this series. In the meantime, the only thing that you need to know is that you can use modules as a way to package and distribute pieces of related functionality.

With the creation of this module we will achieve one thing: We are going to have a place where to keep our symbols hidden from the outside world (the function scope). We will only expose a new SymbolicBarbarian *class* that will use these symbols to obtain *data privacy*:

```
(function(characters){
  characters.SymbolicBarbarian = SymbolicBarbarian;

  // private within this module
  let weapons = Symbol('weapons');

  // the constructor function:
  function SymbolicBarbarian(name){
    this.name = name;
    this["character class"] = "barbarian";
    this.hp = 200;
    this[weapons] = [];
```

```
    }

    // the prototype:
    SymbolicBarbarian.prototype = {
      constructor: SymbolicBarbarian,
      talks: function(){
        console.log("I am " + this.name + " !!!");
      },

      equipsWeapon: function(weapon){
        weapon.equipped = true;
        this[weapons].push(weapon);
          console.log(`${this.name} grabs a ${weapon.name}
    from the cavern floor`);
      },

      saysHi: function (){
        console.log("Hi! I am " + this.name);
      },

      toString: function(){
        if (this[weapons].length > 0)
          return `${this.name} looks angry and wields a
    ${this[weapons].find(w => w.equipped).name}`;
        else
          return `${this.name} looks peaceful`;
      }
    };

    }(window.characters = window.characters || {}))
```

Using the weapons symbol we can create a weapons property that can only be indexed if you have access to the symbol itself. Because the symbol is part of the characters module scope it's only accessible to that function scope and therefore to the SymbolicBarbarian *class* that also lives within it.

As a result the weapons property behaves like a private property of the SymbolicBarbarian *class*:

```
1  var symbolicBarbarian = new characters.SymbolicBarbarian('khaaarg');
2  symbolicBarbarian.equipsWeapon({name: 'katana sword'});
3  // => khaaarg grabs a katana sword from the cavern floor
4
5  console.log(`khaaarg weapons: ${symbolicBarbarian.weapons}`);
6  // => khaaarg weapons: undefined
7
8  console.log(symbolicBarbarian.toString());
9  // => khaaarg looks angry and wields a katana sword
```

Closures vs Symbols with Classes

Closures	ES6 Symbols
Closures let you achieve true privacy.	You cannot achieve true privacy with symbols. A client can use the Object.getOwnPropertySymbols() or Reflect.ownKeys() methods to get access to the symbols of a class and therefore access to its private members.
Because you need to enclose variables with your methods, using closures forces you to move your methods from the *prototype* to the *constructor function*. This requires more memory since these methods are no longer shared by all instances.	With symbols you can keep your methods in the *prototype* and therefore consume less memory.

Static Classes, Members and Methods

Static members and methods in C# are shared across all instances of a given class. They can only access other static members and methods, and are accessed by using the class name followed by the name of the member or method `Class.staticProperty`. They are often used to collect related utility methods that don't require shared state and therefore an instance of class to operate.

You can mimic **static members and methods** in JavaScript by augmenting the *constructor functions* with new properties. For instance, we could create several factory methods in our `Classy-Barbarian` as a convenience to create barbarians with often used presets:

```
// we extend the ClassyBarbarian constructor
// function from previous examples
// with two new properties
ClassyBarbarian.default = function(){
  return new Barbarian('default barbarian');
};

ClassyBarbarian.swordWieldingBarbarian = function(){
  var barbarian = new Barbarian('sword wielding barbarian');
  barbarian.equipsWeapon({name: 'sword'});
  return barbarian;
};
```

Because these are properties of the *constructor function* and not of any instance in particular, they'll only be accessible by having a reference to the *constructor function*.

```
var defaultBarbarian = ClassyBarbarian.default();
console.log(defaultBarbarian.name);
// => default barbarian

var swordWieldingBarbarian =
  ClassyBarbarian.swordWieldingBarbarian();
console.log(swordWieldingBarbarian.name);
// => sword wielding barbarian
```

Additionally, these members or methods will only be able to access other *static* members and methods since they are not tied to any instance in particular.

Static Classes

A **static class** is that which has only static members and methods, is sealed and cannot be instantiated. In a similar way to what you've seen in these examples, you can define a *static class* as a *constructor function* that only has *static members and methods* - that is, properties assigned to the *constructor function* itself.

This is going to give you a similar feeling to using *static classes* in C# but it is a little bit of a stretch. That's because you can still instantiate objects with that *constructor function* and have it be part of an inheritance chain. You can solve both of these problems by throwing an error when the *constructor function* is called:

```
function DateHelpers(){ throw Error('static class'); };
DateHelpers.ToJavaScriptMonth = function(month){
    // JavaScript months are 0 based
    return month - 1;
}
```

Although this may be trying to bring C# into JavaScript way too far and you might enjoy a better solution by using a simple *object initializer*.

Method overloading

In *JavaScript-mancy: Getting Started* we learned how JavaScript doesn't have built-in support for overloading methods. Attempting to overload a method by providing a different implementation of the same method with different arguments only results in overwriting the original method with the overloaded version. There are, however, different patterns that we can follow to achieve the same effect:

- **Argument inspection**: Inspect how many arguments are passed to a function and which are their types then decide what to do.

- **Options object**: Provide an *options* object that contains the arguments to the method. You get the benefits of named parameters and high extensibility.
- **ES6 defaults and destructuring**: *Defaults* let you provide different signatures as default values will be used if some arguments are not passed into the function. *Destructuring* let's you unwrap options objects in a very straightforward fashion.
- **Function Programming and Polymorphic Functions**: Define polymorphic functions by composing several functions that will be called in turn until you get a result from any of them. This solution is extremely extensible.

You can use any of these approaches with the *classes* that we have defined in this chapter so take a look at *Appendix C. Function Overloading* if you need to refresh them.

Mimicking Classical Inheritance in JavaScript

Let's make a summary of what you've learned up to this point:

- We can mimic a single C# *class* with a **constructor function and prototype pair**.
- The *constructor function* often defines the members of each instance and the *prototype* its methods.
- JavaScript doesn't have built-in access modifiers but you can get *private members* by using closures and *ES6 symbols*. Closures force you to move methods from the *prototype* to the *constructor function* before you can use them.
- You can add static members and methods to a *class* by augmenting its *constructor function*.

- JavaScript doesn't have built-in method overloading but there are several techniques that you can use to implement method overloading yourself.

So now we're at this point where we are able to represent a class in JavaScript. But **how do you go from a single class to an inheritance tree and to emulate classical inheritance?**

You can mimic classical inheritance by following these two steps when creating your *classes*:

1. **Call base constructor functions**: Make sure that each *constructor function* calls its base type *constructor function* using call or apply. This will ensure that any instance of a *class* contains all properties defined in each and every base *class* (as they are defined in each *constructor function*)
2. **Use prototypical inheritance**: Use prototypical inheritance to ensure that any instance of a *class* inherits methods from every base *class* (as they are contained within each *prototype*)

Let's see how to achieve *classical inheritance* with an example. Imagine that we were to develop a magic battle simulator to hone our skills as a general and strategist. We could design this battle simulator as a game that would have the following domain model:

```
Creature -> MovingGameObject -> DrawableGameObject -> GameObject
```

Where the different objects in this inheritance tree would have different responsibilities:

- GameObject: Represents any game object within a game scene. It provides functionality to update the status of a game object every game tick of the game loop.

- `DrawableGameObject`: Represents a subset of game objects that are visible within a game scene, like troops within our army. It provides functionality to `draw` these objects in the screen.
- `MovingGameObject`: Represents a subset of drawable game objects that can move within the screen. It provides functionality to move these objects in the screen.
- `Creature`: A specific creature within your armies. It provides specific properties, functionality, graphics, etc... for each creature (a barbarian, a wizard, a shaman, troll, goblin and who knows what else)

In addition to this domain we would have a `GameEngine` class that would control the game loop, gather user input and `update` and `draw` a collection of `GameObject` objects that would represents troops, projectiles, terrain, weather conditions, etc...

A simplified version of part of this domain would look roughly like this. Starting with the `DrawableGameObject`:

```
// Inheritance Hierarchy:
//   MovingGameObject -> DrawableGameObject -> GameObject

function DrawableGameObject(sprite){
    // call base type constructor function
    GameObject.call(this);
    this.sprite = sprite;
}

// establish prototypical inheritance
// between DrawableGameObject and GameObject
DrawableGameObject.prototype =
    Object.create(GameObject.prototype);
DrawableGameObject.prototype.constructor = DrawableGameObject;

// specific DrawableGameObject prototype methods
DrawableGameObject.prototype.draw = function(){
    console.log("drawing sprite: " + this.sprite);
```

```
19      // draw sprite
20  };
```

And continuing with the `MovingGameObject`:

```
1   // Helper Position class
2   function Position(x,y){
3       this.x = x;
4       this.y = y;
5   }
6   Position.prototype.toString = function(){
7       return "[" + this.x + "," + this.y + "]";
8   }
9
10  // GameObject class
11  function MovingGameObject(position, sprite) {
12      // call base type constructor function
13      DrawableGameObject.call(this, sprite);
14      this.position = position;
15  }
16
17  // establish prototypical inheritance
18  // between MovingGameObject and DrawableGameObject
19  MovingGameObject.prototype =
20      Object.create(DrawableGameObject.prototype);
21  MovingGameObject.prototype.constructor = MovingGameObject;
22
23  MovingGameObject.prototype.movesTo = function(newPosition){
24      this.position = newPosition;
25      console.log(`${this} moves to ${newPosition}`);
26  }
```

In this example you have two *classes*, a `DrawableGameObject` which is some object that can be drawn in a screen via a *sprite* (an image) and a `MovingGameObject` that represents some type of object that can move in a two-dimensional space. You can verify how:

1. The `MovingGameObject` *constructor function* calls the parent *class constructor* via `DrawableGameObject.apply(this,`

sprite);. This will ensure that a moving game object will have both a sprite and position properties.
2. The MovingGameObject.prototype object is a new object that in turn has a DrawableGameObject.prototype as prototype. This will ensure that a moving game object will have access to both MovingGameObject and DrawableGameObject *prototype* methods.

We can extend our *inheritance tree* with yet another *class*, the wise Shaman:

```
// Inheritance Hierarchy:
//   Shaman -> MovingGameObject -> DrawableGameObject

function Shaman(name, position, sprite){
  // call base type constructor function
  MovingGameObject.call(this, position, sprite);
  this.name = name;
}

// establish prototypical inheritance
// between Shaman and MovingGameObject
Shaman.prototype = Object.create(MovingGameObject.prototype);
Shaman.prototype.constructor = Shaman;

// Shaman specific methods
Shaman.prototype.toString = function(){
  return this.name;
};
Shaman.prototype.heals = function(target){
  console.log(`${this} heals ${target} (+ 50hp)`);
  target.hp += 50;
}
```

And we can verify that the Shaman works as it is supposed to by creating an instance and taking it for a test drive:

```
1   var koloss = new Shaman("Koloss", new Position(0,0), "koloss.jpg");
2
3   koloss.movesTo(new Position(5,5))
4   // => Koloss moves to [5,5]
5
6   koloss.draw()
7   // => drawing sprite: koloss.jpg
8
9   koloss.heals(conan);
10  // => Koloss heals Conan, the Barbarian
```

Method overriding

You can follow a similar pattern to the one you used in the *constructor function* to override or extend any method defined in a base *class*. That is, **in order to override a method, you call the method from a base *class* using `call` or `apply`.**

Let's override the `heals` method within a new type of shaman, the mysterious `WhiteShaman` who, in addition to healing wounds, can remove all ailments from a comrade like curses, poisons and diseases:

```
1   // constructor function
2   function WhiteShaman(name, position, sprite){
3       // call base type constructor function
4       Shaman.call(this, name, position, sprite);
5   }
6
7   // prototype
8   WhiteShaman.prototype = Object.create(Shaman.prototype);
9   WhiteShaman.prototype.constructor = WhiteShaman;
10
11  // WhiteShaman specific methods
12  WhiteShaman.prototype.castsSlowCurse = function(target){
13      console.log(`${this} casts slow on ${target}.
14      ${target} seems to move slower`);
15      if (target.curses) target.curses.push('slow');
16      else target.curses = ['slow'];
17  };
```

```
18    WhiteShaman.prototype.heals = function(target){
19        // call base class heals method
20        Shaman.prototype.heals.call(this, target);
21
22        console.log(`${this} cleanses all negatives
23            effects in ${target}`);
24        target.curses = [];
25        target.poisons = [];
26        target.diseases = [];
27    }
```

In this example, the `WhiteShaman.prototype.heals` method overrides `Shaman.prototype.heals` and extends it with new functionality to remove curses, poisons and diseases. This bit of code:

```
1    Shaman.prototype.heals.call(this, target);
```

executes the `Shaman.prototype.heals` method in the context of the current object (represented by `this`) and therefore makes sure that the base class implementation is taken into account before `WhiteShaman` specific code is executed.

Let's see how the `WhiteShaman` fares when healing a convalescent patient:

```
1    var khaaar = new WhiteShaman('Khaaar', new Position(0,0),
2        "khaaar.png");
3
4    khaaar.castsSlowCurse(conan);
5    // => Khaaar casts slow on Conan, the Barbarian.
6    //    Conan, the Barbarian seems to move slower
7
8    khaaar.heals(conan);
9    // => Khaaar heals Conan, the Barbarian (from Shaman)
10   // => Khaaar cleanses all negatives effects in Conan, the Barbarian
11   //    (from WhiteShaman)
```

Notice how you are not forced to extend a method. You can also overwrite it completely by merely shadowing it. This takes advantage of the fact that the JavaScript runtime will not call a method in a prototype if it exists in the current object.

Imagine that you want to completely replace the `toString` method for white shamans. You can write a new `toString` method like this:

```
// you don't need to overwrite and extend a method
// you can completely replace it
// the JavaScript runtime will make sure to call the right method:
WhiteShaman.prototype.toString = function(target){
    return `${this.name} the White Shaman`;
}
```

Below you can appreciate how the `toString` method no longer returns `Khaaar` but `Khaaar the White Shaman`:

```
khaaar.castsSlowCurse(conan);
// => Khaaar the White Shaman casts slow on Conan, the Barbarian.
//    Conan, the Barbarian seems to move slower
```

Simplifying Classical Inheritance in ES5

Now that you've arrived at the end of this chapter you may be thinking that writing *classes* in JavaScript is a ton of work. **And you are completely right.** That's why it's helpful to write a helper to make things easier for you and remove the boilerplate code.

Ideally, we would define a helper function that would let us create a *class* by providing all the moving pieces at once:

- a *constructor function*
- a *prototype*
- optionally, a *class* to extend or derive from

This function `newClass` is a possible implementation of such a helper:

```
function newClass({constructor,
                   methods:prototype,
                   extends:BaseClass=Object}){

    // helper function that creates a new constructor function
    // that calls the base class constructor function
    function extendConstructor(ctor, ctorToExtend){
        return function newCtor(...args){
            ctorToExtend.apply(this, args)
            ctor.apply(this, args);
            return this;
        };
    }

    // make sure constructor calls base class constructor
    let extendingConstructor = extendConstructor(constructor, BaseClas\
s);

    // set the class prototype to an object that has
    // the base class prototype as prototype
    extendingConstructor.prototype = Object.create(BaseClass.prototype\
);
    extendingConstructor.prototype.constructor = extendingConstructor;

    // extend the prototype with the *class* methods
    Object.assign(extendingConstructor.prototype, prototype);

    return extendingConstructor;
}
```

The newClass function takes the three ingredients for a *class*: *constructor*, *prototype* and *base class* and assembles them all together for you. It will:

1. Make sure to create a new *constructor function* that calls the base *constructor* before your own class *constructor*.
2. Assemble an appropriate *prototype* by creating an object with the base *class* prototype and combining it with your own *class* prototype.

If you don't provide a base *class* to extend it will use the `Object` *class* as default.

Let's see the `newClass` function in action and define a new `Berserker` *class*:

```
var Berserker = newClass({
  constructor: function(name, position, sprite, animalSpirit){
    this.animalSpirit;
  },
  methods: {
    rageAttack: function(target){
      console.log(`${this} screams and hits ${target}
        with a terrible blow`);
      target.hp -= 100;
    }
  },
  extends: ClassyBarbarian
});
```

Much better right? Now you can start using your `Berserker` *class* to fill your army ranks with fearless (and crazy) warriors:

```
var dwarfBerserker = new Berserker(
                        'Gloin',
                        new Position(0,0),
                        'gloin.png',
                        'badger');

dwarfBerserker.rageAttack("conan");
// => Gloin screams and hits conan with a terrible blow

dwarfBerserker.equipsWeapon({name: 'Double bearded Axe'});
// => Gloin grabs a Double bearded Axe from the cavern floor
```

Concluding

In this chapter you learned how to mimic C# *classes* and *classical inheritance* in JavaScript.

You saw how combining a *constructor function* and a *prototype* object let's you create something comparable to a class, where the *constructor function* defines your *class members* and the *prototype* defines your *class methods*. You then learned about *data privacy* with closures and symbols and how to write *static members, methods and classes* in JavaScript.

We continued extending the scope from a single class to multiple classes and you discovered how to achieve an equivalent experience to C# *classical inheritance*. We could do this by following two steps:

1. Calling a base *class constructor function* for a derived *class constructor* and by,
2. Establishing a *prototypical chain* between each *class* prototype

We wrapped the chapter discussing how to override and extend *class* methods, and how to simplify *class inheritance* in JavaScript using a helper function of our own devise.

If you reflect a little bit about what you've learned in this chapter you'll probably come to wonder: *Really? Does writing a class in JavaScript need to be this hard?*. That's exactly what *ES6 classes* are trying to remedy by providing a much more familiar, simpler and nicer syntax to writing *classes* in JavaScript. Very conveniently, the topic of our next chapter is non other than *ES6 classes*.

```
randalf.says("And that's how you emulate classical " +
    "inheritance in a nutshell");

mooleen.snores();
rat.elbows(mooleen);

mooleen.says("Whaaat? Wha What?");
randalf.says("Did you just fall asleep?");

mooleen.says("What? Oh no, I was pondering that last bit");
randalf.says("I know right, classical inheritance " +
```

```
    "is a little un-idiomatic");

rat.says("I hate to stop your dissertation but... " +
    "can you take a look at the beach?");
mooleen.says("Sweet mother of Jesus");
randalf.says("Mother of Who? What?");
randalf.whistles();

/*
    Where moments ago there were just sand and pebbles a
    humongous army of reddish brutes assembles for battle.

    As their commander shouts a charge and rows after rows
    of warriors start trotting and then running, more and
    more soldiers pour out of two wide portals seemingly
    floating over the beach.
*/

randalf.says("I suggest that you start building an army");
rat.says("Right now");
randalf.says("Bandalf will buy you us some time?");
```

Exercises

Experiment JavaScriptmancer!

You can experiment with these exercises and some possible solutions in this jsFiddle[53] or downloading the source code from GitHub[54].

---

[53]http://bit.ly/javascriptmancy-oop-classical-inheritance-exercises
[54]https://github.com/vintharas/javascriptmancy-code-samples

Take Advantage of the High Terrain with Archers!

Thanks to Bandalf we have some time to prepare a surprise for this host of angry enemies. Create an army of archers to decimate their ranks from the advantageous position on top of the hills.

Create an `Archer` class that inherits from this minion:

```
function Minion(name, hp){
    this.name = name;
    this.hp = hp;
    this.position = {x: 0, y: 0};
}
Minion.prototype = {
    constructor: Minion,
    toString: function(){
        return this.name;
    },
    goesTo: function (x, y){
        console.log(this + " goes to position (" + this.position.x +
                    "," + this.position.y +")");
    }
};
```

The archer should have a method `firesArrowTo` to target an enemy:

```
archer.firesArrowTo(redBrute);
// => archer fires arrow to red brute causing 10 damage
```

Solution

```
// archer -> Minion
function Archer(){
  Minion.call(this, 'archer', 100);
}
Archer.prototype = Object.create(Minion.prototype);
```

```
6    Archer.prototype.constructor = Archer;
7    Archer.prototype.firesArrowTo = function(target){
8      console.log(this + " fires arrow to " + target + " causing 10 dama\
9    ge");
10     target.hp -= 10;
11   }
12
13   // red brutes are coming!!
14   var redBrute = {
15     hp: 100,
16     toString: function(){ return 'red brute';}
17   };
18
19   mooleen.says("I'm almost ready!!!");
20
21   var archer = new Archer();
22   archer.firesArrowTo(redBrute);
23   // => archer fires arrow to red brute causing 10 damage
24
25   randalf.says("Keep them coming!!");
26   randalf.says("There are more coming up the hill!");
27
28   var anotherArcher = new Archer();
29   anotherArcher.firesArrowTo(redBrute);
30   // => archer fires arrow to red brute causing 10 damage
```

Hold Their Charge!! Build a Phalanx!

It looks like your archers have stirred a hornet's nest. A huge column of angry reddish brutes is charging up the hill wielding axes, clubs and humongous double-edged swords. We need to stop their advance before they reach the archers and cut them to pieces. Build a `Phalanx` unit to form an impenetrable and inhospitable wall with shields and lances.

The Phalanx unit should inherit from `Minion` and have these methods:

```
1  phalanx.formsShieldWall();
2  // => Phalanx adopts the shield wall stance +100 defence
3  //    (+100 defence per extra unit in the formation)
4  phalanx.attacksWithLance(redBrute);
5  // => Phalanx pierces red brute with the sharp end of
6  //    her lance causing 50 damage
```

Solution

```
1  function Phalanx(){
2    Minion.call(this, 'Phalanx', 500);
3    this.defense = 100;
4  }
5  Phalanx.prototype = Object.create(Minion.prototype);
6  Phalanx.prototype.constructor = Phalanx;
7  Phalanx.prototype.formsShieldWall = function(){
8    console.log("Phalanx adopts the shield wall stance " +
9    "+100 defense (+100 defense per extra unit in the formation)");
10   this.defense += 100;
11 }
12 Phalanx.prototype.attacksWithLance = function(target){
13   console.log(this + " pierces " + target + " with the " +
14   "sharp end of her lance causing 50 damage");
15   target.hp -= 50;
16 }
17
```

```
18  var phalanx = new Phalanx();
19  phalanx.formsShieldWall();
20  // => Phalanx adopts the shield wall stance +100 defense
21  //    (+100 defense per extra unit in the formation)
22  phalanx.attacksWithLance(redBrute);
23  // => Phalanx pierces red brute with the sharp end of
24  //    her lance causing 50 damage
25
26  randalf.says("Excellent! Form a complete wall! More phalanxes");
27
28  rat.says("errr... guys?");
29  /*
30  A 12 foot tall four-legged horned beast crosses the portal
31  into the beach and roars a blood freezing roar. As it walks
32  each step makes the earth rumble.
33  */
34  mooleen.says('No phalanx is going to stop that');
```

Magic Archers for Magic Beasts

Our archers and phalanxes will be no match for that mighty creature from hell. Create a new `MagicArcher` unit that will be able to enchant and shoot magic arrows at the beast.

The `MagicArcher` should inherit from the `Archer` unit and extend its `firesArrowTo` method. It should also have an `enchantArrow` method to produce magic arrows.

```
1  var fireArrow = magicArcher.enchant('fire', /* damage */ 100);
2  // => Magic archer enchats arrow with fire magic
3  //    (+100 magical damage)
4  magicArcher.firesArrowTo(hellBeast, fireArrow);
5  // => Magic archer fires arrow to hell beast causing 10 damage
6  //    The arrow is a fire arrow that causes additional
7  //    100 magical damage
```

Solution

```javascript
function MagicArcher(){
  Archer.call(this);
  this.name = 'magic archer';
  this.mana = 100;
}
MagicArcher.prototype = Object.create(Archer.prototype);
MagicArcher.prototype.constructor = MagicArcher;
MagicArcher.prototype.enchant = function(magicType, magicalDamage) {
  return {
    magicType: magicType,
    magicalDamage: magicalDamage,
    toString: function(){ return magicType + " arrow";}
  };
}
MagicArcher.prototype.firesArrowTo = function(target, arrow){
  Archer.prototype.firesArrowTo.call(this, target);
  console.log('The arrow is a ' + arrow + ' that causes ' +
    'additional ' + arrow.magicalDamage + ' magical damage');
}

var hellBeast = {
  hp: 20000,
  toString: function(){ return 'hell beast';}
};

var magicArcher = new MagicArcher();
var fireArrow = magicArcher.enchant('fire', 500);
// => magic archer fires arrow to hell beast causing 10 damage
magicArcher.firesArrowTo(hellBeast, fireArrow);
// => The arrow is a fire arrow that causes additional
//    500 magical damage

narrate(`
As the arrow impacts the beast, it roars in pain and rage
and charges up the hill to be welcomed by a shower of magical
arrows that succeed it slowing it and help the phalanx hold
it a bay.
`);

mooleen.says('Uff, that was close');
randalf.says('Great job student!');

rat.says('Hate to be the bearer of bad news, but I think ' +
         'that guy in red just opened two more portals');
```

```
45  mooleen.says('Damn! These spells are to slow to craft, ' +
46      'too complicated, too intricate...');
47  randalf.says("Let me think...");
48
49  randalf.says(`Yes! There's another way, a little bit unproved
50      since it was discovered in the later years but...
51      it might just work. How was it called...
52      Yes! I remember! ES6 classes!`);
```

White Tower Summoning Enhanced: The Marvels of ES6 Classes

Classes are useful in that they
let us represent the world around us
in a simplified abstract manner,
reducing an infinite complex world
to the problem at hand.

Writing summoning spells
for your all-mighty army?
You probably don't need to model
your creatures digestive tract

> \- RaezIm Rurat
> Oracle of Kwarok

White Tower Summoning Enhanced: The Marvels of ES6 Classes

```
/*
The battle rages on and no group seems to have the upper hand.
Brutes and beasts keep pouring out of four great portals
but the advantage of the terrain lets Mooleen defend the hill
with a smaller force.
*/

mooleen.weaves(`new Phalanx()`);
/*
A phalanx materializes and takes his place
reinforcing the third rank.
*/

mooleen.says("Won't they stop coming?");
mooleen.says("I'm starting to get tired");
rat.says("Looks like they're doing a very serious " +
        "attempt at invading the island." +
        "One would say, an effort out of proportion...");

randalf.says("Well, this island is quite a jewel");
randalf.says("It's small, easy to defend and
             a tremendous source of mana");

mooleen.says("Mana?");
randalf.says("Yeah, that's the mysterious energy you " +
             "need to cast spells.")

randalf.says("The more sources of mana you command " +
        "the bigger the armies you can summon " +
        "and the more powerful spells you can cast.");

mooleen.says("That makes sense. I remember feeling a " +
             "sort of euphoria when we vanquised Great.");
randalf.says("Yes, that was the island opening to you.");

mooleen.says("Aha! How can we use that extra power " +
             "to turn the tide of the battle? ");

randalf.says("Hmm, mimicking classical inheritance won't work");
randalf.says("You need to create these units faster " +
             "with ES6 classes!");
```

Create These Units Faster with ES6 Classes!

In the last chapter you learned how to implement *classes* in JavaScript without relying on *ES6 classes*. This puts you in a wonderful position to learn *ES6 classes*:

1. Now you have a deep understanding about the underlying implementation of *ES6 classes* which are just syntactic sugar over *constructor functions* and *prototypes*. This will help you understand not only how *ES6 classes* work but also how they relate to the rest of JavaScript.
2. You have experienced first-hand the tediousness of writing lots of boilerplate code to achieve the equivalent of both *classes* and *classical inheritance*. With this context, the value proposition of *ES6 classes* becomes very clear as they bring a much nicer syntax and developer experience to using *classes* and *classical inheritance* in JavaScript.

Because *ES6 classes* provide a great class developer experience, they are a perfect entry point for developers coming from static typed languages like C#. You can start your JavaScript journey using *classes* just like you would in C#, and little by little learn more about the specific capabilities that JavaScript has to offer.

From ES5 "Classes" to ES6 Classes

 Experiment JavaScriptmancer!!
You can experiment with all examples in this chapter directly within this jsBin[55] or downloading the source code from GitHub[56].

---
[55] http://bit.ly/javascriptmancy-oop-es6-classes
[56] https://github.com/vintharas/javascriptmancy-code-samples

In the previous chapter you learned how to obtain a *class* equivalent by combining a *constructor function* and a *prototype*:

```
// the constructor function:
//    - defines the ClassyBarbarian type
//    - defines the properties a ClassyBarbarian instance
//      is going to have
function ClassyBarbarian(name){
    this.name = name;
    this["character class"] = "barbarian";
    this.hp = 200;
    this.weapons = [];
}

// the prototype:
//    - defines the methods shared across all instances
ClassyBarbarian.prototype = {
    constructor: ClassyBarbarian,
    talks: function(){
        console.log("I am " + this.name + " !!!");
    },
    equipsWeapon: function(weapon){
        weapon.equipped = true;
        this.weapons.push(weapon);
        console.log(`${this.name} grabs a ${weapon.name} ` +
                    ` from the cavern floor`);
    },
    toString: function(){
        return this.name;
    },
    saysHi: function (){
        console.log("Hi! I am " + this.name);
    }
};
```

The transformation between this *class* equivalent to a full blown *ES6 class* is very straightforward. Behold! The mighty `Barbarian` class!

```js
class Barbarian {

  constructor(name){
    this.name = name;
    this["character class"] = "barbarian";
    this.hp = 200;
    this.weapons = [];
  }

  talks(){
    console.log("I am " + this.name + " !!!");
  }

  equipsWeapon(weapon){
    weapon.equipped = true;
    this.weapons.push(weapon);
    console.log(`${this.name} grabs a ${weapon.name} from ` +
                `the cavern floor`);
  }

  toString(){
    return this.name;
  }

  saysHi(){
    console.log("Hi! I am " + this.name);
  }
};
```

The `class` keyword followed by the *class* name now act as a container for the whole *class*. The syntax for the body is very reminiscent of the *shorthand method syntax* of object initializers that you learned in *JavaScript-mancy: Getting Started* (also available in appendix A if you need to take a quick sneak peek):

- The **constructor function** becomes the `constructor` method inside the class
- The **prototype** methods become methods within the body of the class. They are separated by new lines and not by commas like in an object initializer.

- Instead of writing a method with the `function` keyword as in `sayHi: function(){}` we use the shorthand version nearer to C# method syntax `sayHi(){`.
- In addition to methods you can also define *getters* and *setters* just like you would within object literals.

Once defined, you can create *class* instances using the `new` keyword:

```
const conan = new Barbarian('Conan');

console.log(`Conan is a barbarian: ` +
            `${conan instanceof Barbarian}`);
// => Conan is a barbarian: true

conan.equipsWeapon('steel sword');
// => Conan grabs a undefined from the cavern floor
```

Prototypical Inheritance via Extends

Expressing inheritance is equally straightforward when you use *ES6 classes*. The `extends` keyword provides a more declarative approach than the equivalent in *ES5*.

Where in *ES5* we would need to:

1. Make sure to call the base class *constructor function* and,
2. Set the `prototype` property of a *constructor function*

like in this example:

White Tower Summoning Enhanced: The Marvels of ES6 Classes

```
function Berserker(name, animalSpirit){
    // 1) Call base class constructor
    Barbarian.call(this, name);
    this.animalSpirit = animalSpirit;
};

// 2) Set prototype imperatively
Berserker.prototype = Object.create(Barbarian.prototype);
Berserker.prototype.constructor = Berserker;
Berserker.prototype.rageAttack = function(target){
  console.log(`${this} screams and hits ` +
              `${target} with a terrible blow`);
  target.hp -= 100;
};
```

With *ES6 classes* we use the extends keyword in the class declaration:

```
class Berserker extends Barbarian {

    constructor(name, animalSpirit){
        super(name);
        this.animalSpirit = animalSpirit;
    }

    rageAttack(target){
      console.log(`${this} screams and hits ${target} ` +
                  `with a terrible blow`);
      target.hp -= 100;
    }
}
```

The extends keyword ensures that the Berserker class extends (inherits from) the Barbarian class. The super keyword within the constructor let's you call the base class constructor.

If we now instantiate a new maddened Berserker you'll appreciate how it has both Berserker and Barbarian types:

```
const logen = new Berserker('Logen, the Bloody Nine', 'wolf');
console.log(`Logen is a barbarian: ${logen instanceof Barbarian}`);
// => Logen is a barbarian: true
console.log(`Logen is a berserker: ${logen instanceof Berserker}`);
// => Logen is a berserker: true
```

And contains methods from both classes:

```
logen.equipsWeapon({name:'huge rusty sword'});
// => Logen, the Bloody Nine grabs a huge rusty sword
//    from the cavern floor
logen.rageAttack(conan);
// => Logen, the Bloody Nine screams and hits Conan with
//    a terrible blow
```

Infinitely better, isn't it?

Overriding Methods in ES6 Classes

You can also use the `super` keyword to override and extend *class* methods. Remember the `Shaman` and `WhiteShaman` we used in the previous chapter to illustrate method overriding? The example below shows how you can achieve the same thing with ES6 classes. We have taken the original classes, transformed them into very concise ES6 classes and used the `super` keyword to override the `heals` method.

Here is the `Shaman` class:

White Tower Summoning Enhanced: The Marvels of ES6 Classes

```
class Shaman extends Barbarian{
  constructor(name){
    super(name);
  }

  heals(target){
    console.log(`${this} heals ${target} (+ 50hp)`);
    target.hp += 50;
  }
}
```

And here the `WhiteShaman` that overrides and extends the `heals` method with new and improved functionality:

```
class WhiteShaman extends Shaman {

  castsSlowCurse(target){
    console.log(`${this} casts slow on ${target}.` +
                ` ${target} seems to move slower`);
    if (target.curses) target.curses.push('slow');
    else target.curses = ['slow'];
  }

  heals(target){
    // instead of Shaman.prototype.heals.call(this, target);
    // you can use super
    super.heals(target);
    console.log(`${this} cleanses all negatives effects ` +
                `in ${target}`);
    target.curses = [];
    target.poisons = [];
  }
}
```

The `super` keyword provides a great improvement from the ES5 approach where you were required to call the method on the base class prototype:

```
WhiteShaman.prototype.heals = function(target){
  // calling base class implementation
  // omg really?
  Shaman.prototype.heals.call(this, target);

  // etc...
}
```

You can verify how the overridden `heals` method works just as you'd expect:

```
const khaaar = new WhiteShaman('Khaaar');

khaaar.castsSlowCurse(conan);
// => Khaaar casts slow on Conan, the Barbarian.
//    Conan seems to move slower

khaaar.heals(conan);
// => Khaaar cleanses all negatives effects in Conan
```

Static Members and Methods

In addition to per-instance [57] methods, *ES6 classes* provide a syntax to declare static methods. Just prepend the `static` keyword to a method declaration inside a class.

Imagine that we have a `Sword` class to represent swords of different shapes and sizes:

---

[57]This is not entirely true! *What!? Liar!* Let me clarify. Although methods declared within the body of a class may feel like per-instance methods, they are not. They are actually defined as part of the prototype of a class and therefore shared across all instances. The difference with *static* methods is that these are attached to the constructor function.

White Tower Summoning Enhanced: The Marvels of ES6 Classes 149

```
class Sword {
  constructor(material, damage, weight){
    this.material = material;
    this.damage = damage;
    this.weight = weight;
  }

  toString(){
    return `${this.material} sword (+${this.damage})`;
  }
}
```

Within this class we could define a `getRandom()` static method that would allow us to easily forge new swords with random characteristics:

```
class Sword {
  constructor(material, damage, weight){
    this.material = material;
    this.damage = damage;
    this.weight = weight;
  }

  toString(){
    return `${this.material} sword (+${this.damage})`;
  }

  // new static method
  static getRandom(){
    const randomMaterial = 'iron',
        damage = Math.random(Math.random()*10),
        randomWeight = '5 stones';
    return new Sword(randomMaterial, damage, randomWeight);
  }
}
```

You can call a *static method* using the *class* name followed by the method like you would in C#. Voila a new sword!

```
const randomSword = Sword.getRandom();

console.log(randomSword.toString());
// => iron sword (+4)
```

Unlike with methods, *ES6 classes* don't offer a declarative syntax to declare *static members*. Fortunately, you can still use the approach you learned in the previous chapter, that is, you can augment the *constructor function* (the class identifier) with the *static member*.

Let's say that we want to make our previous sword generator algorithm a little bit more configurable by providing a list of available materials. We can store this list of allowed materials in a static member:

```
Sword.materials = ['wood', 'iron', 'steel'];

console.log(Sword.materials);
// => ['wood', 'iron', 'steel']
```

Now we can update the getRandom *static method* to use this list of allowed materials. Since they are both *static* they can freely access each other:

```
static getRandom(){
    // super complex randomness algorithm
    // to pick a material :) cheater!
    const randomMaterial = Sword.materials[0],
        damage = Math.random(Math.random()*10),
        randomWeight = '5 stones';

    return new Sword(randomMaterial, damage, randomWeight);
}
```

ES6 Classes and Information Hiding

When it comes to *ES6 classes* and *information hiding* we are in the same place[58] as we were prior to *ES6*: Every property inside the constructor of a class and every method within the class declaration body is public. **You need to rely on closures or *ES6 symbols* to achieve data privacy.**

Just like with *ES5 classes*, if you want to use closures to declare private members or methods you'll need to move the method consuming these private members inside the *class* constructor. This will ensure that the method can enclose the private member or method.

For instance, we can make the weapons member private just like we did in the previous chapter:

```
class PrivateBarbarian {

  constructor(name){
    // private members
    const weapons = [];

    // public members
    this.name = name;
    this["character class"] = "barbarian";
    this.hp = 200;

    this.equipsWeapon = function (weapon){
      weapon.equipped = true;

      // the equipsWeapon method encloses
      // the weapons variable
      weapons.push(weapon);

      console.log(`${this.name} grabs a ${weapon.name} ` +
                  `from the cavern floor`);
```

---

[58]You'll be happy to know that there is an active proposal to bring class members and private fields to JavaScript. Wiii!

```
    };

    this.toString = function(){
      if (weapons.length > 0) {
        return `${this.name} wields a ` +
                `${weapons.find(w => w.equipped).name}`;
      } else return this.name
    };
  }

  talks(){
    console.log("I am " + this.name + " !!!");
  }

  saysHi(){
    console.log("Hi! I am " + this.name);
  }
};
```

In the example above we have defined weapons as a normal variable inside the constructor scope. We have then moved the equipsWeapon and toString methods inside the constructor and rewritten them to enclose the weapons variable. Now we can verify how weapons effectively becomes a private member of the PrivateBarbarian class:

```
const privateBarbarian = new PrivateBarbarian('timido');
privateBarbarian.equipsWeapon({name: 'mace'});
// => timido grabs a mace from the cavern floor

console.log(`Barbarian weapons: ${privateBarbarian.weapons}`);
// => Barbarian weapons: undefined

console.log(privateBarbarian.toString())
// => timido wields a mace
```

Alternatively, you can use symbols just like with *ES5 classes*:

White Tower Summoning Enhanced: The Marvels of ES6 Classes 153

```
// this should be placed inside a module
// so only the SymbolicBarbarian has access to it
const weapons = Symbol('weapons');

class SymbolicBarbarian {

  constructor(name){
    this.name = name;
    this["character class"] = "barbarian";
    this.hp = 200;
    this[weapons] = [];
  }

  talks(){
    console.log("I am " + this.name + " !!!");
  }

  equipsWeapon(weapon){
    weapon.equipped = true;
    this[weapons].push(weapon);
    console.log(`${this.name} grabs a ` +
                `${weapon.name} from the cavern floor`);
  }

  toString(){
    if(this[weapons].length > 0) {
      return `${this.name} wields a ` +
             `${this[weapons].find(w => w.equipped).name}`;
    } else return this.name;
  }

  saysHi(){
    console.log("Hi! I am " + this.name);
  }
};
```

Which also results in weapons being private [59]:

---

[59] Remember that you can get access to all symbols used within an object via getOwnPropertySymbols and therefore *symbols* don't offer true privacy like *closures* do.

```
1  const symbolicBarbarian = new SymbolicBarbarian('simbolo');
2  symbolicBarbarian.equipsWeapon({name: 'morning star'});
3  // => timido grabs a mace from the cavern floor
4
5  console.log(`Barbarian weapons: ${symbolicBarbarian.weapons}`);
6  // => Barbarian weapons: undefined
7
8  console.log(symbolicBarbarian.toString())
9  // => timido wields a morning star
```

Which to choose? That depends on what style you prefer. Just know that closures and *symbols* have the same trade-offs with *ES6 classes* than with *ES5 classes*:

Closures	ES6 Symbols
Let's you achieve true privacy.	You cannot achieve true privacy because a client could use getOwnPropertySymbols to obtain to your symbols and therefore your private variables.
Because you need to enclose variables with your methods, using closures forces you to move your methods from the *prototype* to the *constructor function*. This requires more memory since these methods are no longer shared by all instances.	With symbols you can keep your methods in the *prototype* and therefore consume less memory.

ES6 Classes Behind the Curtain

If you've been attentive during this chapter about ES6 classes you may have noticed one thing. Because ES6 classes are just syntactic sugar over JavaScript existing OOP constructs, we can fill in the gaps left by lacking features using vanilla ES5 solutions like we did with static members or data privacy.

This is a hint that we can use *ES6 classes* just like we would use a *constructor function* and a *prototype* pair. For instance, we can augment an *ES6 class* prototype at any time with new capabilities and all instances of that class will get instant access to those features (via the *prototype chain*).

For instance, let's bless all our barbarians with a mysterious god mode:

```
Barbarian.prototype.entersGodMode = function(){
    console.log(`${this} enters GOD MODE!!!!`);
    this.hp = 99999;
    this.damage = 99999;
    this.speed = 99999;
    this.attack = 99999;
};
```

After executing this bit of code, the instances that we created earlier like conan the *Barbarian,* logen the *Berserker* and khaaar the *Shaman* all obtain the new ability to enter god mode:

```
conan.entersGodMode();
// => Conan enters GOD MODE!!!!
logen.entersGodMode();
// => Logen, the Bloody Nine enters GOD MODE!!!!
khaaar.entersGodMode();
// => Khaaar enters GOD MODE!!!!
```

Freaky.

Concluding

ES6 classes are a result of the natural evolution of JavaScript's object oriented programming paradigm. The evolution from the rudimentary *class* support we had in *ES5* where we needed to write a lot of boilerplate code to the much better native support in *ES6*.

They resemble C# classes and can be created using the `class` keyword. They have a `constructor` function where you declare the *class* members and have a very similar syntax to that of shorthand object initializers.

ES6 classes provide support for method overriding via the `super` keyword, static methods via the `static` keyword and they can easily express inheritance trees (prototype chains) in a declarative way by using the `extends` keyword.

It is important that you understand that *ES6* classes are just syntactic sugar over the existing inheritance model. Wielding that knowledge you can take advantage of what you learned in previous chapters to implement static members, data privacy via closures and symbols, augment a *class* prototype at runtime, and anything you can imagine.

Now that you know how to write OOP in JavaScript using a C# style it's time to move beyond *classical inheritance* and embrace JavaScript's dynamic nature and flexibility. Up next! Mixins and Object Composition!

```
/*
    A new portal appears on top of the hill flanking
    Mooleen, Randalf and rat's position. In the blink
    of an eye, a throng of brutes charge from within
    the portal.
*/

mooleen.says("When I thought things couldn't " +
             "get any worse...");
rat.says("Things can and will always get worse");
mooleen.says("Yeah but can't we ever have the " +
             "upper hand? Just once?");

randalf.says("You know? Imminent death is approaching" +
    " and the only thing I can think of is... damn! " +
    " These people sweat profusely. What a reek!");
```

```
rat.says('That was mean Randalf. Shame on you');

mooleen.says("Imminent death?! Not if I can prevent it!");
```

Exercises

 Experiment JavaScriptmancer!

You can experiment with these exercises and some possible solutions in this jsFiddle[60] or downloading the source code from GitHub[61].

---

[60] http://bit.ly/javascriptmancy-oop-es6-classes-exercises
[61] https://github.com/vintharas/javascriptmancy-code-samples

White Tower Summoning Enhanced: The Marvels of ES6 Classes

 Prevent Imminent Death!

Quick! There are seconds separating us from the Netherworld. Create a `SandGolem` class that inherits from the same `Minion` from the previous chapter.

```
function Minion(name, hp){
  this.name = name;
  this.hp = hp;
  this.position = {x: 0, y: 0};
}
Minion.prototype = {
  constructor: Minion,
  toString: function(){
    return this.name;
  },
  goesTo: function (x, y){
    this.position.x = x;
    this.position.y = y;
    console.log(this + " goes to position (" +
      this.position.x + "," + this.position.y + ")");
  }
};
```

The `SandGolem` should have two methods `bash` and `absorb`, the first one to bash enemies heads and the second one to stop them in their tracks by absorbing their attacks inside its body of sand.

```
sandGolem.bash(redBrute);
// => Sand golem bashes red brute with
//    terrible force causing 30 damage
sandGolem.absorb(redBrute);
// => Sand golem absorbs red brute into its body of sand.
//    The red brute can't move
```

Solution

```
function Minion(name, hp){
```

White Tower Summoning Enhanced: The Marvels of ES6 Classes

```
 2      this.name = name;
 3      this.hp = hp;
 4      this.position = {x: 0, y: 0};
 5   }
 6   Minion.prototype = {
 7     constructor: Minion,
 8     toString: function(){
 9       return this.name;
10     },
11     goesTo: function (x, y){
12       this.position.x = x;
13       this.position.y = y;
14       console.log(this + " goes to position (" +
15           this.position.x + "," + this.position.y + ")");
16     }
17   };
18
19   var redBrute = {
20     hp:100,
21     toString(){ return 'red brute';}
22   };
23
24   class SandGolem extends Minion {
25     constructor(name='Sand Golem', hp=200){
26       super(name, hp);
27     }
28     bash(target){
29       console.log(`${this} bashes ${target} with ` +
30           `terrible force causing 30 damage`);
31       target.hp -= 30;
32     }
33     absorb(target){
34       console.log(`${this} absorbs ${target} into its ` +
35           `body of sand. The ${target} can't move`);
36     }
37   }
38
39   const sandGolem = new SandGolem();
40   sandGolem.goesTo(1, 1)
41   // => sand golem goes to position (1,1)
42   sandGolem.bash(redBrute);
43   // => sand golem bashes red brute with terrible
44   //    force causing 30 damage
45   sandGolem.absorb(redBrute);
46   // => Sand golem absorbs red brute into its body.
47   //    The red brute can't move
48
```

```
49  mooleen.says('Aha! Look how I combined the sand golem' +
50               'with my old Minion!');
51  rat.says('Majestic!');
52  randalf.says("And it looks like it's working to stop " +
53               "the tide of barbarians! Awesome!");
54
55  mooleen.says("And now for the final number... GIANTS!!");
```

GIANTS!!!!

Let's deliver our last blow to this army of red barbarians. Create a SandGiant that extends the SandGolem with two new methods: A bash method that destroys enemies and a stomp method that makes the earth shake.

```
1  sandGiant.bash(redBrute);
2  // => Sand giant bashes brute and turns it into a pulp
3  sandGiant.stomp();
4  // => Sand giant stomps the ground in fury. The earth
5  //    shakes stopping everyone around the giant.
```

Solution

```
1   class SandGiant extends SandGolem {
2     constructor(name='Sand giant', hp=9999){
3       super(name, hp)
4     }
5     bash(target){
6       console.log(`${this} bashes ${target} ` +
7                   `and turns it into a pulp`);
8       target.hp = 0;
9     }
10    stomp(){
11      console.log(`${this} stomps the ground in fury. ` +
```

```
12        `The earth shakes stopping everyone around the giant.`);
13      }
14    }
15
16    const sandGiant = new SandGiant();
17    sandGiant.goesTo(2,2);
18    // => Sand giant goes to position (2,2)
19    sandGiant.bash(redBrute);
20    // => Sand giant bashes red brute and turns it into a pulp
21    sandGiant.stomp();
22    // => Sand giant stomps the ground in fury. The earth
23    //    shakes stopping everyone around the giant.
24
25    /*
26
27    The sudden appearance of the sand giants turns the
28    battlefield into chaos. The brute army tries to
29    rally and mount an attack but they are overwhelmed.
30
31    One by one the portals start fading and disappear.
32
33    */
34
35    mooleen.says('Enemies! Tremble upon my wrath!');
36    rat.says('moahahaha');
37    randalf.says('moahahaha');
38    bandalf.says('moahahaha');
39    mooleen.says('moahahaha');
40
41    mooleen.says('Wait, where have you been all this time?');
42    bandalf.says("I was entertaining the red wizard, in an " +
43                 "epic insult sword fighting duel");
44    mooleen.says("Insult sword fighting... " +
45                 "that sounds vaguely familiar...");
```

Black Tower Summoning: Objects Interweaving Objects with Mixins

I used to think that the important
innovation of JavaScript was prototypal inheritance.

Upon more reflection, I think that it is
class free object oriented programming.

It is JavaScript's gift to humanity.

> - Glas Ford,
> JavaScript-Mancy: A missunderstood art, Meditations

Black Tower Summoning: Objects Interweaving Objects with Mixins

```
/* The wind blows atop a sandy hill, a deep thick silence
   envelops everything, as if there was nothing left alive
   walking the world. Bodies piled on top of more bodies.
   The sick aftermath of a terrible battle.

   Suddenly a muffled sound. A ever so slight shift within
   a pile. A vibration. Something definitely alive.
*/

redBrute.shouts("aaaaarrghhhh!");

/*
   From a pile of bodies raises a huge red figure muscles bulging.
   In his right hand a monstruous two handed longsword that may
   or may not have impaled two or more bodies on its way up.
*/

redBrute.coughsWithAnUncharacteristiclyHighPitchCough();

/*
   With his left hand he reaches inside his furs and takes a
   pair of thin-framed glasses that he carefully places in his
   face over his nose.
*/

redBrute.says("That was most inconvenient");

/*
   If you were an inhabitant of a planet called Earth you
   may have compared the accent of this barbarian to that
   of a British aristocrat.

   The red brute is quickly surrounded by a circle of lances.
*/

redBrute.says("Dear gentlemen, I appreciate your consideration " +
              "but I'm not in the need of a toothpick." +
              "I'd be delighted if you'd be so kind to " +
              "bring your general.");

mooleen.says("That happens to be me");

redBrute.says("Aha!");

/*
   The barbaric figure lunges towards Mooleen with a warcry
   wielding the immense sword and...
*/
```

```
    ...smashes it into a rock breaking it into pieces

    ...that is, the sword not the rock
*/

redBrute.kneels();
mooleen.looksPuzzled();
randalf.looksPerplexed();
bandalf.looksAmused();
rat.looksLikeRatsLook();

redBrute.says("Milady. As the ancient laws of my people demand" +
    " and having being utterly defeated by your superior " +
    " commanding prowess, I hereby pledge fealty to you " +
    " until I can prove myself and gain my honor back ");

mooleen.says("wat");
mooleen.says("Wait, how do I know that you won't stab me" +
    " in the back at the slightest chance?");

redBrute.says("Oh, that's easy, if anything were to happen " +
    "to you before I regained my honor I'd never be able to " +
    "gain entrance to Walhala. I'd be a pariah condemned " +
    "to walk the darklands for eternity, my innards " +
    "chewed by rats and my flesh and eyes picked by crows.");

rat.says("yum");
randalf.says("I'm not convinced...");

redBrute.says("I also happen to know where you can find that " +
    "twat of the Red Hand and how you can crush him " +
    "and all his chronies before they rally their " +
    "unending hosts and exterminate you.");

mooleen.says("I'm listening");

redBrute.says("The problem with classes and classical inheritance...\
")
```

The Problem With Classes and Classical Inheritance...

The world we live in is unbelievably complex. Creating software that handles this infinite degree of complexity and detail is a futile endeavor. Object Oriented Programming attempts to solve this problem by abstracting the world inside a problem space and creating representations of reality that are simplified and that let us solve very specific problems. Thus turning the impossible into something, if not simple, at least manageable.

These OOP representations are usually done with the aid of *classes* and *objects*. A class represents a blueprint of something, some entity in reality that we want to abstract and use in our programs. It determines the properties that we will use to represent this entity and which actions it can perform. An *object* represents a particular instance of that blueprint, of that class, something that exists, has a particular state and can be operated on.

This is all well and good. We live in a complex world and OOP helps us manage that complexity through simplified versions of reality called *classes* and *objects*.

A side effect of using *classes* is that it creates a *taxonomy* or a *classification* of the entities in the world around us. This classification, because of the nature of classes and inheritance, tends to be a very rigid one that doesn't tolerate change well. *Change* not strictly in the sense of adding a new property to a class but in accommodating the system of *classes* to new knowledge about the domain at hand.

We saw an example of this particular problem in the introduction to this book where we defined these three classes `Minion`, `Wizard` and `Thief`:

```
class Minion {
  constructor(name, hp){
    this.name = name;
    this.hp = hp;
  }
  toString(){
    return this.name;
  }
}

class Wizard extends Minion {
  constructor(element, mana, name, hp){
    super(name, hp);
    this.element = element;
    this.mana = mana;
  }
  toString(){
    return super.toString() + ", the " + this.element +" Wizard";
  }
  castsSpell(spell, target){
    console.log(this + ' casts ' + spell + ' on ' + target);
    this.mana -= spell.mana;
    spell(target);
  }
}

class Thief extends Minion {
  constructor(name, hp){
    super(name, hp);
  }
  toString(){
    return super.toString() + ", the Thief";
  }
  steals(target, item){
    console.log(`${this} steals ${item} from ${target}`);
  }
}
```

Our problem space was represented by a world in which we have a `Wizard` as someone who can cast spells, and a `Thief` as someone who can steal. Within this context we learned something new about our domain: The existence of *Bards* as creatures of myth and legend

Black Tower Summoning: Objects Interweaving Objects with Mixins 167

that could both casts spells, steal, and even play an instrument!

But the system of *classes* that we had created, our current taxonomy that represents our view of the world right now doesn't accommodate very well the idea of a Bard... is it a Wizard? Is it a Thief? Is it something else? It cannot be both! Can it!?

And so in order to bring this knowledge into our system, we need to do a major redesign of our *classes*, redefine our whole taxonomy, or duplicate code and forsake the benefits that could come from polymorphism.

So classes create taxonomies. Taxonomies are rigid and don't tolerate change well. *Is there anything else we need to take into account?* Well there's also a problem with the **when**, when do we create these classes and taxonomies? And how does that affect how we work?

A very wise person [62] reflected over this and realized that we build these taxonomies when we start a project, which is the moment when we least know about our domain and problem space. We are creating these very rigid systems to represent a domain we are usually not familiar with. Systems that will inevitably need to change as we find out more about the domain, but which are not well suited to adapt to that change.

Is there a better way?

Well, yes sir/madam there is. It is **class-free object oriented programming** and this gentleman calls it the single most important contribution of JavaScript to humanity. In this and the upcoming chapters we will focus in how you can achieve this approach to object oriented programming, where *classes* disappear and we just focus on *objects*. Sounds exciting doesn't it?

---

[62] Douglas Crockford talks about this idea of class-free inheritance in his excellent talk at nordic.js http://bit.ly/douglas-crockford-nordicjs

Free Yourself From Classes With Object Composition and Mixins

Experiment JavaScriptmancer!!

You can experiment with all examples in this chapter directly within this jsBin[63] or downloading the source code from GitHub[64].

In the introduction to this book you had a taste of *class-free inheritance* when you learned how to compose objects with each other using `Object.assign`. In that particular implementation of *class-free* inheritance we defined behaviors as objects `canBeIdentifiedByName`, `canCastSpells`, `canSteal` and `canPlayMusic`:

```
const canBeIdentifiedByName = {
  toString(){
    return this.name;
  }
};

const canCastSpells = {
  castsSpell(spell, target){
    console.log(this + ' casts ' + spell + ' on ' + target);
    this.mana -= spell.mana;
    spell(target);
  }
};

const canSteal = {
  steals(target, item){
    console.log(`${this} steals ${item} from ${target}`);
  }
};
```

---

[63] http://bit.ly/javascriptmancy-oop-object-composition-mixins
[64] https://github.com/vintharas/javascriptmancy-code-samples

```
const canPlayMusic = {
  playsMusic(){
    console.log(`${this} grabs his ${this.instrument} and starts pla\
ying music`);
  }
};
```

And we composed them together to build more complex objects:

```
// and now we can create our objects by composing this behaviors tog\
ether
function Wizard(element, mana, name, hp){
  const wizard = {element,
                  mana,
                  name,
                  hp};
  Object.assign(wizard,
                canBeIdentifiedByName,
                canCastSpells);
  return wizard;
}

function Thief(name, hp){
  const thief = {name,
                 hp};
  Object.assign(thief,
                canBeIdentifiedByName,
                canSteal);
  return thief;
}

function Bard(instrument, mana, name, hp){
  const bard = {instrument,
                mana,
                name,
                hp};
  Object.assign(bard,
                canBeIdentifiedByName,
                canCastSpells,
                canSteal,
                canPlayMusic);
```

```
33      return bard;
34  }
```

That work just like you would expect of a wizard:

```
1   const lightningSpell = (target) => {
2     console.log(`A bolt of lightning electrifies ` +
3                 `${target} (-10hp)`);
4     target.hp -= 10;
5   };
6   lightningSpell.mana = 5;
7   lightningSpell.toString = () => 'lightning spell';
8
9   const orc = {
10    name: 'orc',
11    hp: 100,
12    toString(){ return this.name }
13  };
14
15  const wizard = Wizard('fire', 100, 'Randalf, the Red', 10);
16  wizard.castsSpell(lightningSpell, orc);
17  // => Randalf, the Red casts lightning spell on orc
18  // => A bolt of lightning electrifies orc(-10hp)
```

A thief:

```
1   const thief = Thief('Locke Lamora', 100);
2   thief.steals('orc', /*item*/ 'gold coin');
3   // => Locke Lamora steals gold coin from orc
```

And a bard:

Black Tower Summoning: Objects Interweaving Objects with Mixins 171

```
1  const bard = Bard('lute', 100, 'Kvothe', 100);
2  bard.playsMusic();
3  // => Kvothe grabs his lute and starts playing music
4
5  bard.steals('orc', /*item*/ 'sandwich');
6  // => Kvothe steals sandwich from orc
7
8  bard.castsSpell(lightningSpell, orc);
9  // => Kvothe casts lightning spell on orc
10 // =>A bolt of lightning electrifies orc(-10hp)
```

The objects that encapsulate a piece of reusable behavior (canSteal, canPlayMusic, etc) are what we call **mixins**. We compose them, or *mix* them, with other objects to augment them with additional behavior.

Note that you don't need to use a *factory function* like in the previous examples, you can compose a simple object if so you wish:

```
1  const orcMagician = Object.assign(
2      {name: 'orc mage', hp: 100, mana: 50},
3      canBeIdentifiedByName,
4      canCastSpells);
5
6  orcMagician.castsSpell(lightningSpell, wizard);
7  // => orc mage casts lightning spell on Randalf, the Red
8  // => A bolt of lightning electrifies Randalf, the Red(-10hp)
9  // sweet vengeance moahahahaha
```

The *factory function* just adds that extra level of convenience to create many objects.

Let's continue strengthening this idea of object composition and flexibility with a new example. Imagine that you want to be able to see your legions displayed on a map so that you can take better strategic decisions in your path to ruling the known universe.

You can define a canBePositioned object that encapsulates this new behavior of positioning stuff:

```
const canBePositioned = {
    x : 0,
    y : 0,
    movesTo(x, y) {
        console.log(`${this} moves from ` +
            `(${this.x}, ${this.y}) to (${x}, ${y})`);
        this.x = x;
        this.y = y;
    }
};
```

And augment all of our minions with that functionality:

```
Object.assign(wizard, canBePositioned);
Object.assign(thief, canBePositioned);
Object.assign(bard, canBePositioned);
Object.assign(orcMagician, canBePositioned);
```

All of the sudden we can position and move them to our heart's content. And if we define a very simple ASCII two-dimensional map like this one:

```
function Map(width, height, creatures){

    function paintPoint(x,y){
        const creatureInPosition = creatures
            .find(c => c.x === x && c.y === y);
        if (creatureInPosition)
            return creatureInPosition.name[0];
        return '_';
    }

    return {
        width,
        height,
        creatures,
        paint() {
            let map = '';
            for(let y = 0; y < height; y++) {
                for (let x = 0; x < width; x++)
```

```
            map += paintPoint(x,y);
            map += '\n';
        }
        return map;
    }
}
```

We can combine the Map capability of drawing stuff and the minions capability of positioning themselves and moving around to get a tactical representation of our army:

```
wizard.movesTo(10,10);
// => Randalf, the Red moves from (0, 0) to (10, 10)
thief.movesTo(5,5);
// => Locke Lamora moves from (0, 0) to (5, 5)
bard.movesTo(15,15);
// => Kvothe moves from (0, 0) to (15, 15)

const worldMap = Map(50, 20, [wizard, thief, bard, orcMagician]);
console.log(worldMap.paint());

/* =>
O_____




       L










        R







       K


*/
```

You may be thinking... *Well, I can do this with C# and classical inheritance any day.* And indeed you can, but some interesting ideas about the object composition approach are that:

- **We don't need any upfront design effort to make our application extensible.** In C# you need to define the extensibility points of a system because you need to use the right artifacts like interfaces, composition over inheritance, design patterns like strategy, etc. In JavaScript we don't need to over-architect our solution, or carefully design our application for extensibility purposes. You get a new feature, you define a new behavior, compose it with your existing objects and start using it.
- **Object composition happens at runtime.** You have your program running, your objects doing whatever objects do and all of the sudden *BOOM!* Object composability and your objects get new features and can do new interesting things. New things like changing from a text representation to a 2D representation or a 3D representation and who knows what more.
- **It doesn't need to affect the original objects at all.** You can keep your objects as they are, clone them and apply the composition on the clones. This can enable interesting approaches like having different bounded contexts (like in DDD[65]) with slightly diverse domain models adapted to a particular context needs and goals.
- **You can compose an object with many other objects representing different behaviors** (like a multiple inheritance of sorts). This tends to be harder to do in classical inheritance

---

[65]Domain Driven Design (http://bit.ly/wiki-ddd)

based languages like C# where you are limited to a single base class or to a flavor of composition that requires a lot of boilerplate code, forward planning and design.

With object composition we achieve this true plug and play solution where you can combine domain objects with behaviors in very interesting and flexible ways. This type of *object composition* is another type of *prototypical inheritance* that we introduced as the mysterious *concatenative inheritance* earlier in the book.

Limitations of Mixins as Objects

As wonderful as *mixin* objects are they have some severe limitations:

- They don't support data privacy
- They can create undesired coupling between objects
- They are subject to name collisions

Let's take a closer look at each of these.

Mixin objects don't support true data privacy because they don't support closures. An alternative is to use *ES6 symbols* and keep your symbols tucked away within a module where you define your *mixins*. This won't give you true privacy but will at least give you the appearance of it.

If you are not careful, **mixin objects can create undesired coupling between disparate objects.** For instance, if you use the same *mixin* to extend several other objects, because the *extending* consists in copying properties, you can end up having several objects that have a reference to the same object property. This will result in undesired side-effects and possibly a horrible source of bugs.

You can clearly appreciate this problem when we do a small tweak in the canBePositioned mixin that we used in previous examples. Instead of describing a position using two separate properties x and y we will use a position object that'll contain these very same properties:

```
const canBePositionedWithGotcha = {
    position: {x: 0, y: 0},
    movesTo(x, y) {
        console.log(`${this} moves from (${this.position.x}, ${this.\
position.y}) to (${x}, ${y})`);
        this.position.x = x;
        this.position.y = y;
    }
};
```

This change may seem harmless and inocuous but it is not! If you now compose the wizardOfOz and tasselhof with this *mixin* the position object is shared between them both. This results in any minion moving affecting the other, a characteristic that you most definitely want to avoid:

```
const wizardOfOz = Wizard('oz', 100, 'Wizard of Oz', 10);
const tasselhof = Thief('Tasshelhof B.', 20);

Object.assign(wizardOfOz, canBePositionedWithGotcha);
Object.assign(tasselhof, canBePositionedWithGotcha);

wizardOfOz.movesTo(2,2);
// => Wizard of Oz moves from (0, 0) to (2, 2)

tasselhof.movesTo(6,6);
// => Tasshelhof B. moves from (2, 2) to (6, 6)
// wait... from (2,2)?????
```

Object mixins are also subject to property name collisions. Trying to compose an object with two *mixins* with the same properties but different interfaces can lead to errors:

Black Tower Summoning: Objects Interweaving Objects with Mixins

```
const canBePositionedIn3Dimensions = {
    x: 0,
    y: 0,
    z: 0,
    movesTo(x, y, z) {
        console.log(`${this} moves from (${this.x}, ${this.y}, ${thi\
s.z}) to (${x}, ${y}, ${z})`);
        this.x = x;
        this.y = y;
        this.z = z;
    }
};

const raist = Wizard('death', /*mana*/ 1000, 'Raistlin', /*hp*/ 1);
Object.assign(raist, canBePositioned, canBePositionedIn3Dimensions);

// we used the movesTo method thinking about the canBePositioned mix\
in
// and we get an unexpected result z becomes undefined
raist.movesTo(10, 20);
// => Raistlin moves from (0, 0, 0) to (10, 20, undefined)
```

Is there a way to surpass these limitations? Indeed there is! Behold! **Functional mixins!**

Functional Mixins

Functional mixins are *mixins* that are implemented as functions instead of objects. Because they are functions they:

- naturally support *data privacy* through closures and,
- can easily avoid undesired coupling between objects by working as factories of *mixins*

Let's see how we can turn our previously defined behaviors from *mixin* objects to *functional mixins*:

```
const canCastSpellsFn = (state) => ({
  castsSpell(spell, target){
    console.log(`${state.name} casts ${spell} on ${target}`);
    state.mana -= spell.mana;
    spell(target);
  }
});

const canStealFn = (state) => ({
  steals(target, item){
    console.log(`${state.name} steals ${item} from ${target}`);
  }
});

const canPlayMusicFn = (state) => ({
  playsMusic(){
    console.log(`${state.name} grabs his ${state.instrument} and sta\
rts playing music`);
  }
});
```

In this example the `canCastSpell` *mixin* and its companions have been rewritten as functions. These functions take a `state` argument that represents the state of the object that the *mixins* are going to extend and use it to augment it with new functionality. This functional implementation comes with two advantages:

- Because the `state` object is passed as a argument to the *mixin* it can remain private between object and *mixin*.
- Because each time the *functional mixin* object is called it returns a new object we solve the problem of coupling state between objects.

Having redefined our behaviors we can also redefine the wizards, thiefs and bards in terms of them:

```javascript
function TheWizard(element, mana, name, hp){
  // private state
  const state = {element,
                 mana,
                 name,
                 hp};

  // public API
  return Object.assign({},
              canBeIdentifiedByNameFn(state),
              canCastSpellsFn(state));
}

function TheThief(name, hp){
  const state = {name,
                 hp};

  return Object.assign({},
              canBeIdentifiedByNameFn(state),
              canStealFn(state));
}

function TheBard(instrument, mana, name, hp){
  const state = {instrument,
                 mana,
                 name,
                 hp};

  return Object.assign({},
              canBeIdentifiedByNameFn(state),
              canCastSpellsFn(state),
              canStealFn(state),
              canPlayMusicFn(state));
}
```

And use them as we have done in previous examples:

```
const landaf = TheWizard('light', 100, 'Landaf the light', 100);
landaf.castsSpell(lightningSpell, orc);
// => Landaf the light casts lightning spell on orc
// => A bolt of lightning electrifies orc(-10hp)

const lupen = TheThief('Lupen', 200);
lupen.steals(orc, 'rusty copper ring');
// => Lupen steals rusty copper ring from orc

const bart = TheBard('lute', 200, 'Bart', 100);
bart.playsMusic();
// => Bart grabs his lute and starts playing music
bart.steals(lupen, 'rusty copper ring');
// => Bart steals rusty copper ring from Lupen
bart.castsSpell(lightningSpell, landaf);
// => Bart casts lightning spell on Landaf the light
// => A bolt of lightning electrifies Landaf the light(-10hp)
// Wow Bart is mean!
```

In this use case for functional mixins we have separated the internal state of every object, represented by the state object, from its public *API* which is returned by the factory function.

The internal state of the object is passed as an argument to the different *functional mixins* so that they can access it thereafter.

The public API is defined by extending an empty object with the objects resulting from applying the different *functional mixins* to the state object. This empty object could also include a subset or all of the variables contained in state and, in that case, they would become public:

```
function TheBard(instrument, mana, name, hp){
  // internal state
  const state = {instrument,
                 mana,
                 name,
                 hp};

  // public API
  // exposing entire state publicly
  return Object.assign(state,
                       canBeIdentifiedByNameFn(state),
                       canCastSpellsFn(state),
                       canStealFn(state),
                       canPlayMusicFn(state));
}
```

As you've appreciated in these examples, *functional mixins* solve the limitations of *mixin* objects in terms of data privacy and coupling between extended objects.

There's still one limitation to contend with which are name collisions, that is, the possibility that two *mixins* provide behaviors with the same name. You can handle name collisions in two ways: live with them or use namespacing.

Since `Object.assign` works overwriting object properties from right to left you can be aware of this feature when working with mixins and even embrace it and take advantage of it when you need to replace behaviors with new ones:

```js
const canCastSpellsOnMany = {
  castsSpell(spell, ...many){
    many.forEach(target => {
            console.log(this + ' casts ' + spell + ' on ' + target);
            this.mana -= spell.mana;
      spell(target);
    });
  }
}

Object.assign(bard, canCastSpellsOnMany);
bard.castsSpell(lightningSpell, orc, orcMagician, landaf);
// => Kvothe casts lightning spell on orc
// => A bolt of lightning electrifies orc (-10hp)
// => Kvothe casts ligtning spell on orcmag
// => A bolt of lightning electrifies orcmag (-10hp)
// => Kvothe casts lightning spell on Landaf the light
// => A bolt of lightning electrifies Landaf the light(-10hp)
```

Alternatively, you can prevent name collisions from happening by namespacing each *mixin* that is composed with an object. This will result in a less natural and more verbose API for the resulting objects:

```js
const canEat = {
  food: {
    eats(foodItem) {
      console.log(`${this} eats ${foodItem}`);
      this.hp += foodItem.recoverHp;
    }
  }
};
// bard.food.eats({
//   name: 'banana', recoverHp: 10,
//   toString(){return this.name;}
// });

const canEatMany = {
  foods: {
    eats(...foodItems) {
      foodItems.forEach(f => {
```

Black Tower Summoning: Objects Interweaving Objects with Mixins

```
            console.log(`${this} eats ${f}`);
            this.hp += f.recoverHp;
        });
      }
    }
};

// bard.foods.eats([
//     name: 'banana', recoverHp: 10,
//     toString(){return this.name;}
//   }, {
//     name: 'sandwich', recoverHp: 20,
//     toString(){return this.name;}
//   }]);
```

Combining Mixins with ES6 Classes

If you are still not convinced about the usefulness and simplicity of vanilla objects and *mixins* you can continue using *ES6 classes* and combine them with *mixins*. **That way you get a comfortable path from C# into JavaScript, a familiar pattern for defining your domain model and additionally you gain a fantastic way to reuse code and behaviors via mixins.**

You have two options when combining *ES6 classes* with *mixins*. You can either compose your already instantiated objects with a *mixin* on a *per-case* basis, or you can compose your *class* prototype with a *mixin* and automatically provide all existing and future instances of that *class* with new behaviors.

Let's imagine we have a `Warrior` class to help us illustrate this with an example:

```js
class Warrior {

  constructor(name, hp=500) {
    this.name = name;
    this.hp = hp;
    this.weapons = [];
  }

  equipsWeapon(weapon) {
    weapon.isEquipped = true;
    this.weapons.push(weapon);
    console.log(`${this} picks ${weapon} from the ground ` +
                `and looks at it appreciatively`);
  }

  attacks(target) {
    if (this.weapons.length === 0) {
      console.log(`${this} attacks ${target} with ` +
                  `his bare arms`);
    } else {
      console.log(`${this} attacks ${target} with ` +
                  `${this.weapons.find(w => w.isEquipped)}`);
    }
  }

  toString() {
    return this.name;
  }

}
```

The first option is very straightforward because we are just composing an object with another object. We can instantiate a new fearful warrior `caramon`:

```js
const caramon = new Warrior('Caramon', 1000);
```

And now, if we want this specific warrior to be able to steal, we compose it with the `canSteal` *mixin* from previous examples:

```
Object.assign(caramon, canSteal);

caramon.steals(bard, 'lute');
// => Caramon steals lute from Kvothe
```

Alternatively, we can compose the Warrior *class* prototype with a *mixin* and provide all existing and future instances of this class with new functionality. This is an excellent way to define a series of reusable behaviors and compose them with our domain model classes as we see fit.

For instance, let's make all warriors capable of being positioned in a map via the canBePositioned *mixin*:

```
Object.assign(Warrior.prototype, canBePositioned);
```

We can easily verify how indeed both already defined warriors like caramon and new warriors like riverwind can move around in a two dimensional space:

```
// existing instances of Warrior now can be positioned
caramon.movesTo(10,10);
// => Caramon moves from (0, 0) to (10, 10)
// Crazy!

// and new ones as well
const riverwind = new Warrior('Riverwind', 300);
riverwind.movesTo(20,20);
// => Riverwind moves from (0, 0) to (20, 20)
```

Object.assign in Depth

We've used Object.assign a lot during this chapter and even in previous chapters. We know that it copies properties from several source objects into a target object. *But does it copy all properties? What about the properties within an object prototype? Does it do a deep copy of the source objects? Or just a shallow copy?* That's what we'll answer to in this section.

The Object.assign method is a new Object static method in *ES6* that **lets you copy all enumerable own properties** from one or several *source* objects into a single *target* object.

```
// copy properties from one object to another
const companyOfTheRing = { aHobbit: 'frodo'};
const companyPlusOne = Object.assign(
    /* target */ companyOfTheRing,
    /*source*/ { aWizard: 'Gandalf'}
);
console.log(companyOfTheRing);
// => [object Object] {
//     aHobbit: "frodo", aWizard: "Gandalf"
// }

// merge serveral objects into one
Object.assign(companyOfTheRing,
    {anElf: 'Legolas'},
    {aDwarf: 'Gimli'}
);
console.log(companyOfTheRing);
// => [objetc Object] {
//     aHobbit: "frodo", ... anElf: "Legolas", aDwarf: "Gimli"
// }
```

The target object is the first argument passed to Object.assign but it is also returned by it:

```
// the returned object is the same as the target object
console.log(`companyPlusOne and companyOfTheRingt ` +
    `are the same: ${companyPlusOne === companyOfTheRing}`);
// => companyPlusOne and companyOfTheRing are the same: true
```

If you don't want to mutate any of your existing objects, you can use a new object {} as *target*:

Black Tower Summoning: Objects Interweaving Objects with Mixins

```
// clone an object (shallow-copy)
const clonedCompany = Object.assign(
  /*target*/ {},
  /*source*/ companyOfTheRing
);
console.log(clonedCompany);
// => [objetc Object] {
//     aHobbit: "frodo", ... anElf: "Legolas", aDwarf: "Gimli"
// }
```

Object.assign only copies properties from the *source* object itself and not from its prototype:

```
const newCompanyWithPrototype = Object.assign({
  '__proto__': {
    destroyTheRing(){
      console.log('The mighty company of the ring successfully' +
                  'destroys the ring and saves Middle Earth');
    }
  }
}, companyOfTheRing);

const companyOfTheBracelet = Object.assign(
    /* target */ {},
    /* source */ newCompanyWithPrototype);
console.log(`companyOfTheBracelet.destroyTheRing: ` +
            `${companyOfTheBracelet.destroyTheRing}`);
// => companyOfTheBracelet.destroyTheRing: undefined
// prototype method was not assigned!
```

It performs a shallow copy of the *source* object properties. That is, if your *source* object has a property that is an object, the *target* object will gain a new property that will reference that same object.

```
1  companyOfTheRing.equipment = ['bread', 'rope', 'the one ring'];
2
3  const companyOfTheSash = Object.assign({}, companyOfTheRing);
4  companyOfTheSash.equipment.push('sash');
5
6  console.log(companyOfTheRing.equipment);
7  // => ["bread", "rope", "the one ring", "sash"]
8  // ooops!
```

> ### Enumerable Properties?
>
> Enumerability is an internal characteristic of object properties in JavaScript. It determines whether or not an object property can be enumerated via the for/in loop. When you create an object with an *object initializer* or a *constructor function* all properties are enumerable.
>
> You'll learn more about enumerability in the *Object Internals* chapter later within the book.

Object.assign Alternatives for ES5 JavaScript-mancers

This chapter has relied heavily in the use of `Object.assign`, a new method in *ES6* that lets you extend an target object with many other objects. *Does that mean that you cannot use mixins and object composition if you are not using ES6?* No! You can definitely use object composition and mixins if you haven't made the jump to *ES6* yet.

Chances are that you are already using a library that offers a similar functionality to `Object.assign`. For instance, *jQuery* has the `$.extend` method, *underscore* the `_.extend` and `_.assign` methods and so does *lodash*:

- **jQuery extend ($.extend)**: Copies all properties even from prototypes. It can perform deep-copy by using a flag (the source objects is traversed recursively and copied over the target object, this avoids coupling source and target objects)
- **underscore extend (_.extend)**: Copies all enumerable properties even from prototypes
- **underscore assign (_.assign)**: Copies only own enumerable properties (not properties inherited from prototypes)
- **lodash extend and assign (_.extend, _.assign)**: Copies only own enumerable properties

If you are not using any of these libraries don't worry, you can also implement your own version of Object.assign using this code example below:

```
function assign(){
  const args = Array.prototype.slice.call(arguments, 0),
        target = args[0],
        sources = args.slice(1);

  return sources.reduceRight(assignObject, target);

  function assignObject(target, source){
    for (let prop in source)
      if (source.hasOwnProperty(prop))
        target[prop] = source[prop];

    return target;
  }
}
```

This new assign method works just like Object.assign:

```
1  const thor = new Warrior('Thor', 2000);
2  assign(thor, canCastSpells);
3  thor.castsSpell(lightningSpell, orc);
4  // => Thor casts lightning spell on orc
5  // => A bolt of lightning electrifies orc (-10hp)
6  // poor orc
```

Not familiar with the `reduceRight` function yet? Worry not! We will take a look at this method and others in the functional programming tome later in the series. The only thing you need to know right now is that `reduceRight`:

1. traverses the `sources` array from right to left,
2. it applies the `assignObject` function to each item within the array,
3. accumulates the results in the `target` object which is fed back into the `assignObject` function for the next item.

Concluding

Developing software is a complex trade. We try to model the world around us by creating abstractions and simplifications that only have enough detail to solve the problem at hand. Object-Oriented Programming attempts to help reduce the complexities of developing software by defining classes that represent simplified versions of real world entities. However, using classes result in rigid taxonomies that aren't well suited to absorbing change.

Class-free object oriented programming appears as an alternative solution to classic OOP that is more adaptable to change and more flexible. An example of *class-free* OOP is object composability through *mixins*. Mixins are objects or functions that encapsulate a reusable piece of functionality or behavior. You can apply these *mixins* to your domain model objects by using `Object.assign` and what is known as *concatenative inheritance* (the second type of

Black Tower Summoning: Objects Interweaving Objects with Mixins   191

prototypical inheritance we discussed in earlier chapters of the book).

You can represent *mixins* as objects or functions. Function *mixins* are better than object mixins because they support *data privacy* and prevent coupling via shared references. Both types of *mixins* have problems with name collisions because object composition consists in copying properties from one object to the next.

Object.assign is a new Object method in *ES6* that lets you copy enumerable own properties from one or several *source* objects into a *target* object. If you are not using *ES6*, you can use alternatives from popular JavaScript libraries like *jQuery* or *underscore*, or write your own implementation of Object.assign.

In the next chapters we will look at other interesting approaches to achieving *class-free object oriented programming*: traits and stamps.

```
redBrute.says("And that's how you can elengantly" +
    "share behaviors amongst many objects");

randalf.says("That's very interesting");
mooleen.says("Yeah I can think of a thousand ways to " +
    "use that");

mooleen.says("Wait... " +
    "How do you know so much about javascriptmancy?" +
    "You didn't use a scrap of magic in the battle");

redBrute.says("You insult me?");
redBrute.says("Magic is for tinfers");

randalf.says("tinder?");
redBrute.says("tinfers!... the inferior races");
redBrute.says("Weaklings whose natural biological " +
    "limits force them to cheat and rely on external " +
    "help... like magic");

mooleen.says("Why learn magic then?");
redBrute.says("The pursue of knowledge is a virtue." +
    "An excellent mental exercise." +
```

```
    "We Turians hone our superior natural talents " +
    "in the pursuit of perfection... and honor");

mooleen.says("Well, if you are so superior," +
    "Why serve The Red Hand?");
/*
A flash of anger transfixes the otherwise cold
expression of the barbarian for just a fraction
of a second
*/
redBrute.says("That's a long and unfortunate story " +
    "that I may share with you in the future...");
redBrute.says("Now let's get you to The Red Stronghold!" +
    "In the clouds of the Everstorm");
```

Exercises

 ### Experiment JavaScriptmancer!

You can experiment with these exercises and some possible solutions in this jsFiddle[66] or downloading the source code from GitHub[67].

---

[66] http://bit.ly/javascriptmancy-oop-mixins-exercises
[67] https://github.com/vintharas/javascriptmancy-code-samples

Volareeee Oh oH!

The Red Stronghold stands in the depths of Everstorm within crimson clouds, fire and lightning. To get there you'll need to fly, moreover your army will need to fly as well.

Create a `canFly` functional mixin that encapsulates the flying behavior and which can be used to give the wondrous ability of flying to your now summoned army. It should provide the following API.

```
sandGolem.raise(10);
// => Sand Golem raises 10 feet into the air
sandGolem.dive(10);
// => Sand Golem dives 10 feet down through the air
sandGolem.fliesTo(100);
// => Sand Golem flies to 100 feet above sea level
sandGolem.position.z
// => 100
```

Tip: Use the `SandGolem` class from the previous chapter to create sand golems that you can extend with this new mixin `canFly`

Solution

```
/* Creature classes */
class Minion {
  constructor(name, hp){
    this.name = name;
    this.hp = hp;
    this.position = {x: 0, y: 0};
  }
  toString(){
    return this.name;
  }
  goesTo(x, y){
    this.position.x = x;
    this.position.y = y;
    console.log(`${this} goes to position (` +
```

```
      `${this.position.x},${this.position.y})`);
    }
  }


class SandGolem extends Minion {
  constructor(name="Sand golem", hp=200){
    super(name, hp);
  }
  bash(target){
    console.log(`${this}  bashes ${target} with terrible ` +
      `force causing 30 damage`);
    target.hp -= 30;
  }
  absorb(target){
    console.log(
        `${this} absorbs ${target} into its body of sand.` +
                `The ${target} can't move`);
  }
}

/* Mixin */
function canFlyFn(state){
  const canFly = {
    fliesTo(height){
      this.position.z = height;
      console.log(`${this} flies to ${height} feet above sea level`);
    },
    raise(height){
      this.position.z += height;
      console.log(`${this} raises ${height} feet into the air`);
    },
    dive(height){
      this.position.z -= height;
      console.log(`${this} dives ${height} feet through the air`);
    }
  }
  Object.assign(state, canFly);
  // assuming the target object has a position property
  state.position.z = 0;
}


let sandGolem = new SandGolem();
canFlyFn(sandGolem);

sandGolem.raise(10);
```

Black Tower Summoning: Objects Interweaving Objects with Mixins 195

```
62  // => Sand Golem raises 10 foot into the air
63  sandGolem.dive(10);
64  // => Sand Golem dives 10 foot down through the air
65  sandGolem.fliesTo(100)
66  // => Sand Golem flies to 100 foot above sea level
67  sandGolem.position.z
68  // => 100
69
70  mooleen.says("haha! Look at that, there they fly!");
71  rat.says("Yippie!");
72
73  redBrute.says("Sloppy work...");
74  randalf.says("but it works");
75  redBrute.says("What if the golem didn't have a position?");
76
77  mooleen.says("What if you were a mighty warrior " +
78                "of a vast superior race and you " +
79                "had lost a battle and a complete army " +
80                "in the process?");
81
82  redBrute.says('...');
83  redBrute.says('still sloppy work')
```

Labeling and Tactics!

As your army grows you'll need to group your soldiers into companies, batallions, brigades and divisions to better control them and guide them into battle. A way to keep order into chaos is to label these groupings and give them colors that they can display in their armor, flag and standards.

Create a new functional mixin `canBeLabeled` that allows you to label your troops with a name and color for their company. It should provide the following API:

```
1  sandGolem.companyName
2  // => "Scarlett salamanders"
3  sandGolem.companySymbol
4  // => "s"
5  sandGolem.companyColor
6  // => "red"
```

Bonus! As a bonus exercise you can update the map generator in this chapter to display companies instead of individual soldiers

Solution

```
1   function canBeLabeledFn(state, name, symbol, color){
2     const canBeLabeled = {
3       companyName: name,
4       companySymbol: symbol,
5       companyColor: color
6     };
7     return Object.assign(state, canBeLabeled);
8   }
9
10  canBeLabeledFn(sandGolem, "Scarlett salamanders", "s", "red");
11
12  console.log(sandGolem.companyName);
13  // => "Scarlett salamanders"
```

Black Tower Summoning: Objects Interweaving Objects with Mixins 197

```
14    console.log(sandGolem.companySymbol);
15    // => "s"
16    console.log(sandGolem.companyColor);
17    // => "red"
18
19    // bonus
20    console.log(`
21
22    === Bonus Exercise: Generate map of labels ===
23
24    `);
25    function LabeledMap(width, height, creatures){
26
27        function paintPoint(x,y){
28            var creatureInPosition = creatures
29                .find(c => c.position.x === x && c.position.y === y);
30            if (creatureInPosition)
31                return creatureInPosition.companySymbol;
32            return '_';
33        }
34
35        return {
36            width,
37            height,
38            creatures,
39            paint() {
40                console.log("Generating map of companies...")
41                let map = '';
42                for(let y = 0; y < height; y++) {
43                    for (let x = 0; x < width; x++)
44                        map += paintPoint(x,y);
45                    map += '\n';
46                }
47                return map;
48            }
49        }
50    }
51
52    const anotherSandGolem = new SandGolem();
53    canBeLabeledFn(anotherSandGolem, "Dark Fiends", "d", "black");
54    anotherSandGolem.goesTo(2, 2);
55
56    const myLabeledMap = new LabeledMap(10,10,
57                            [sandGolem, anotherSandGolem]);
58    console.log(myLabeledMap.paint());
59    /*
60        Generating map of companies...
```

```
61    s_____
62     _____
63    _d_____
64     _____
65     _____
66     _____
67     _____
68     _____
69     _____
70     _____
71    */
72
73    mooleen.says("good... now I'll have a better " +
74                "control of my batallions");
75    mooleen.says("I think everything's ready");
76    mooleen.says("All that remains is to fly");
77    mooleen.says("How long will it take us to get " +
78                "to the Red Stronhold?");
79
80    redBrute.says("Hmm...");
81    redBrute.slicksTheTopOfAFingerAndRaisesItToTheAir();
82    redBrute.says("It'll take between... 2 to 3 weeks");
83
84    randalf.says("And we'll be flying all the time");
85    bandalf.says("And eating, sleeping...");
86    redBrute.says("Who needs to eat? Sleep? You weaklings...");
87
88    rat.says("Doing ...the thing you know... no toilet");
89    redBrute.says("Gravity will take care of it, " +
90                 "just don't fly atop each other");
91
92    mooleen.says("Hmm showering");
93    redBrute.says("Now, that is something!" +
94        "I can relate to the magic properties of a bubble bath");
95
96    mooleen.says("Yeah, we'll need a transport, a big one");
```

Conquest in Comfort with a Zeppelin!

Flying is awesome but it can be impractical and inconvenient at times. Like when you need to use a toilet or take a bubble bath. When forced to conquer why not conquer in the comfort of a giant flying fortress in the shape of a Zeppelin? With the basics for transporting a huge army with provisions while including all the amenities of a first-class ticket?

Write a factory function that creates Zeppelins by composing a state object with the mixins from previous exercises canFlyFn, canBeLabeledFn and a new one canTransportFn. The canTransportFn mixin should provide the following API:

```
zeppelin.load(mooleen);
// => The zeppelin is loaded with Mooleen
zeppelin.load(randalf);
// => The zeppelin is loaded with Randalf
zeppelin.showLoad();
// => The zeppelin is loaded with: Mooleen, Randalf
let load = zeppelin.unload();
// => The zeppelin unloads Mooleen and Randalf
console.log(load)
// [ "Mooleen", "Randalf" ]
```

Solution

```
function Zeppelin(name, hp=1000){
  let state = {
    name,
    hp,
    position: {x: 0, y: 0},
    toString(){
      return `Zeppelin "${this.name}"`
    },
    floatsTo(x,y){
```

```
10        this.position.x = x;
11        this.position.y = y;
12        console.log(`${this} floats to position ` +
13          `(${this.position.x},${this.position.y})`);
14      }
15    };
16
17    return Object.assign(state,
18      canFlyFn(state),
19      canBeLabeledFn(state, 'Armada', 'a', 'black'),
20      canTransportFn(state))
21  }
22
23  function canTransportFn(state){
24    const canTransport = {
25      contents: [],
26      load(...newContent){
27        this.contents.push(...newContent);
28        console.log(`${this} is loaded with ${newContent}`);
29      },
30      showLoad(){
31        console.log(`${this} is loaded with: ${this.contents}`);
32      },
33      unload(){
34        console.log(`${this} unloads ${this.contents.join(' and ')}`);
35        const contents = [...this.contents];
36        this.contents = [];
37        return contents;
38      }
39    };
40
41    return Object.assign(state, canTransport);
42  }
43
44  let zeppelin = Zeppelin("HMS Intrepid");
45  zeppelin.fliesTo(20);
46  // => Zeppelin "HMS Intrepid" flies to 20 feet above sea level
47
48  zeppelin.floatsTo(9, 9);
49  // => Zeppelin "HMS Intrepid" floats to position (10,10)
50  myLabeledMap.creatures.push(zeppelin);
51  console.log(myLabeledMap.paint());
52  /*
53  Generating map of companies...
54  s_____
55  _____
56  __d_____
```

```
57     _____
58     _____
59     _____
60     _____
61     _____
62     _____
63     _____a
64     */
65
66     zeppelin.load(mooleen, redBrute);
67     // => Zeppelin "HMS Intrepid" is loaded with Mooleen,Red brute
68     zeppelin.load(randalf);
69     // => Zeppelin "HMS Intrepid" is loaded with Randalf, the Red
70     zeppelin.showLoad();
71     // => Zeppelin "HMS Intrepid" is loaded with:
72     //    Mooleen,Red brute,Randalf, the Red
73     zeppelin.unload();
74     // => Zeppelin "HMS Intrepid" unloads
75     //    Mooleen and Red brute and Randalf, the Red
76
77     randalf.says("And now we're ready");
78     mooleen.says('Assemble the Army!');
79     mooleen.says('To the Zeppelin!');
80
81     rat.standsOnTwoLegsAndStartsMarching();
```

Black Tower Summoning: Safer Object Composition with Traits

Humans are flawed.
Take that into consideration
when designing a tool.

Within your tool, create a path
to guide your user to success.
Her failure is your failure.

       - Iamnos Ydad
       Spellsmith, 1st Age

Black Tower Summoning: Safer Object Composition with Traits

```
/*
    The sunset as viewed from the zeppelin is a sight to behold.
    A crimson ball of incandescent fire that ever so slowly
    creeps into the horizon and bathes the world in a mystical
    orange light.

    At this very moment, the world consists on a teeny tiny
    zeppelin surrounded in all directions by a seemingly infinite
    ocean.

    On the bridge of the flying ship two figures confer.
*/

redBrute.says("The Red Hand's armies are vast as" +
    " this ocean that surround us");
mooleen.says("That's... encouraging");

redBrute.says("...as the sky that extends in every direction");
mooleen.says("I get it");

mooleen.says("I need to expand our force. It looks like " +
    "lady luck finally smiles upon me because we have " +
    "several weeks ahead of us before we arrive to that " +
    "dreaded Red Stronghold of yours");
redBrute.says("Then you better get started");

mooleen.says("I know, I know... it is just that " +
    "sometimes I wonder how the hell I got here");
rat.says("You summoned a zeppelin, then jumped on it");

mooleen.says("ehr... How I got to this world, " +
    "How I saved the people of Asturi from Great," +
    "How I ended up commanding an army to conquer " +
    "The Red Hand..." +
    "I just wanted to find my way back home");
redBrute.says("Well, if what the old man says " +
    "is true you may find some answers in the " +
    "library of Orrile. But to ever get a chance " +
    "to get there you'll need to become stronger. " +
    "The Tatians are fierce enemies".);

mooleen.says("Then let's better get started");
mooleen.says("I've been experimenting with something new");
mooleen.says("An improvement over mixins...");
```

An Improvement Over Mixins

In the last chapter you learned about *mixins* and how you can use them to encapsulate reusable units of behavior that you can later compose with your domain objects or classes.

Mixins, while awesome, have some limitations. In particular, conflicting *mixin* methods and properties are overwritten when using Object.assign. To add insult to injury, you don't get any warning when this happens. Updating a *mixin* with new functionality at some point in time can inadvertently change the behavior of some of your objects and lead to unexpected results.

Traits offer a solution to this problem by providing a safer and more structured way to do object composition.

 Experiment JavaScriptmancer!!
You can experiment with all examples in this chapter directly within this jsBin[68] or downloading the source code from GitHub[69].

Traits

The idea of *Traits* appeared as a natural response to the problems and limitations that exist in more traditional OOP practices like classical inheritance, multiple inheritance and mixins. Let's examine these issues one by one before we round back to Traits and their characteristics.

---
[68] http://bit.ly/javascriptmancy-oop-traits
[69] https://github.com/vintharas/javascriptmancy-code-samples

The Problem with Classes

Classes in *classical inheritance* perform two distinct functions with conflicting goals. They work as:

1. Factories that **create objects**
2. A mechanism of **code reuse** through inheritance

The first goal of object creation requires a class to be complete so that you use it to instantiate objects. The second goal of code reuse truly shines when you have small reusable units. These goals conflict with each other as complete classes beget large reusable units, and small reusable units beget incomplete classes.

As a result of this dichotomy designing a domain model using classes leaves you with few options as we've seen in earlier chapters: You can use inheritance as a method of *code reuse* where you inherit everything, you can incur in *code duplication* between different classes, or you require a lot of boilerplate to delegate behaviors to other classes.

The Issue With Multiple Inheritance

Multiple inheritance improves the *code reuse* factor from the single-class inheritance approach but comes with its own host of problems.

With multiple inheritance you can define smaller classes and make new classes reuse functionality from these smaller units. However, problems arise as several paths of the inheritance tree can provide conflicting functionality and overriding features with super can be ambiguous: *Which super class where you referring to, my dear?*.

The Plight Of Mixins

Mixins excel at *code reuse* by defining small reusable units that you can compose with your existing classes and objects. Unlike *classes* a mixin doesn't have the goal of being a factory for objects and therefore can be incomplete (and small and focused).

On the minus side, because of the mechanism used to compose classes and objects with mixins, there are no guarantees that the resulting objects will be correct:

- The target class or object may not meet a mixin requirements, i.e. the composed class may lack a property the mixin depends upon
- Mixins may conflict with each other in unexpected ways, i.e. when two mixins provide methods with the same name

Furthermore, there are no warnings when we fail at composing objects or when mixin features conflict with each other.

Traits to The Rescue

Traits attempt to solve all these problems existing in previous techniques. They do so by providing a way to reuse code and behavior just like we do with *mixins* but in a safer fashion that will let us:

- handle conflicts between traits and be warned when conflicts occur
- define requirements in our traits that must be satisfied before certain features can be used

Let's see how you can get started using traits in JavaScript.

Traits with traits.js

 Open Source Alert!

We are going to be using traits.js[70], a traits JavaScript library for the remainder of the article. Note that there are other trait implementations in JavaScript like light-traits[71] and simple-traits[72] so you can pick the one you like the most when you are ready to experiment yourself.

Trait.js[73] is an open source library that brings the beauty of traits into JavaScript. Using *traits.js* we can define reusable pieces of behavior - **traits** - and then compose them together to build objects.

Let's imagine that we want to represent the ability of being positioned in a two-dimensional space using a trait `TPositionable`. Traits.js lets us define a new trait by using a factory function (`Trait`) and passing in an object that contains the behavior that we're interested in:

```
const TPositionable = Trait({
  x: 0,
  y: 0,
  location(){
    console.log(`${this} is calmly resting ` +
                `at (${this.x}, ${this.y})`);
  }
});
```

---

[70] https://github.com/traitsjs/traits.js
[71] https://github.com/Gozala/light-traits
[72] https://github.com/YR/simple-traits
[73] http://soft.vub.ac.be/~tvcutsem/traitsjs/

> Much in the same way that we use the letter I in front of interfaces in C#, it is common to use the letter T as a convention when defining traits.

In this particular case, the `TPositionable` trait is composed by two properties x and y that represent a position, and a method `location` which prints the current position.

Now that we have defined our first trait we can start creating new objects that are expressed in terms of that trait. Behold a very sparse minion!

```
function MinionWithPosition(){
  const methods = {
    toString(){ return 'minion';}
  };

  const minion = Object.create(
      /* prototype */ methods,
      /* traits (object properties) */ TPositionable);
  return minion;
}
```

In this example we have a factory function `MinionWithPosition` that creates minions with the ability of being positioned.

We use `Object.create` to create an instance of a minion that will have the following characteristics:

- A prototype that contains a single method `toString`
- A set of properties reflected by the `TPositionable` trait

This is interesting because it highlights the fact that we can combine JavaScript's *prototypical inheritance* with traits. We can verify that the resulting minion works as we would expect:

```
const minionWithPosition = MinionWithPosition();

minionWithPosition.location();
// => minion is calmly resting at (0, 0)
```

A minion that rests in the same place for eternity is not very useful. Let's see how we can truly tap into the power of traits by giving this minion more behaviors.

Composing Traits

Let's define a new trait that will represent the behavior of moving from one place to another TMovable:

```
const TMovable = Trait({
    // required properties
    x: Trait.required,
    y: Trait.required,

    movesTo(x,y){
        console.log(`${this} moves from ` +
            `(${this.x}, ${this.y}) to (${x}, ${y})`);
        this.x = x;
        this.y = y;
    }
});
```

This new trait is going to be composed of two parts:

- **The moving behavior** represented by the movesTo method that will allow our minions to perform the actual moving around.
- **A set of requirements** that the target object needs to fulfill for the movesTo method to work. In this case, these will be two properties x and y since it doesn't make sense for someone to move if you cannot be in any position in the first place.

Notice how Trait.js lets us define required properties by using the static property `Trait.required`. These required properties will be factored in when we try to instantiate a new object later on.

Now that we have two traits let's compose them to create a more useful minion. You can compose traits together using the `Traits.compose` method which will result in a new composite trait:

```
function MovingMinion(){
  const methods = {
    toString() { return 'moving minion';}
  };

  const minion = Object.create(/* prototype */ methods,
      Trait.compose(TPositionable, TMovable));
  return minion;
}
```

Now we can see how a moving minion can be *positioned* and also *move around*:

```
const movingMinion = MovingMinion();

movingMinion.location();
// => moving minion is calmly resting at (0, 0)

movingMinion.movesTo(2,2);
// => moving minion moves from (0, 0) to (2, 2)
movingMinion.location();
// => moving minion is calmly resting at (2, 2)
```

In the previous example, we used the new composite trait directly within the `Object.create` method which made it pass by a little bit unnoticed. Notice that you can save composite traits for later, compose them further and build richer and more detailed traits like we illustrate in this example:

```
const TPositionableAndMovable =
  Trait.Compose(TPositionable, TMovable);

const TDrawable = Trait({...drawing behavior...});

const T2DCapable =
  Trait.Compose(TPositionableAndMovable, TDrawable);

// etc
```

What Happens When You Miss Required Properties?

Let's try creating a new object with the `TMovable` trait that doesn't meet its requirements. We'll devise a `ConfusedMinion` who can move around but doesn't know where it is exactly:

```
function ConfusedMinion(){
  const methods = {
    toString() { return 'confused minion'; }
  };

  const minion = Object.create(/* prototype */ methods,
                               /* properties */ TMovable);
  return minion;
}

const confusedMinion = ConfusedMinion();
confusedMinion.movesTo(1,1);
// => confused minion moves from
//    (undefined, undefined) to (1, 1);
// => TypeError: Cannot assign to
//    read only property 'x' of [object Object]
```

As you can appreciate in this example when the requirements of a specific trait haven't been met you get some nice feedback.

Calling `Object.create` with a trait that misses required properties results in an object that has these requirements as read-only properties. If you try to set these properties to a new value you will get

an exception which will warn you about the fact that your object is
not composed correctly. This is a great improvement from *mixins*
where missing expected properties could result in unexpected side-
effects.

> **Assigning to Read-only Properties Only Throws in Strict Mode**
>
> Notice that you need to enable *strict mode* for read-only
> properties to throw exceptions when assigning values to them.
> Otherwise the assign operation will just fail silently.

Resolving Name Conflicts

Unlike *mixins* which only support linear composition where later
mixins overwrite the previous ones, *Traits* composition order is
irrelevant. With traits, conflicting methods or properties must be
resolved explicitly.

Let's imagine that we now want to be able to position our minions
in a three dimensional space. We define a `TPositionable3D` trait
like this:

```
const TPositionable3D = Trait({
  x: 0, // conflict
  y: 0, // conflict
  z: 0,

  location(){ // conflict
    console.log(`${this} is calmly resting at
               (${this.x}, ${this.y}, ${this.z})`);
  }
});
```

Since we want to retain the ability to position our minion in a two dimensional space (we want to be able to switch between a map view and a real-world view) we define our new minion like the following:

```
function ConflictedMinion(){
  const methods = {
    toString() { return 'conflicted minion'; }
  };

  const minion = Object.create(
      /* prototype */ methods,
      /* props */ Trait.compose(TPositionable,
                                TPositionable3D));
  return minion;
}
```

If we now attempt to create a conflicted minion and access any of its conflicting properties we will get an exception:

```
const conflictedMinion = ConflictedMinion();
conflictedMinion.location();
// => Error: Conflicting property: location
```

This will give us great feedback whenever there are name collisions between our traits properties and methods, again an important advantage over *mixins*. This behavior will be particularly helpful when updating an existing trait results in name collisions within existing objects inside your application (which otherwise would have gone unnoticed).

Traits provide different strategies that you can use to resolve name conflicts:

- **Aliasing or renaming properties**: Use when you want to conserve the functionality in either of the conflicting traits. Renaming the conflicting properties will result in objects

containing both the original properties plus the renamed ones.
- **Excluding properties**: Use when you don't care about a particular trait functionality. The excluded properties won't be taken into account when creating the new object
- **Overriding properties**: Use when you want a trait to completely override another.

Trait.js offers the `Trait.resolve` function to help you resolve name conflicts using any of the strategies that we have detailed above. For instance, you can *rename* a property by using `Trait.resolve` to map a property to another name:

```
function AliasedMinion(){
  const methods = {
    toString() { return 'aliased minion'; }
  };

  const minion = Object.create(/* prototype */ methods,
      Trait.compose(TPositionable,
                    Trait.resolve(/* mappings */ {
                            x: 'x3d',
                            y: 'y3d',
                            location: 'location3d'
                    }, TPositionable3D)));
  return minion;
}
```

`Trait.resolve` takes two arguments, first an object that describes the conflicting property mappings and second the trait whose properties we want to rename. In the example above we have renamed `x` to `x3d`, `y` to `y3d` and the `location` method to `location3d`.

After resolving the conflicts we can instantiate a new minion without problems:

```
const aliasedMinion = new AliasedMinion();

aliasedMinion.location3d();
// => aliased minion is calmly resting at (0, 0, 0)

aliasedMinion.location();
// => aliased minion is calmly resting at (0, 0)
```

Using this renaming approach the object composed from the traits will keep all the properties from the original traits:

```
console.log(aliasedMinion);
/* => [object Object] {
  toString: function toString() {
    return 'aliased minion';
  },
  x: 0,
  x3d: 0,
  y: 0,
  y3d: 0,
  z: 0,
}
*/
```

Note how the methods defined by the traits location and location3d do not appear when logging the object. The reason for this is that methods created through traits are not enumerable, that is, they cannot be enumerated by using the *for/in* loop. This can be helpful when you want to enumerate the properties of an object and you are only interested about its data members (its state).

We can verify that both of these methods location and location3d are part of the aliasedMinion object by logging them directly:

```
console.log(aliasedMinion.location);
// => function location() {
//   console.log(this + " is calmly resting at (" +
//              this.x + ", " + this.y + ")");
// }
console.log(aliasedMinion.location3d);
// => function location() {
//   console.log(this + " is calmly resting at (" +
//      this.x + ", " + this.y + ", " + this.z + ")");
// }
```

This example above highlights something important that you may have missed: Renaming a trait property doesn't rename a reference to that same property within the body of a function. You can appreciate this if you take a look at the body of location3d which still refers to this.x and this.y. This places an important limitation that you need to keep in mind when resolving conflicts in *traits.js* through aliasing.

Alternatively you can exclude specific properties using the Trait.resolve function and setting the value of a property mapping to undefined:

```
function LeanMinion(){
  const methods = {
    toString() { return 'lean minion'; }
  };

  const minion = Object.create(/* prototype */ methods,
        Trait.compose(TPositionable, TMovable
                Trait.resolve({
                        x: undefined,
                        y: undefined,
                        location: 'location3d'
                }, TPositionable3D)));
  return minion;
}
```

This will create a lean minion where the x and y properties of the TPositionable3D properties have been excluded. In the resulting

Black Tower Summoning: Safer Object Composition with Traits   217

object, the `location3d` method is effectively using the x and y properties from the original `TPositionable` trait:

```
const leanMinion = LeanMinion();
leanMinion.location3d();
// => lean minion is calmly resting at (0, 0, 0)
leanMinion.location();
// => lean minion is calmly resting at (0, 0)

console.log(leanMinion);
/*
[object Object] {
  toString: function toString() {
    return 'lean minion';
  },
  x: 0,
  y: 0,
  z: 0
}
*/
```

Finally you can use the `Trait.override` method to override conflicting properties between traits. `Trait.override` works in a similar way to `Object.assign` but the precedence is taken from left to right - that is, in the opposite order.

Following this order the properties within the first trait will override those of the second trait, the properties within the second trait will override those of the third trait and so on:

```
function OverridenMinion(){
  const methods = {
    toString() { return 'overriden minion'; }
  };

  const minion = Object.create(/* prototype */ methods,
      Trait.compose(TMovable,
                    Trait.override(TPositionable3D,
                                   TPositionable)));
  return minion;
}
```

In the resulting minion all properties from TPositionable have been overwritten by TPositionable3D:

```
const overridenMinion = OverridenMinion();
overridenMinion.location();
// => overriden minion is calmly resting at (0, 0, 0)

overridenMinion.movesTo(1,2);
// => overriden minion moves from (0, 0) to (1, 2)
overridenMinion.location();
// => overriden minion is calmly resting at (1, 2, 0)

console.log(overridenMinion);
/* =>
[object Object] {
  toString: function toString() {
    return 'overriden minion';
  },
  x: 1,
  y: 2,
  z: 0
}
*/
```

Traits and Data Privacy

Just like with other JavaScript constructs, you can achieve data privacy with traits by taking advantage of closures.

Black Tower Summoning: Safer Object Composition with Traits 219

Because traditionally, traits are just objects, you will need to wrap them inside a function so that you can define a new scope where to place the private variables. The resulting functions will work like trait factories.

For instance, here we have two factories of `TPositionable` and `TMovable` traits where the `position` property is meant to be a private member:

```
const TPositionableFn = function(state){
  const position = state.position;

  return Trait({
    location(){
      console.log(`${this} is calmly resting at (${position.x}, ${po\
sition.y})`);
    }
  });
}

const TMovableFn = function(state) {
  const position = state.position;

  return Trait({
    movesTo(x,y){
      console.log(`${this} moves from (${position.x}, ${position.y})\
 to (${x}, ${y})`);
      position.x = x;
      position.y = y;
    }
  });
}
```

The *positionable* and *movable* traits above define a single method each: `location` and `movesTo`. These methods enclose the variable `state` that is going to be passed to either function as an argument and which will represent the private state of an object.

Having defined these trait factories we can now represent a new kind of minion in terms of them:

```
function PrivateMinion(){
  const state = { position: {x: 0, y: 0} },
    methods = { toString: () => 'private minion' };

  const minion = Object.create(/* prototype */ methods,
      Trait.compose(TPositionableFn(state), TMovableFn(state)));
  return minion;
}
```

The PrivateMinion is going to have a series of private members defined by the state variable. When instantiating a new object, the factory method will share this private state with the traits but it won't let it be accessed from the outside world:

```
const privateMinion = PrivateMinion();

// we can access the public API as usual
privateMinion.movesTo(1,1);
// => private minion moves from (0, 0) to (1, 1)
privateMinion.location();
// => private minion is calmly resting at (1, 1)

// but the private state can't be accessed
console.log(privateMinion.state);
// => undefined
```

Using closures with traits we get:

1. true data privacy and the ability to use private members within an object and its traits
2. required properties and name conflict handling for the public interface of an object

What about Symbols?

You may be wondering *what happens with symbols*. Unfortunately the current implementation of *traits.js* does not support symbols.

High Integrity Objects With Immutable Traits

Up until this point we have instantiated our objects using the Object.create method and passing a prototype and a trait (or a composite trait) as arguments. This results in a new object with the following characteristics:

- **If all requirements are met and there are no conflicts:** The resulting object will contain all properties and methods defined within the traits and will have as prototype whichever object we passed to Object.create
- **If not all requirements have been met:** The resulting object has these requirements as read-only properties. Attempting to modify these results in an exception
- **If there are unresolved naming conflicts:** The resulting object throws an exception when conflicting properties or methods are accessed

We are getting much better feedback about the consistency of our composed object than when we used *mixins* but it could be much better: We could get this feedback sooner. Like directly when creating the object and not when accessing inconsistent properties or methods.

Trait.js offers another method Trait.create that lets you instantiate high integrity objects. Objects created using Trait.create will:

- Throw an exception if there are requirements that haven't been satisfied
- Throw an exception if there are unresolved naming conflicts
- Have all their methods bound to themselves
- Be immutable

Let's use `Trait.create` with some of the traits we defined previously in this chapter. For instance, we can instantiate a positionable minion taking advantage of `TPositionable`:

```
function ImmutableMinionWithPosition(){
  const methods = {
    toString(){ return 'minion';}
  };
  const minion = Trait.create(/* prototype */ methods,
                              /* traits */ TPositionable);

  return minion;
}

const immutableMinion = new ImmutableMinionWithPosition();
immutableMinion.location();
// => minion is calmly resting at (0, 0)
```

The resulting `immutableMinion` is an immutable object. Attempting to change, delete or add new properties will result in an exception (that applies to *strict mode* otherwise it will fail silently):

```
immutableMinion.x = 10;
// => TypeError: Cannot assign to read only property 'x

delete immutableMinion.x;
// => TypeError: Cannot delete property 'x'

immutableMinion.health = 100;
// => TypeError: Can't add property health, object is not extensible
```

As we introduced earlier, if we attempt to create an object with missing requirements `Trait.create` will let us know immediately by throwing a composition exception.

For example, if we attempt to create a new minion with the `TMovable` trait which requires the `x` and `y` properties without providing such properties:

Black Tower Summoning: Safer Object Composition with Traits 223

```
function ConfusedMinionThatThrows(){
  const methods = {
    toString() { return 'confused minion'; }
  };

  // The TMovable trait requires two properties: x and y
  const minion = Trait.create(/* prototype */ methods, TMovable);
  return minion;
}

const confusedMinionThatThrows = ConfusedMinionThatThrows();
// => Error: Missing required property: x
```

This will also be the case when trying to create an object with unresolved conflicts, like when combining the `TPositionable` and `TPositionable3D` traits:

```
function ConflictedMinionThatThrows(){
  const methods = {
    toString() { return 'conflicted minion'; }
  };
  const minion = Trait.create(/* prototype */ methods,
    Trait.compose(TPositionable, TPositionable3D));
  return minion;
}

const conflictedMinionThatThrows = ConflictedMinionThatThrows();
// => Error: Remaining conflicting property: location
```

In general, you'll find that `Trait.create` offers a better developer experience than `Object.create` and will help you create high integrity objects that are immutable. But how do you build an application if all your objects are immutable? How can you make a minion move if you cannot change its state? You have a couple of choices:

1. Separate mutable and immutable states
2. Embrace immutability

Separate Mutable and Immutable States

A straightforward way to enjoy the great developer experience Trait.create provides and allow for the type of mutable state that is common in object oriented programming is to separate mutable from immutable state.

You can achieve this by keeping your mutable state inside the scope of a function and using closures to access and transform it. If mutable state needs to be accessed by other traits or users of the final object you'll need to make it available via getters and setters.

Let's redefine TPositionable to separate mutable state from public immutable state. We'll start by wrapping the trait inside a function that will act as a factory for positionable traits and will allow these to have their own state:

```
function TPositionable(x, y){
  return Trait({
    location(){
      console.log(`${this} is calmly resting at (${x}, ${y})`);
    }
  });
}
```

The next step is to make the mutable state x, y accessible to other traits using getters and setters:

Black Tower Summoning: Safer Object Composition with Traits

```
function TPositionable(x, y){
  return Trait({
    // now other traits can define requirements
    // based on these properties
    // and even access them.
    // So can object users
    get x() { return x; },
    set x(value) { x = value; },
    get y() { return y; },
    set y(value) { y = value; },

    location(){
      console.log(`${this} is calmly resting at (${x}, ${y})`);
    }
  });
}
```

We can now define another trait `TMovable` that requires the x and y properties in the target object and provides behavior that allows any object to move via the `movesTo` method:

```
function TMovable(){
  return Trait({
    x: Trait.required,
    y: Trait.required,

    movesTo(newX, newY){
      console.log(`${this} moves from (${this.x}, ${this.y}) to (${n\
ewX}, ${newY})`);
      this.x = newX;
      this.y = newY;
    }
  });
}
```

Finally, a `StatefulMinion` can be composed by using both of these traits as follows:

```
function StatefulMinion(x, y){
  const methods = {
    toString(){ return 'minion';}
  };

  const minion = Trait.create(/* prototype */ methods,
                              /* traits */ Trait.compose(
                                TPositionable(x,y),
                                TMovable()));
  return minion;
}
```

This faithful servant would now be able to be positioned and move around:

```
const statefulMinion = StatefulMinion(1, 1);

statefulMinion.location();
// => minion is calmly resting at (1, 1)
statefulMinion.movesTo(2, 2);
// => minion moves from (1,1) to (2,2)
statefulMinion.location();
// => minion is calmly resting at (2, 2)
```

Great! Now we get both the mutable state handling familiar to object oriented programming and if we were to forget some properties or define new traits with conflicting ones, Trait.create would warn us in an instant. Wohooo!

Embrace Immutability

Option number two is to embrace immutability. In traditional functional programming, where this practice is common, the answer is to rewrite methods that change state to create new objects reflecting the new state instead. In this context, a movesTo method wouldn't just change the position of the current object, it would re-create a complete new object reflecting the new position. However, since

Black Tower Summoning: Safer Object Composition with Traits

traits are not complete objects but just slivers of functionality this approach would prove challenging as it would impose the necessity for a trait to know about the shape of its complete composed object. A possible solution would be to use a Redux-like [74] architecture where a trait method wouldn't instantiate a new object but trigger an action representing the desired change and that would eventually result in the new state been created from scratch with all traits being considered in a centralized repository. But that would require a longer discourse that lies outside the scope of this chapter.

> ### Interested in Immutability?
>
> In another book in the series - *Functional Programming: Immutability* - we will do a deep dive into immutability, its advantages, uses cases and how you can use it in your applications.

Below you can find a summarized comparison between using `Object.create` and `Trait.create`:

Object.create	Trait.create
Can create objects even if there are unmet requirements or unresolved conflicts.	Cannot create objects when there are unmet requirements or unresolved conflicts.
Unmet requirements result in read-only property. Read-only properties throw when you try to change them in strict mode.	Unmet requirements cause an exception as soon as we try to instantiate an object.
Properties with unresolved conflicts throw an exception when accessed.	Unresolved conflicts cause an exception as soon as we try to instantiate an object.

---

[74]Redux is a state management framework for JavaScript applications that is very popular in the React community

Object.create	Trait.create
The object created doesn't have its methods bound. The object created can be be modified and augmented with new properties.	The object created has all its methods bound. The object created is immutable. You cannot augment it with new properties, remove properties nor modify existing ones.

Traits vs Mixins

Mixins	Traits
Class-free inheritance based on object composition via Object.assign. Let's you encapsulate functionality and behavior, and easily reuse them.	Class-free inheritance based on trait composition. Let's you encapsulate functionality and behavior, and easily reuse them.
Mixins don't have a way to express requirements. A mixin may expect a property or method in the composed object but it doesn't have a way to represent it. If a requirement is not met, unpredictable side-effects may occur.	Traits can express that they require specific properties or methods for functioning. Failing to meet requirements will result in errors being thrown either when trying to assign to an unexisting required property or upon object creation (Trait.create).
Only allow linear composition. Later composed mixins overwrite previous mixins.	Can be composed freely because they require that you resolve any conflict explicitly.
	Conflicts can be resolved by renaming, excluding properties, or by overriding traits.

Mixins	Traits
	Unresolved conflicts will result in exceptions being thrown when accessing conflicting properties or methods, or on object creation (with Trait.create)
Support data privacy with closures and symbols.	Support data privacy with closures and symbols. Trait.js doesn't support symbols but that's more of an implementation detail than traits themselves not supporting symbols.
Object mixins can lead to state being coupled between different objects composed from the same mixin.	Traits can also lead to state being between composed objects. In order to avoid that, wrap your trait inside a trait factory function. That will ensure that new objects are composed from new state.
Functional mixins provide a solution to this problem by doubling as an object factory and ensuring that each new object is composed with new state.	
Mixins usually extend existing objects or classes.	Traits create new objects from scratch by composing many traits together instead of extending existing objects or classes.
	Supports the easy creation of high integrity objects using Trait.create.

Concluding

Traits are a *class-free* object oriented programming alternative to *mixins*. Just like *mixins* they encapsulate reusable pieces of behavior that can be composed together to create complex objects. They are an improvement over *mixins* because they let you express requirements within your traits and actively resolve conflicts. Both of these features result in code that is less error prone because composition mistakes don't fail silently and cause unwanted side-effects like with *mixins*.

Traits.js is a library that brings traits to JavaScript. It lets you define traits via the `Trait` factory method, compose traits with `Trait.compose`, define requirements using `Trait.required` and resolve conflicts via `Trait.resolve`.

Traits.js offers two ways to instantiate objects from traits: `Object.create` and `Trait.create`. The first one, which is native to JavaScript, creates vanilla JavaScript objects that can be mutated and augmented. With `Object.create` unmet requirements result in read-only properties and accessing properties with unresolved conflicts results in exceptions. `Trait.create` offers a high integrity alternative to `Object.create` that provides a shorter feedback loop. It throws on object creation when requirements are missing or there are unresolved conflicts. `Trait.create` returns immutable objects which we cannot augment with new properties and whose properties cannot be changed nor deleted.

```
redBrute.says("That's an extremely interesting technique...");
mooleen.says("Thank you Red. Can I call you Red?");

red.says("Since I'm dishonored I have no name. " +
    "You can call me what you please until I reclaim my " +
    "honor and rise again as a new person with a new name.");
mooleen.says("Interesting... Who chooses your new name then?");

red.says("Destiny! A new name comes with a legendary feat. " +
```

Black Tower Summoning: Safer Object Composition with Traits

```
                "The right name should be obvious then.");
    mooleen.says("So it's basically you who choose your new name...");
    red.says("Ehr... Pretty much, yes");

    rat.says("So if you were to make a legendary bagel... " +
             "Could we call you **Bagel**?");
    red.says("...");

    /*
    An arrow lodges itself beside Mooleen stopping this completely
    nonsensical conversation before it goes too far and you stop
    reading this book.
    */

    mooleen.says("We're under attack! Raise the alarm!");
    rat.says("What happened to our scouts?");
    mooleen.says("Well, they're no use now. Defend the bridge!");
    mooleen.says("Red! You'll guard me while I cast");
    /* silence */
    mooleen.says("Red?");
```

Exercises

 Experiment JavaScriptmancer!

You can experiment with these exercises and some possible solutions in this jsFiddle[75] or downloading the source code from GitHub[76].

---

[75] http://bit.ly/javascriptmancy-oop-traits-exercises
[76] https://github.com/vintharas/javascriptmancy-code-samples

Repel the Boarders With Ballistas!

There's enemies on the bridge! Build several Ballistas to clean the deck before it is overran!

You'll need to define several traits to build a ballistas:

- `TNameable` that represents something that can be named and described
- `TPlaceable` that represents something that can be positioned in a two dimensional space
- `TShootable` that represents something that can be shot

An object composed from these traits would satisfy the following interface:

```
let b = Ballista('vera', 1, 1);

// Interface provided by TNameable
console.log(b.name); // => ballista 'vera'
console.log(b) // => ballista 'vera'

// Interface provided by TPlaceable
console.log(b.x); // => 1
console.log(b.y); // => 1
console.log(b.position); // => (1,1)
b.place(2, 2);
// => You place ballista 'vera' in position (2,2)

// Interface provided by TShootable
b.shoot(draconianWarrior)
// => You shoot draconian warrior with ballista
//    'vera' causing 25 damage
```

Come on! Hurry before it's too late!

Solution

Black Tower Summoning: Safer Object Composition with Traits

```
1   /* the enemy */
2   let draconianWarrior = {
3     hp: 50,
4     toString(){
5       return 'draconian warrior';
6     }
7   };
8
9   /* Traits */
10  function TNameable(name){
11    return Trait({
12      name,
13      toString(){
14        return this.name;
15      }
16    });
17  }
18
19  function TPlaceable(x=0, y=0){
20    return Trait({
21      get x(){ return x;},
22      set x(newX){ x = newX;},
23
24      get y(){ return y;},
25      set y(newY) { y = newY;},
26
27      get position(){ return `(${x}, ${y})`;},
28
29      place(x, y) {
30        this.x = x;
31        this.y = y;
32        console.log(`You place ${this} in (${this.x},${this.y})`);
33      }
34    });
35  }
36
37  function TShootable(damage){
38    return Trait({
39      shoot(target){
40        console.log(`You shoot ${target} with ${this}` +
41                    ` causing ${damage} damage`);
42        target.hp -= damage;
43      }
44    });
45  }
46
47  function Ballista(name, x=0, y=0){
```

```js
    return Trait.create(
        /* proto */ Object.prototype,
        /* traits */ Trait.compose(
            TNameable(`Ballista '${name}'`),
            TPlaceable(x, y),
            TShootable(25)));
}

let ballista = Ballista('Vera', 1, 1);
console.log(ballista.name);
// => Ballista 'Vera'
console.log(ballista.position);
// => (1 , 1)
ballista.shoot(draconianWarrior);
// => You shoot draconian warrior with
//    Ballista 'Vera' causing 25 damage

mooleen.says("Yes! More ballistas! Let's kick'em out!");
/*
Mooleen summons more ballistas and you quickly drive the
Draconian assault from the deck of the Zeppelin
*/
rat.says("Hmm... Are those draconian warriors?");
rat.says("They are extremely devious creatures " +
         "perfectly adapted to air warfare");

mooleen.says("That's discomforting...");
rat.says("Yep... may I be so blunt as to say that all this " +
         "has the bitter smell of betrayal?");
mooleen.says("... so it does, you can tell me 'I told you so' if " +
             " we both survive");

rat.says("Oh, familiars are immortal");
rat.says("That's one of the perks of the job");
mooleen.stepsOn(rat.tail);
rat.says("Ouch!!");

phalanx.says("Milady they are about to board us " +
             "with small flying vessels!");
/*
A crash, a boom, the deck of the Zeppelin lurking and the sound of
wood breaking  and splintering. Shouts and a mass of Turians
jumping off the small wreckage, and hacking and slashing into
a disconcerted phalanx platoon.
*/
```

Now Prevent More Soldiers From Boarding With Siege Ballistas!

The smaller ballistas will take care of the boarders and the draconian flying around the Zeppelin. Now you need to build bigger ballistas to prevent the Turians, who are formidable at close quarters, from boarding your ship.

Siege Ballistas are heavier and slower than the smaller units. In addition to using the `TNameable` a `TPositionable` traits you'll need two new traits:

- `TAimable` that describes something that can be aimed at a target
- `TFireable` that describes something that can be fired after having being aimed. This trait requires a property `target` in the composed object.

An object composed from these traits would satisfy the following interface:

```
let siegeBallista = SiegeBallista('Dora', 1, 1);

/* TAimable */
siegeBallista.aimAt(troopTransport);
// => you aim the Siege Ballista 'Dora' at troop transport

/* TFireable */
siegeBallista.fire();
// => you fire the Siege Ballista 'Dora' at troop transport
//    causing 100 damage
```

Solution

```
let troopTransport = {
```

```
  2    hp: 200,
  3    toString(){ return 'flying troop transport';},
  4    load: [
  5      /* many Turians */
  6    ]
  7  };
  8  let moreTuriansOnTheDeck = {
  9    toString: () => 'more turians on the deck'
 10  };
 11
 12  function TAimable(){
 13    const state = { target: undefined };
 14
 15    return Trait({
 16      get target() { return state.target; },
 17      aimAt(target) {
 18        state.target = target;
 19        console.log(`You aim ${this} at ${target}`);
 20      }
 21    });
 22  }
 23
 24  function TFireable(damage){
 25    return Trait({
 26      target: Trait.required,
 27      fire(){
 28        if (this.target){
 29          console.log(`You fire ${this} at ${this.target}` +
 30                      ` causing ${damage} damage`);
 31          this.target.hp -= damage;
 32        } else {
 33          console.log(`${this} doesn't have a target`);
 34        }
 35      }
 36    })
 37  }
 38
 39  function SiegeBallista(name){
 40    return Trait.create(
 41      /* proto */ Object.prototype,
 42      /* traits */ Trait.compose(
 43                     TNameable(`Siege Ballista '${name}'`),
 44                     TPlaceable(),
 45                     TAimable(),
 46                     TFireable(100)
 47                   ));
 48  }
 49
```

Black Tower Summoning: Safer Object Composition with Traits 237

```
50  var siegeBallista = SiegeBallista('Brutus', 2, 2);
51  siegeBallista.aimAt(troopTransport);
52  // => You aim Siege Ballista 'Brutus' at flying troop transport
53  siegeBallista.fire();
54  // => You fire Siege Ballista 'Brutus' at flying troop transport
55  //    causing 100 damage
56
57  mooleen.says('Good! Rally the troops!');
58
59  /*
60   The new ballistas succeed at keeping the transports at bay
61   */
62  mooleen.says("Looks like we've repelled the attack...");
63  rat.screams("Behind!");
64
65  /* Moolen turns in time to see an angry red brute
66   * wielding an axe towards her. It's way too late to cast a spell
67   */
68
69  red.shields(mooleen);
70
71  /*
72   The axe falls down for what it feels like an eternity
73   and it suddenly comes to a halt. All of the sudden, Red stands
74   between Mooleen and the brute, muscles bulging, roars, lifts the
75   opposing Turian from the ground and throws him off the deck of
76   the ship.
77   */
78
79  red.laughs();
80  red.charges(moreTuriansOnTheDeck);
81
82  rat.says("Hmmm... that whole thing was very odd");
83
84  /*
85   *  An explosion above, the flying ship lurks and starting
86   *  losing altitude
87   */
88
89  mooleen.says("Damn... If they can't board us they'll sink us...");
```

Protect the Zeppelin From the Heights!

The draconian force has started attacking the Zeppelin itself in an effort to sink it into oblivion. You must summon floating ballistas that can protect the Zeppelin from all heights.

Given a trait `TPlaceable3D` that looks like this:

```
function TPlaceable3D(z=0){
  return Trait({
    x: Trait.required,
    y: Trait.required,
    get z() { return z;},
    set z(value) { z = value; },
    place(x, y, z){
      this.x = x;
      this.y = y;
      this.z = z;
      console.log(
        `You place ${this} in (${this.x},${this.y}, ${this.z})`);
    }
  })
}
```

Define a `FloatingBallista` composed using the following traits `TNameable`, `TPlaceable`, `TPlaceable3D`, `TShootable`.

Tip: You'll need to explicitly handle the conflict with the `place` method. The resulting object sould be able to be placed at an arbitrary height.

Solution

```
function TPlaceable3D(z=0){
  return Trait({
    x: Trait.required,
    y: Trait.required,
    get z() { return z;},
```

```
 6      set z(value) { z = value; },
 7      place(x, y, z){
 8        this.x = x;
 9        this.y = y;
10        this.z = z;
11        console.log(`You place ${this} in position ` +
12                    `(${this.x},${this.y}, ${this.z})`);
13      }
14    });
15  }
16
17  function FloatingBallista(name, x=0, y=0, z=0){
18    return Trait.create(
19      Object.prototype,
20      Trait.compose(
21        TNameable(`Floating Ballista '${name}'`),
22        Trait.override(TPlaceable3D(z), TPlaceable(x,y)),
23        TShootable(50)
24      )
25    );
26  }
27
28  let floatingBallista = FloatingBallista("Ursa", 1, 1, 20);
29  floatingBallista.shoot(draconianWarrior);
30  // => You shoot draconian warrior with Floating Ballista 'Ursa'
31  //    causing 50 damage
32  floatingBallista.place(1, 2, 50);
33  // => You place Floating Ballista 'Ursa' in position (1,2, 50)
34
35  /*
36   * The last enemy forces retreats as the sun
37   * raises in the sky again announcing a new beautiful day.
38   */
39
40  mooleen.says('Did we fight all night?');
41  red.says('Yes! And it was glorious!');
42  rat.says('Epic!');
43  red.says('Legendary');
44
45  randalf.yawns();
46  randalf.says('What a beautiful morning!');
47
48  mooleen.says("Don't tell me you slept through everything...");
49  randalf.says("everything?");
50
51  bandalf.yawns();
52  bandalf.says('What a beautiful day!');
53
```

```
54  randalf.says("Bandalf... don't tell me you slept " +
55                "through everything...");
56  bandalf.says("everything?");
57
58  mooleen.facepalms();
59  // => mooleen epicly facepalms
```

Black Tower Summoning: Next Level Object Composition With Stamps

Favor composition
over inheritance

> - Gill Of Fyra
> Designer of the Pattern

Black Tower Summoning: Next Level Object Composition With Stamps   242

```
/*
A broken Zeppelin flies slightly sideways in a desolated
cloudless sky. A countless number of ropes fall down
from the board as the crew hurriedly repairs the hull
and the rigging of the flying vessel. On the bridge several
figures discuss heatedly and decide what will be the
future of the expedition.
*/

randalf.says("I think we need to go back to Asturi");
bandalf.says("Yes, we have a strong position there");
rat.says("The villagers really love us...");

red.says("That is utter nonsense. You need to strike... " +
"Strike now they're weak and demoralized after " +
"been defeated twice.");

mooleen.says("Hmm... I don't know. This last attack " +
"has me worried. They may have expected us to attack. " +
"But how did they know where to find us " +
"in all the unending miles of sky that surround us?");

red.says("Well either they got lucky... " +
"or someone stabbed you in the back.");

mooleen.says("Disturbing... No one knew this route " +
"but you Red");
randalf.says("You deceitful imp... She spared your life!");
bandalf.says("Phalanx put this man in shackles!!");

/*
The soldiers surround Red fearfuly but he doesn't
seem to react to their approach. One gathers the
courage to hit him in the head with the butt of his
spear and Red drops to the ground. They shackle him
and bring him beneath.
*/

randalf.says("Now we can stop this nonsense and go back");
bandalf.says("Regroup");
randalf.says("Strengthen our position");

mooleen.says("No");
mooleen.says("If we go back I'll never get home. " +
"I'll just get trapped in that teeny tiny island for ever.");
mooleen.says("We're pushing through.");
```

Black Tower Summoning: Next Level Object Composition With Stamps   243

```
randalf.says("but...");

mooleen.says("Don't worry. I have a trick down my sleeve");
mooleen.says("Our troops will be unstoppable!!")
mooleen.says("I've been adapting this object composition " +
    "technique to make extra weapons, armors and potions.");
mooleen.says("I call them stamps");
```

I Call Them Stamps

In the last two chapters you learned about two great alternatives to classical object oriented programming: *mixins* and *traits*. Both techniques embrace the dynamic nature of JavaScript. Both encourage creating small reusable components that you can either mix with your existing objects or compose together to create new objects from scratch.

Object and functional *mixins* are the simplest approach to object composition. Together with `Object.assign` they make super easy to create small units of reusable behavior and augment your domain objects with them.

Traits continue the tradition of composability of *mixins* adding an extra layer of expressiveness and safety on top. They let you define required properties, resolve naming conflicts and they warn you whenever you've failed to compose your traits properly.

In this chapter you'll learn a new technique to achieve class-free inheritance through object composition. This particular technique embraces not only the dynamic nature of JavaScript but also its many ways to achieve code reuse: prototypes, mixins and closures. Behold! **Stamps**[77]!

---

[77] Stamps were initially devised by a mythical figure in the JavaScript world: Eric Eliott. If you have some time to spare go check his stuff at ericelliottjs.com or JavaScript Scene.

Experiment Javascriptmancer!!
You can experiment with all examples in this chapter directly within this jsBin[78] or downloading the source code from GitHub[79].

 Open Source Alert! Stampit!
We are going to be using stampit[80] (version 3) for the remainder of the article. Stampit is a library that follows the stamp specification and allows you to use stamps in JavaScript. If you're curious and eager to learn more about it, I encourage you to visit the GitHub page[81] and the stamp specification[82].

What are Stamps?

Stamps are composable factory functions. Just like regular factory functions they let you create new objects but, lo and behold, they also have the earth shattering ability to compose themselves with each other. Factory composition unlocks a world of possibilities and a whole new paradigm of class-free object oriented programming as you'll soon see.

Imagine that you have a factory function to create swords that you can *wield*:

---

[78] http://bit.ly/javascriptmancy-oop-stamps
[79] https://github.com/vintharas/javascriptmancy-code-samples
[80] https://github.com/stampit-org/stampit
[81] https://github.com/stampit-org/stampit
[82] https://github.com/stampit-org/stamp-specification

Black Tower Summoning: Next Level Object Composition With Stamps   245

```
const Sword = () =>
  ({
    description: 'common sword',
    toString(){ return this.description;},
    wield(){
      console.log(`You wield ${this.description}`);
    }
  });

const sword = new Sword();
sword.wield();
// => You wield the common sword
```

And another one that creates deadly knives that you can *throw*:

```
const Knife = () =>
  ({
    description: 'rusty knife',
    toString(){ return this.description},
    throw(target){
      console.log(`You throw the ${this.description} ` +
                  `towards the ${target}`);
    }
  });

const knife = new Knife();
knife.throw('orc');
// => You throw the rusty knife towards the orc
```

Wouldn't it be great to have a way to combine that *wielding* with the *throwing* so you can *wield* a knife? Or *throw* a sword? That's exactly what *stamps* let you do. With *stamps* you can define factory functions that encapsulate pieces of behavior and later compose them with each other.

Before we start composing, let's break down both `Sword` and `Knife` into the separate behaviors that define them. Each of these behaviors will be represented by a separate stamp that we'll create with the aid of the `stampit` function, the core API of the `stampit` library[83].

So, we create stamps for something that can be wielded:

```
// wielding something
const Wieldable = stampit({
  methods: {
    wield(){
      console.log(`You wield ${this.description}`);
    }
  }
});
```

Something that can be thrown:

```
// throwing something
const Throwable = stampit({
  methods: {
    throw(target){
      console.log(`You throw the ${this.description} ` +
                  `towards the ${target}`);
    }
  }
});
```

And something that can be described:

---

[83] https://github.com/stampit-org/stampit

```
 1  // or describing something
 2  const Describable = stampit({
 3    methods: {
 4      toString(){
 5        return this.description;
 6      }
 7    },
 8    // default description
 9    props: {
10      description: 'something'
11    },
12    // let's you initialize description
13    init({description=this.description}){
14      this.description = description;
15    }
16  });
```

In the examples above, we use the stampit function to create three different stamps: Wieldable, Throwable and Describable. The stampit function takes a **configuration object** that represents how objects should be created and produces a factory that uses that configuration to create new objects.

In our example we use different properties of the *configuration object* to create our stamps:

- methods: allows us to define the methods that an object should have like wield, throw and toString
- props: lets us set a default value for an object description
- init: allows stamp consumers initialize objects with a given description

As a result, the Wieldable *stamp* creates objects that have a wield method, the Throwable *stamp* creates objects with a throw method and so on.

Once you have defined these *stamps* you can compose them together into yet another *stamp* that represents a weapon by using the compose method:

```
const Weapon = stampit()
  .compose(Describable, Wieldable, Throwable);
```

Now you can use this *stamp* Weapon, that works just like a factory, to create (or stamp) new mighty weapons that you'll be able to *wield*, *throw* and *describe*.

Let's start with a mighty sword:

```
const anotherSword = Weapon({description: 'migthy sword'});

anotherSword.wield();
// => You wield the mighty sword
anotherSword.throw('ice wyvern');
// => You throw the mighty sword towards the ice wyvern
```

Notice how we pass an object with a description property to the stamp? This is the description that will be forwarded to the init method of the Describable stamp we defined earlier.

And what about a sacrificial knife?

```
const anotherKnife = Weapon({description: 'sacrificial knife'});

anotherKnife.wield();
// => You wield the sacrificial knife
anotherKnife.throw('heart of the witch');
// => You throw the sacrificial knife towards the heart of the witch
```

Yey! We did it! Using stamps we were able to create factories for stuff that can be wielded, thrown and described, and compose them together to create a sword and a knife that can be both wielded and thrown. These examples only scratch the surface of the capabilities of *stamps*. There's much more in store for you. Let's continue!

Stamps OOP Embraces JavaScript

A very interesting feature of *stamps* that differentiates them from other existing approaches to object composition is that they truly embrace JavaScript strengths and idioms. *Stamps* use:

- **Prototypical inheritance** so that you can take advantage of prototypes to share methods between objects.
- **Mixins** so that you can compose pieces of behavior with your stamps, use defaults, initialize or override properties.
- **Closures** so that you can achieve data privacy and only expose it through the interface of your choice.

Moreover, stamps wrap all of this goodness in a very straightforward declarative interface:

```
const stamp = stampit({
  // methods inherited via prototypical inheritance
  methods: {...},

  // properties and methods mixed in via Object.assign (mixin)
  props: {...},

  // properties and methods mixed in through a recursive algorithm
  // (deeply cloned mixin)
  deepProps: {...}

  // closure that can contain private members
  init: function(arg0, context){...},
});
```

Stamps By Example

Let's continue with the example of the swords and the knives - we need to arm our army after all if we want to defeat *The Red Hand* - and go through each of the different features provided by *stamps*.

In the upcoming sections, we will define the weapon *stamp* from scratch using new *stamp* options as the need arises and showcasing how *stamps* take advantage of different JavaScript features.

Prototypical Inheritance and Stamps

We will start by defining some common methods that could be shared across all weapons and therefore it makes sense to place them in a *prototype*. In order to do that we use the `methods` property you saw in previous examples:

```
const AWeapon = stampit({
  methods: {
    toString(){
      return this.description;
    },
    wield(target){
      console.log(`You wield the ${this} ` +
                  `and attack the ${target}`);
    },
    throw(target){
      console.log(`You throw the ${this} ` +
                  `at the ${target}`);
    }
  }
});
```

We now have a AWeapon stamp with three methods `toString`, `wield` and `throw` that we can use to instantiate new weapons like this sword:

```
const aSword = AWeapon({description: 'a sword'});
aSword.wield('giant rat');
// => You wield the sword and attack the giant rat
```

You can verify that all these methods that we include within the `methods` property are part of the `aSword` object prototype using `Object.getPrototypeOf()`:

Black Tower Summoning: Next Level Object Composition With Stamps   251

```
1  console.log(Object.getPrototypeOf(aSword));
2  // => [object Object] {
3  //    throw:...
4  //    toString:...
5  //    wield:...}
```

The `Object.getPrototypeOf` method returns the prototype of the `aSword` object which, as we expected, includes all the methods we are looking for: `throw`, `wield` and `toString`.

Mixins and Stamps

The `props` and `deepProps` properties let you define the properties or methods that will be part of each object created via *stamps* [84]. Both properties define an **object mixin** that will be composed with the object being created by the *stamp*:

- Properties within the `props` object are merged using `Object.assign` and thus copied over the new object as-is.
- Properties within the `deepProps` object are deeply cloned and then merged using `Object.assign` which guarantees that no state is shared between objects created via the *stamp*. This is very important if you have properties with objects or arrays since you don't want state changes in one object affecting other objects.

We can expand the previous weapon example using `props` and `deepProps` to add new functionality to our weapon. The abilities to:

1. obtain a detailed description when under thorough examination (`examine`)
2. enchant the weapon with powerful spells and enchantments (`enchant`)

---

[84]These properties or methods are part of the object itself as opposed to being part of the prototype. Therefore they won't be shared across all instances created using a stamp.

```js
const AWeightedWeapon = stampit({
  props: {
    // 1. props part of examining ability
    weight: '4 stones',
    material: 'iron',
    description: 'weapon'
  },
  deepProps: {
    // 2. deep props part of the enchanting ability
    enchantments: []
  },
  methods: {
    /*
    // collapsed to save space
    toString(){...},
    wield(target){...},
    throw(target){...},
    */
    examine(){
      console.log(`You examine the ${this}.
It's made of ${this.material} and ${this.examineWeight()}.
${this.examineEnchantments()}.`)
    },
    examineWeight(){
      const weight = Number.parseInt(this.weight);
      if (weight > 5) return 'it feels heavy';
      if (weight > 3) return 'it feels light';
      return 'it feels surprisingly light';
    },
    examineEnchantments(){
      if (this.enchantments.length === 0)
        return 'It is not enchanted.';
      return `It seems enchanted: ${this.enchantments}`;
    },
    enchant(enchantment){
      console.log(`You enchant the ${this} with ${enchantment}`);
      this.enchantments.push(enchantment)
    }
  },
  init({description = this.description}){
    this.description = description;
  }
});
```

Now we can examine our weapons that, from this moment forward, will have a weight and be made of some material:

```
const aWeightedSword = AWeightedWeapon({
  description: 'sword of iron-ness'
});

aWeightedSword.examine();
// => You examine the sword of iron-ness.
//    It's made of iron and it feels light.
//    It is not enchanted.
```

And even enchant them with powerful spells:

```
aWeightedSword.enchant('speed +1');
// => You enchant the sword of iron-ness with speed +1

aWeightedSword.examine();
// => You examine the sword of iron-ness.
//    It's made of iron and it feels light.
//    It seems enchanted: speed +1.
```

It is interesting to point out that the object passed as an argument to the *stamp* function when creating a new object will be passed forward to all defined initializers (init methods). For instance, in the example above we called the AWeightedWeapon stamp with the object {description: 'sword of iron-ness'}. This object was passed to the stamp init method and used to initialize the weapon description for the resulting aWeightedSword object. Had there been more stamps with init methods, this object would have been passed as an argument to each one of them.

In addition to using props and deepProps to define the shape of an object created via stamps, we can use them in combination with the same *mixins* we saw in previous chapters. That is, we can take advantage of previously defined mixins that represent a behavior and compose them with our newly created stamps.

For instance, we could have defined a reusable madeOfIron *mixin*:

```
const madeOfIron = {
    weight: '4 stones',
    material: 'iron'
};
```

And passed it as part of the props object:

```
const AnIronWeapon = stampit({
    props: madeOfIron,
    ...
});
```

This *object composition* is even easier to achieve using the *stamp* fluent API that we'll examine in detail in later sections:

```
const AnHeavyIronHolyWeapon =
    // A weighted weapon
    AWeightedWeapon
    // compose with madeOfIron mixin
    .props(madeOfIron)
    // compose with veryHeavyWeapon mixin
    .props(veryHeavyWeapon)
    // compose with deeply cloned version of holyEnchantments mixin
    .deepProps(holyEnchantments);
```

Data Privacy and Stamps

Let's imagine that we don't want to expose to everyone how we have implemented the enchanting weapons engine, so that, we can change and optimize it in the future. *Is there a way to make that information private?* Yes, indeed there is. *Stamps* support data privacy by using closures through the init property.

Let's take the previous weapon example and make our enchantment implementation private. We'll do that by moving the enchantments property from the public API (props) into the init function where it'll be isolated from the outside world. Since the manner of accessing this private enchantments property is via closures, we'll need to

Black Tower Summoning: Next Level Object Composition With Stamps 255

move all methods that need to have a access to the property inside the `init` function as well (`examineEnchantments` and `enchant`):

```
const APrivateWeapon = stampit({
  methods: {
    /*
      like in previous examples
      toString(){...},
      wield(target){...},
      throw(target){...},
    */
    examine(){
      console.log(`You examine the ${this}.
It's made of ${this.material} and ${this.examineWeight()}.
${this.examineEnchantments()}.`)
    },
    examineWeight(){
      const weight = Number.parseInt(this.weight);
      if (weight > 5) return 'it feels heavy';
      if (weight > 3) return 'it feels light';
      return 'it feels surprisingly light';
    }
  },
  props: {
    weight: '4 stones',
    material: 'iron',
    description: 'weapon'
  },
  init: function({description=this.description}){
    // this private variable is the one being enclosed
    const enchantments = [];
    this.description = description;

    // augment object being created
    // with examineEnchantments and enchant
    // methods
    Object.assign(this, {
      examineEnchantments(){
        if (enchantments.length === 0) return 'It is not enchanted.';
        return `It seems enchanted: ${enchantments}`;
      },
      enchant(enchantment){
```

```
        console.log(`You enchant the ${this} with ${enchantment}`);
        enchantments.push(enchantment)
    }
  });
 }
});
```

The init function will be called during the creation of an object with the object itself as context (this). This will allow us to augment the object with the examineEnchantments and enchant methods that enclose the enchantments property. As a result, when we create an object using this stamp, it will have a private variable enchantments that can only be operated through these methods.

Having defined this new stamp we can verify how indeed the enchantments property is now private:

```
const aPrivateWeapon = APrivateWeapon({
  description: 'sword of privacy'
});

console.log(aPrivateWeapon.enchantments);
// => undefined;

aPrivateWeapon.examine();
// => You examine the sword of privacy.
//It's made of iron and it feels light.
//It is not enchanted.

aPrivateWeapon.enchant('privacy: wielder cannot be detected');
// => You enchant the sword of privacy with privacy:
//    wielder cannot be detected

aPrivateWeapon.examine();
// => You examine the sword of privacy.
//    It's made of iron and it feels light.
//    It seems enchanted: privacy: wielder cannot be detected.
```

In addition to helping you with information hiding, the init function adds an extra degree of flexibility by allowing you to provide additional arguments that affect object creation.

The init function takes two arguments:

1. The first argument passed to the stamp during object creation. This is generally an options object with properties that will be used when creating an object.
2. A context object with these three properties:

```
{
  instance, // the instance being created
  stamp,    // the stamp
  args      // arguments passed to the stamp during object creation
}
```

So we can redefine our init function to, for instance, limit the number of enchantments allowed for a given weapon:

```
const ALimitedEnchantedWeapon = stampit({
  methods: {
    /*
        // Same as in previous examples
        toString(){...},
        wield(target){...},
        throw(target){...},
        examine(){...},
        examineWeight(){...}
    */
  },
  props: {
    weight: '4 stones',
    material: 'iron',
    description: 'weapon'
  },
  init: function({ /* options object */
                  description = this.description,
                  maxNumberOfEnchantments = 10
                }){
    // this private variable is the one being enclosed
    const enchantments = [];
```

```
    this.description = description;

    Object.assign(this, {
      examineEnchantments(){
        if (enchantments.length === 0) return 'It is not enchanted.';
        return `It seems enchanted: ${enchantments}`;
      },
      enchant(enchantment){
        if(enchantments.length === maxNumberOfEnchantments) {
          console.log('Oh no! This weapon cannot ' +
                     'be enchanted any more!');
        } else {
          console.log(`You enchant the ${this} with ${enchantment}`);
          enchantments.push(enchantment);
        }
      }
    });
  }
});
```

In this example we have updated the init method to unwrap the arguments being passed to the *stamp* function. The method now expects the first argument to be an options object that contains:

- a description
- a maxNumberOfEnchantments variable that will determine how many enchantments a weapon can hold. If it hasn't been defined it defaults to a value of 10

So now, we can call the *stamp* passing a configuration of our choosing:

```
const onlyOneEnchanmentWeapon = ALimitedEnchantedWeapon({
  description: 'sword of one enchanment',
  maxNumberOfEnchantments: 1
});
```

As we mentioned earlier, this options object will be passed in to the init function as its first argument resulting in a weapon that can only hold a single enchantment:

```
1   onlyOneEnchanmentWeapon.examine();
2   // => You examine the sword of privacy.
3   //It's made of iron and it feels light.
4   //It is not enchanted.
5
6   onlyOneEnchanmentWeapon.enchant('luck +1');
7   // => You enchant the sword of one enchanment with luck +1
8
9   onlyOneEnchanmentWeapon.enchant(
10    'touch of gold: everything you touch becomes gold');
11  // => Oh no! This weapon cannot be enchanted any more!
```

As you could appreciate in this example, the `init` function adds a lot of flexibility to your stamps as it allows you to configure them via additional parameters during creation such as `maxNumberOfEnchantments`.

Stamp Composition

Stamps are great at composition. On one hand you compose *prototypes*, *mixins* and *closures* to produce a single *stamp*. On the other, you can compose *stamps* with each other just like you saw in the introduction to this chapter with the words, knives, the wielding and the throwing.

Let's take a closer look at stamp composition. Following the *weapons* example from previous sections, imagine that all of the sudden we need a way to represent *potions* and *armors*.

What do we do?

Well, we can start by factoring the *weapon* stamp into smaller reusable behaviors also represented as *stamps*. We have the `Throwable`, `Wieldable` and `Describable` behaviors we defined at the beginning of the chapter:

```
const Throwable = stampit({
  methods: {
    throw(target){
      console.log(`You throw the ${this.description} ` +
                  `towards the ${target}`);
    }
  }
});

// wielding something
const Wieldable = stampit({
  methods: {
    wield(target){
      console.log(`You wield the ${this.description} ` +
                  `and attack the ${target}`);
    }
  }
});

// or describing something
const Describable = stampit({
  methods: {
    toString(){
      return this.description;
    }
  },
  props: {
    description: 'something'
  },
  init({description=this.description}){
    this.description = description;
  }
});
```

We can define new Weighted and MadeOfMaterial stamps to represent something that has weight and something which is made of some sort of material:

Black Tower Summoning: Next Level Object Composition With Stamps

```
const Weighted = stampit({
  methods: {
    examineWeight(){
      const weight = Number.parseInt(this.weight);
      if (weight > 5) return 'it feels heavy';
      if (weight > 3) return 'it feels light';
      return 'it feels surprisingly light';
    }
  },
  props: {
    weight: '4 stones'
  },
  init({weight=this.weight}){
    this.weight = weight;
  }
});

const MadeOfMaterial = stampit({
  methods: {
    examineMaterial(){
      return `It's made of ${this.material}`;
    }
  },
  props: {
    material: 'iron'
  },
  init({material=this.material}){
    this.material = material;
  }
});
```

And finally an `Enchantable` stamp to represent something that can be enchanted:

```
const Enchantable = stampit({
  init: function({maxNumberOfEnchantments=10}){
    // this private variable is the one being enclosed
    const enchantments = [];

    Object.assign(this, {
      examineEnchantments(){
        if (enchantments.length === 0) return 'It is not enchanted.';
        return `It seems enchanted: ${enchantments}`;
      },
      enchant(enchantment){
        if(enchantments.length === maxNumberOfEnchantments) {
          console.log('Oh no! This weapon cannot be enchanted ' +
                      'any more!');
        } else {
          console.log(`You enchant the ${this} with ${enchantment}`);
          enchantments.push(enchantment);
        }
      }
    });
  }
});
```

Now that we have identified all these reusable behaviors we can start composing them together. We could wrap the most fundamental behaviors in an `Item` *stamp*:

```
const Item = stampit()
              .compose(Describable, Weighted, MadeOfMaterial);
```

And define the new `AComposedWeapon` *stamp* in terms of it:

Black Tower Summoning: Next Level Object Composition With Stamps

```
const AComposedWeapon = stampit({
  methods: {
    examine(){
      console.log(`You examine the ${this}.
${this.examineMaterial()} and ${this.examineWeight()}.
${this.examineEnchantments()}.`)
    },
  }
}).compose(Item, Wieldable, Throwable, Enchantable);
```

This reads very nicely. A Weapon is an **Item** that you can **Wield**, **Throw** and **Enchant**.

If we define a weapon using this new *stamp* we can verify how everything works just like it did before the factoring:

```
// now we can use the new weapon as before
const swordOfTruth = AComposedWeapon({
  description: 'The Sword of Truth'
});

swordOfTruth.examine();
// => You examine the The Sword of Truth.
//    It's made of iron and it feels light.
//    It is not enchanted.."

swordOfTruth.enchant("demon slaying +10");
// => You enchant the The Sword of Truth with demon slaying +10

swordOfTruth.examine();
// => You examine the The Sword of Truth.
//    It's made of iron and it feels light.
//    It seems enchanted: demon slaying +10.
```

Now we can combine these behaviors together with new ones to define the `Potion` and `Armor` *stamps*.

A *potion* would be something that can be drunk and which has some sort of effect on the drinker. For instance, if we create a new stamp to represent something that can be drunk:

```
const Drinkable = stampit({
  methods: {
    drink(){
      console.log(`You drink the ${this}. ${this.effects}`);
    }
  },
  props: {
    effects: 'It has no visible effect'
  },
  init({effects=this.effects}){
    this.effects = effects;
  }
});
```

We can define a potions as follows: An **Item** that you can **Throw** and **Drink**.

```
const Potion = stampit().compose(Item, Throwable, Drinkable);
```

We can verify that the potion works as we want it to:

```
const healingPotion = Potion({
  description: 'Potion of minor healing',
  effects: 'You heal 50 hp (+50hp)!'
});

healingPotion.drink();
// => You drink the Potion of minor healing. You heal 50 hp (+50hp)!
```

On the other hand, an *armor* would be something that you could wear and which would offer some protection. Let's define a Wearable behavior:

```
const Wearable = stampit({
  methods: {
    wear(){
      console.log(`You wear ${this} in your ` +
          `${this.position} gaining +${this.protection} ` +
          `armor protection.`);
    }
  },
  props: { // these act as defaults
    position: 'chest',
    protection: 50
  },
  init({position=this.position, protection=this.protection}){
    this.position = position;
    this.protection = protection;
  }
});
```

And now an **Armor** is an **Item** that you can **Wear** and **Enchant**:

```
const Armor = stampit().compose(Item, Wearable, Enchantable);
```

Let's take this Armor for a test run and create a powerful steel breastplate of fire:

```
const steelBreastPlateOfFire = Armor({
  description: 'Steel Breastplate of Fire',
  material: 'steel',
  weight: '50 stones',
});

steelBreastPlateOfFire.enchant('Fire resistance +100');
// => You enchant the Steel Breastplate of Fire with
//    Fire resistance +100

steelBreastPlateOfFire.wear();
// => You wear Steel Breastplate of Fire in your chest
//    gaining +50 armor protection.
```

In the two previous examples we have added two behaviors - drinking and wearing something - as part of the Potion and Armor stamps. Using this type of approach allows us to create a rich domain model with behaviors that we reuse and compose to our heart's content. These stamps result in the vocabulary of a domain specific language of sorts that allows us to express one stamp in terms of other stamps, one idea or concept in our domain model in terms of other ones:

```
const Armor = stampit().compose(Item, Wearable, Enchantable);
// => an armor is an item that you can wear and that can be enchanted

const Weapon = stampit().compose(Item, Throwable, Wieldable);
// => a weapon is an item that you can throw or wield

const Potion = stampit().compose(Item, Drinkable, Throwable);
// => a potion is an item that you can drink or throw
```

Pretty cool right? You end up with a very declarative, readable, flexible and extensible way to work with objects. Now imagine how much work and additional code you would have needed to implement the same solution using classical inheritance.

Prototypical Inheritance When Composing Stamps

You may be wondering... *What happens with prototypical inheritance when you compose two stamps? Does stampit create multiple prototypes and establish a prototype chain between them?*

The answer is no, whenever you compose *stamps* all the different methods assigned to the methods property in each *stamp* are flattened into a singular *prototype*.

Let's illustrate this with an example. Imagine that you want to define elemental weapons that let you perform mighty elemental attacks. In order to do this you compose the existing AComposedWeapon stamp with a new stamp that has the elementalAttack method:

Black Tower Summoning: Next Level Object Composition With Stamps   267

```
const ElementalWeapon = stampit({
  methods: {
    elementalAttack(target){
      console.log(`You wield the ${this.description} and perform ` +
                  `a terrifying elemental attack on the ${target}`);
    }
  }
}).compose(AComposedWeapon);
```

When you instantiate a new sword of fire you can readily verify how the aFireSword object does not have a prototype with a single elementalAttack method. Instead, the prototype contains all methods defined in all *stamps* that have being composed to create ElementalWeapon:

```
const aFireSword = ElementalWeapon({
  description: 'magic sword of fire'
});

console.log(Object.getPrototypeOf(aFireSword));
// => [object Object] {
//   elementalAttack: ...
//   examine: ...
//   examineMaterial: ...
//   examineWeight: ...
//   throw: ...
//   toString: ...
//   wield: ...
// }
```

If there are naming collisions between composed *stamps* the last one wins and overwrites the conflicting method, just like with Object.assign.

Data Privacy When Composing Stamps

Another interesting advantage of using closures to define private data and being able to later compose *stamps* with each other is that private data doesn't collide. If you have a private member with the same name in two different *stamps* and you compose them together they will act as two completely different variables.

Let's illustrate this with another example (example craze!!). If you remember from previous sections the `AComposedWeapon` stamp allowed weapons to be enchanted (via the `Enchanted` stamp) and stored these magic spells inside a private variable called `enchantments`. *What would happen if we were to rewrite our elemental weapon to also have a private property called enchantments?*

```
// We redefine the elemental weapon to store its
// elemental properties as enchantments of some sort:

const AnElementalWeapon = stampit({
  init({enchantments=[]}){
    Object.assign(this, {
      elementalAttack(target){
        console.log(`You wield the ${this.description} and ` +
          `perform a terrifying elemental attack of ` +
          `${enchantments} on the ${target}`);
      }
    });
  }
}).compose(AComposedWeapon);
```

In this example we have redefined the element weapon to store its powers like an enchantment (that is, inside an `enchantments` array). We moved the `elementalAttack` method from the `methods` properties to the `init` property so that it will enclose the `enchantments` private member that will, from now on, store the elemental attack.

We go ahead and create a new super elemental weapon: an igneous lance!

```
const igneousLance = AnElementalWeapon({
  description: 'igneous Lance',
  enchantments: ['fire']
});
```

But what happens with this lance that effectively has two enchantments private members (from the `AnElementalWeapon` and `Enchanted` stamps)? Well, we can easily verify that they do not affect each other by putting the lance into action:

```
igneousLance.elementalAttack('rabbit');
// => You wield the igneous Lance and perform a
//    terrifying elemental attack of fire on the rabbit

igneousLance.enchant('protect + 1');
// => You enchant the igneous Lance with protect + 1

igneousLance.elementalAttack('goat');
// => You wield the igneous Lance and perform a
//    terrifying elemental attack of fire on the goat
```

Why don't the `enchantments` variables collide? Even though I often use the word private members to refer to these variables, the reality is that they are not part of the object being created by the *stamps*. Different `enchantments` variables are enclosed by the `enchant` and `elementalAttack` functions and it is these two different values that are used when calling these two functions. Since they are two different variables that belong to two completely different scopes no collision takes place even though both variables have the same name.

Stamp Fluent API

In addition to the API that we've used in the previous examples where you pass a configuration object to the `stampit` method:

```
const stamp = stampit({

    // methods inherited via prototypical inheritance
    methods: {...},

    // properties and methods mixed in via Object.assign (mixin)
    props: {...},

    // closure that can contain private members
    init(options, context){...},

    // properties and methods mixed in through a recursive algorithm
    // (deeply cloned mixin)
    deepProps: {...}
});
```

You can use the fluent interface if it is more to your liking:

```
const stamp = stampit().
    // methods inherited via prototypical inheritance
    methods({...}).

    // properties and methods mixed in via Object.assign (mixin)
    props({...}).

    // closure that can contain private members
    init(function(options, context){...}).

    // properties and methods mixed in through a recursive algorithm
    // (deeply cloned mixin)
    deepProps({...}).

    // compose with other stamps
    compose(...);
```

For instance, we can redefine the Armor *stamp* as a chain of methods using this new interface:

Black Tower Summoning: Next Level Object Composition With Stamps

```
const FluentArmor = stampit()
  .methods({
    wear(){
      console.log(`You wear ${this} in your ` +
        `${this.position} gaining +${this.protection} ` +
        `armor protection.`);
    }})
  .props({
    // these act as defaults
    position: 'chest',
    protection: 50
  })
  .init(function init({
              position=this.position,
              protection=this.protection}){
    this.position = position;
    this.protection = protection;
  })
  .compose(Item, Enchantable);
```

Which works just like you'd expect:

```
const fluentArmor = FluentArmor({
  description: 'leather jacket',
  protection: 70
});

fluentArmor.wear();
// => You wear leather jacket in your chest
//    gaining +70 armor protection
```

It is important to understand that each method of the fluent interface returns a new *stamp*. That is, you don't modify the current *stamp* but go creating new *stamps* with added capabilities as you go adding more methods. **This makes the fluent interface particularly useful when you want to build on top of existing stamps or behaviors.**

Concluding: Stamps vs Mixins vs Traits

Stamps are like mixins on steroids. They offer a great declarative API to create and compose your factories of objects (*stamps*) with baked in support for composing prototypes, mixing in features, deep copying composition and private variables.

Stamps truly embrace the nature of JavaScript and take advantage of all of its object oriented programming techniques: prototypical inheritance, concatenative inheritance with mixins and information hiding through closures.

The only drawback in comparison with *mixins* is that they require that you use a third party library whereas `Object.assign` is native to JavaScript.

In relation to *traits*, these still offer a safer composition experience with support for required properties and proactive name conflict resolution.

Be it mixins, traits or stamps, they are all awesome techniques to make your object oriented programming more modular, reusable, flexible and extensible, really taking advantage of the dynamic nature of JavaScript.

This chapter wraps the different object composition techniques that I wanted to offer to you as an alternative to classical object oriented programming. I hope you have enjoyed learning about them and are at least a little bit curious to try them out in your next project.

```
randalf.says("That's indeed an amazing technique");
bandalf.says("It could give us an edge");
randalf.says("Enough edge to conquer The Red Stronghold");

mooleen.grins();
mooleen.says("Haha not so crazy now eh?");
rat.says("Always humbled by your prowess my master");
```

Black Tower Summoning: Next Level Object Composition With Stamps

```
mooleen.reddens();
mooleen.says("Ok, let's get to work");
mooleen.says("I'll be down in my cabin forging weapons");
mooleen.says("Let me know if you come up with any " +
    "crazy ideas...");

bandalf.says("What about a helmet where you can put your " +
    "mead flask so you can have your hands free " +
    "for eating? ");

mooleen.says("hmm interesting... although I fail to see " +
    "how that could tip the war to our side");

randalf.says("Well it could keep the troops hydrated " +
    "during a long hard battle");

mooleen.says("...with mead?!?");

bandalf.says("... and it would act as a normal helmet " +
    "as well, protecting the heads of our troops.");
randalf.says("You're a genious brother");
bandalf.says("You're not so bad yourself");

/*
Bandalf and Randalf continue congratulating each other
until they disappear into the hull of the ship.
*/

mooleen.says("Oh my god");
rat.says("I know. But you don't need to feel intimidated " +
    "by their brilliance. They've got far more experience " +
    "than you. You'll get there. You'll see.");

mooleen.doesAnEpicEyeRoll();
```

Exercises

 Experiment Javascriptmancer!
You can experiment with these exercises and some possible solutions in this jsFiddle[85] or downloading the source code from GitHub[86].

---
[85] http://bit.ly/javascriptmancy-oop-stamps-exercises
[86] https://github.com/vintharas/javascriptmancy-code-samples

Spells For Everyone! Scrolls of Power!

Mooleen just had a brilliant idea to vanquish The Red Hand: Scrolls of power! Imagine any normal having the ability to cast terrible spells and inflicting chaos and destruction upon our enemies.

A scroll of power should be something:

- Describable: It has a name and can be described
- Inscribable: It can be inscribed with a spell with a maximum number of charges. Once it has been inscribed, it can be read to cast a spell and consume one charge.

And it should satisfy the following interface:

```
var scrollOfLightning = Scroll();
scrollOfLightning.describe();
// => You see an ancient parchment scroll. It's empty.
scrollOfLightning.read();
// => You try to read the scroll but it is empty.

scrollOfLightning.inscribe({
  spell: {
    name: 'Lightning',
    cast(target) {
      console.log(`${target} is striken by lightning (50 damage)`);
      target.hp -= 50;
    }
  },
  charges: 1
});
// => You inscribe the scroll with a spell of Lightning

scrollOfLightning.describe();
// => You see an ancient parchment scroll.
//    Using your knowledge in the runic language you
//    decipher its contents, it seems to be a scroll of Lightning
scrollOfLightning.read("Troll");
// => Troll is striken by lightning (50 damage)
// => After you cast the spell the scroll dissolves into dust
scrollOfLightning.read("Troll");
// => You can't read dust
```

Tip: Define two stamps - Describable and Inscribable - and compose them to create a Scroll stamp.

Solution

```javascript
// Describable
const Describable = stampit({
  props: {
    name: 'scroll'
  },
  methods: {
    describe(){
      if (this.name === 'scroll'){
        console.log("You see an ancient parchment scroll. " +
                    "It's empty.");
      } else {
        console.log(`You see an ancient parchment scroll. Using your\
 knowledge in the runic language you decipher its contents, it seems\
 to be a scroll of ${this.name}`);
      }
    }
  }
});

// Inscribable
const Inscribable = stampit({
  props: {
    spell: undefined,
    charges: 1
  },
  methods: {
    inscribe({spell, charges}){
      this.spell = spell;
      if (spell) this.name = spell.name;
      if (charges) this.charges = charges;
      console.log(`You inscribe the scroll with a ` +
                  `spell of ${this.name}`);
    },
    read(...args){
      if (this.spell && this.charges) {
        this.charges--;
        console.log(`You start reading the scroll slowly ` +
                    `entonating each rune... Klaatu barada nikto...`);
        this.spell.cast(...args);
        if (this.charges === 0)
          console.log('...after you cast the spell the ' +
                      `scroll dissolves into dust');
      } else if(this.spell && !this.charges) {
        console.log("You can't read dust");
```

```
45        } else {
46          console.log('You try to read the scroll but it is empty');
47        }
48      }
49    }
50  });
51
52  // The Scroll stamp!
53  const Scroll = stampit().compose(Describable, Inscribable);
54
55
56  // Let's test that it works
57  var scrollOfLightning = Scroll();
58
59  scrollOfLightning.describe();
60  // => You see an ancient parchment scroll. It's empty.
61
62  scrollOfLightning.read();
63  // => You try to read the scroll but it is empty.
64
65  scrollOfLightning.inscribe({
66    spell: {
67      name: 'Lightning',
68      cast(target) {
69        console.log(`${target} is striken by lightning (50 damage)`);
70        target.hp -= 50;
71      }
72    },
73    charges: 1
74  });
75  // => You inscribe the scroll with a spell of Lightning
76
77  scrollOfLightning.describe();
78  // => You see an ancient parchment scroll.
79  //    Using your knowledge in the runic language you
80  //    decipher its contents, it seems to be a scroll of Lightning
81
82
83  scrollOfLightning.read("Inkwell");
84  // => Inkwell is striken by lightning (50 damage)
85  // => After you cast the spell the scroll dissolves into dust
86
87  scrollOfLightning.read("Inkwell");
88  // => You can't read dust
89
90  mooleen.says("Die you evil inkwell!!!");
91  mooleen.laughs();
```

```
 92  mooleen.says("haha I have so much fun on my own");
 93
 94  rat.says("wasn't that the inkwell I got you to celebrate" +
 95          " our monthiversary as master and familiar?");
 96  mooleen.says("Hmm... no...?");
 97  mooleen.says("I left that in the... Caves of Mist..." +
 98          "it's too valuable to bring to war.");
 99  mooleen.breathesASighOfRelieve();
100
101  rat.says('Btw, did you notice your method for ' +
102          'assigning charges is very insecure?');
```

Charges are Insecure!

The current definition of `Inscribable` is not very secure. Anyone with a pinch of deviousness could tamper with it an create itself a scroll of power with unlimited charges by just doing this:

```
1  spell.charges = 10000;
2  // moahahahahaha
```

Rewrite the `Inscribable` stamp to not allow setting charges once they've been defined. Tip: use the `init` property in stamps.

Solution

```
1  // Inscribable
2  const SecureInscribable = stampit({
3    init() {
4      let _spell,
5          chargesRemaining;
6
7      this.inscribe = function inscribe({spell, charges=1}){
8        _spell = spell;
```

Black Tower Summoning: Next Level Object Composition With Stamps 279

```javascript
          if (spell) this.name = spell.name;
          chargesRemaining = charges;
          console.log(`You inscribe the scroll with a ` +
                      `spell of ${this.name}`);
        };

        this.read = function read(...args){
          if (_spell && chargesRemaining) {
            chargesRemaining--;
            console.log(`You start reading the scroll slowly ` +
                        `entonating each rune... Klaatu barada nikto...`);
            _spell.cast(...args);
            if (chargesRemaining === 0) {
              console.log('...after you cast the spell the ` +
                          `scroll dissolves into dust');
          } else if(_spell && !chargesRemaining) {
            console.log("You can't read dust");
          } else {
            console.log('You try to read the scroll but it is empty');
          }
        };
      }
    });

    // The Scroll stamp!
    const ScrollOfPower = stampit()
                        .compose(Describable, SecureInscribable);


    // Let's test that it works
    var scrollOfLightningV2 = ScrollOfPower();

    scrollOfLightningV2.describe();
    // => You see an ancient parchment scroll. It's empty.

    scrollOfLightningV2.read();
    // => You try to read the scroll but it is empty.

    scrollOfLightningV2.inscribe({
      spell: {
        name: 'Lightning',
        cast(target) {
          console.log(`${target} is striken by lightning (50 damage)`);
          target.hp -= 50;
        }},
      charges: 1
    });
```

```
56    // => You inscribe the scroll with a spell of Lightning
57
58    scrollOfLightningV2.read("Ashtray");
59    // => Ashtray is striken by lightning (50 damage)
60    // => After you cast the spell the scroll dissolves into dust
61
62    scrollOfLightningV2.read("Ashtray");
63    // => You can't read dust
64
65    scrollOfLightningV2.charges = 10000;
66
67    scrollOfLightningV2.read("Ashtray");
68    // => You can't read dust
69
70    mooleen.says('Aha!');
71    mooleen.says('No more sneaky extending scroll charges');
72    mooleen.says('Thank you rat!');
73
74    rat.says("Wasn't that the ashtray I got you for your birthday?");
75    rat.says("The one I made with my bare pawns and tail?");
76
77    mooleen.says("Errr... no...?");
78    mooleen.says("I keep that in... inside my chest of awesomeness!");
79    mooleen.says("Yes! In the Caves of Mist where I keep my most " +
80                 "precious posessions! Yes!");
81
82    rat.says("That makes me so happy");
83    rat.smilesWithJoy();
84
85    mooleen.says("Ok, now let's try to formalize some spells...");
```

What's a Spell?

Hmm how to define a Spell... Let's start with the basics! It is something... a power within the universe that you can harness, shape and **cast** forward to produce a desired effect in the real world. So it's something that:

- Can be described with a name and a describe method
- Can be casted into the world to produce an effect

Write a Spell stamp that fulfills the following:

```
let spell = Spell({
  name: 'Fire',
  describe: () => 'A spell of Fire',
  spell: () =>
    console.log('A flame surges from the palm of your hand')
});

spell.describe();
// => A spell of Fire

spell.cast();
// => You cast spell of Fire
// => A flame surges from the palm of your hand
```

Solution

```
// this is a more generic and configurable
// Describable stamp than the one we used before
const GenericDescribable = stampit({
  props: {
    name: 'something'
  },
  methods: {
```

```
        describe(){
          console.log(this.toString());
        },
        toString(){
          return this.name;
        }
      },
      init({name, describe}){
        if (name) this.name = name;
        if (describe) this.toString = describe;
      }
    });

    const Thing = stampit().compose(GenericDescribable);

    let fryingPan = Thing({name: 'A frying pan'});
    fryingPan.describe();
    // => A frying pan

    let fork = Thing({
      name: 'a fork',
      describe(){ return `You see ${this.name}`;}
    });
    fork.describe();
    // => You see a fork


    // Castable
    const Castable = stampit({
      props: {
        spell() { console.log('nothing happens'); }
      },
      methods: {
        cast(...args) {
          console.log(`You cast spell of ${this.name}`);
          this.spell(...args);
        }
      },
      init({spell}){
        if (spell) this.spell = spell;
      }
    });

    const Spell = stampit().compose(Thing, Castable);

    let spell = Spell({
      name: 'Fire',
```

Black Tower Summoning: Next Level Object Composition With Stamps

```
55    describe: () => 'A spell of Fire',
56    spell: () => console.log('A flame surges from the palm of your han\
57  d')
58    });
59
60  spell.describe();
61  // => A spell of fire
62
63  spell.cast();
64  // => You cast spell of Fire
65  // => A flame surges from the palm of your hand
66
67  mooleen.says('Ok ok, that sets some basics');
68  rat.says('Indeed indeed a very good start');
69
70  mooleen.says("Now let's get serious");
71  mooleen.says("What makes a damaging spell?...");
```

 ## What Makes a Damaging Spell?

Now let's make a serious spell. Something that you can use in the heat of battle to destroy a foe. A Damaging spell is like a normal spell that you can describe and cast but in addition to that it should damage the target you cast it upon. For instance:

```
1   const magicArrowSpell = DamagingSpell({
2     name: 'Magic Arrow',
3     damage: 20,
4     incantation(target){
5       console.log(`A magic arrow flies from your hand ` +
6                   `and impacts ${target} (${this.damage} damage)`);
7     }
8   })
9   magicArrowSpell.cast('the wall');
10  // => A magic arrow flies from your hand and
11  //    impacts the wall (20 damage)
```

Create a new stamp `DamagingSpell` that fulfills the example above.

Solution

```javascript
// Damaging
const Damaging = stampit({
  props: {
    damage: 50,
    // default incantation
    inchantation(target){
      console.log(`You do ${this.damage} to ${target}`)
    },
    // the spell encapsulates the damaging behavior
    spell(target){
      this.incantation(target);
      target.hp -= this.damage;
    }
  },
  init({damage, incantation}){
    if (damage) this.damage = damage;
    // you can personalize the incantation for each spell
    if (incantation) this.incantation = incantation;
  }
});

const DamagingSpell = stampit().compose(Spell, Damaging);

const magicArrowSpell = DamagingSpell({
  name: 'Magic Arrow',
  damage: 20,
  incantation(target){
    console.log(`A magic arrow flies from your hand ` +
                `and impacts ${target} (${this.damage} damage)`);
  }
})
magicArrowSpell.cast('the wall');
// => A magic arrow flies from your hand and
//    impacts the wall (20 damage)

mooleen.laughsWithGlee();
rat.says('Wow! That was amazing master!');
mooleen.says('haha Thank you!');

mooleen.says('Now for the final touch! An elemental spell ' +
             'that we can inscribe in a powerfull scroll');
rat.says('uyuyuyuyuy');
rat.says("This is really going to turn the tides!");
```

An Elemental Spell and The Mighty Scroll of Fireball

Let's take things one step further. We will build on top of the damaging spell and make an elemental spell. A type of spell that has an element associated to it and which can inflict double the damage to creatures that are weak to that element (or half the damage to creatures with element resistance).

A fireball spell could look like the following:

```
const fireballSpell = ElementalSpell({
  name: 'Fireball',
  damage: 100,
  element: 'fire'
});

const waterWisp = {
  toString: () => 'Water Wisp',
  hp: 100,
  weaknesses: ['fire']
};

fireballSpell.cast(waterWisp);
// => You cast the spell of Fireball
// => The Water Wisp has fire weakness!!! x2 Damage!!
// => The Fireball impacts the water wisp with 200 damage
```

Tip: Remember to inscribe a scroll of power from the previous examples with the fireballSpell. Test one with 2 charges!

Solution

```
// Elemental
const Elemental = stampit({
  props: {
    element: 'fire',
    spell(target){
```

```
  6        let elementalDamage = this.calculateElementalDamage(target)
  7        target.hp -= elementalDamage;
  8        console.log(`The ${this.name} impacts the ${target}` +
  9                    ` with ${elementalDamage} damage`);
 10      }
 11    },
 12    methods: {
 13      calculateElementalDamage(target){
 14        if (target.resistances
 15            && target.resistances.includes(this.element)){
 16          console.log(`The ${target} has ${this.element}` +
 17                      ` resistance! /2 damage!!`);
 18          return this.damage/2;
 19        }
 20        else if (target.weaknesses
 21            && target.weaknesses.includes(this.element)){
 22          console.log(`The ${target} has ${this.element} ` +
 23                      `weakness! x2 damage!!`)
 24          return this.damage*2;
 25        }
 26        return this.damage;
 27      }
 28    },
 29    init({spell, element}){
 30      if (spell) this.spell = spell;
 31      if (element) this.element = element;
 32    }
 33  });
 34
 35
 36  const ElementalSpell = stampit().compose(Spell, Damaging, Elemental);
 37
 38  const fireballSpell = ElementalSpell({
 39    name: 'Fireball',
 40    damage: 100,
 41    element: 'fire'
 42  });
 43
 44  const waterWisp = {
 45    toString: () => 'Water Wisp',
 46    hp: 100,
 47    weaknesses: ['fire']
 48  };
 49
 50  fireballSpell.cast(waterWisp);
 51  // => You cast the spell of Fireball
 52  // => The Water Wisp has fire weakness!!! x2 Damage!!
```

```
53  // => The Fireball impacts the water wisp with 200 damage
54
55  // Put spells inside a scroll for normals to cast
56  var fireballScroll = ScrollOfPower();
57  fireballScroll.inscribe({spell: fireballSpell, charges: 2});
58  // => You inscribe the scroll with a spell of Fireball
59
60  fireballScroll.read(waterWisp);
61  // => You cast spell of Fireball
62  //    The Water Wisp has fire weakness! x2 damage!!
63  //    The Fireball impacts the Water Wisp with 200 damage
64
65  rat.says('Poor wisp...');
66  mooleen.says('Poor wisp indeed..');
67
68  // simultaneoulsy
69  rat.says("wait...");
70  mooleen.says("wait...")
71
72  mooleen.says("What's a water wisp doing here?");
73  rat.says('Bew....'); // gurgling sounds...
74
75  narrate(`
76  Something hard smacks Mooleen in the back of her head and she drops \
77  to the floor. Before she loses consciousness she feels a coldness sl\
78  owly enveloping her hands, her wrists, her arms...
79  `);
```

Object Internals: The Secrets of Objects

Shaping the world
is a noble pursuit,

Shaping the shaping,
Crafting the crafting,
is the mark of masters

> \- Sylo Peskimn
> Master Artificer

Object Internals: The Secrets of Objects

```
/*
 * A dark and damp cell in the deepest dungeon...
 */

mooleen.regainsConsciousness();
mooleen.says("Aaaaa");

rat.says('Nice to see you back!');
mooleen.says("Ooooo");

rat.says("I have some bad news for you master...");
moleen.says("Eeeee");

rat.says("We've been kidnapped, detained and shackled");
mooleen.says("Uuuuu");

rat.says("I praise your eloquence... " +
         "As always you know the right thing to say" +
         " in every situation");
mooleen.chuckles();

mooleen.says("Very... strong... headache");
rat.says("Well that would match the symptoms " +
         "of being smacked " +
         "in the head with a cudgel");

/*
    A noise comes from the least dark corner of
    this pitch black cell. A door screeches open
    and you hear steps approaching.
*/

stranger.says("Welcome to the Red Stronghold " +
              "our most esteemed guest");
stranger.says("You've been very problematic...");
stranger.says("Taking over Asturi..." +
    "Frustrating our attempts to control it... " +
    "Destroying our advanced party to Tates... ");
stranger.says("But that has come to an end...");

mooleen.says("I know... I know the drill... " +
    "now you're going to ask me to join you...");
stranger.says("What?!?");
mooleen.says("Yeah! This is the part where " +
    "you say... why oppose us when you can join us? " +
    "I'm shackled and not dead after all");
```

Object Internals: The Secrets of Objects   290

```
stranger.says("Oh that! We are still deciding on your " +
    "method of execution my dear. " +
    "Decapitation... Burning at the stake... " +
    "Skinning... Strangling... Hanging... " +
    "One doesn't just defy The Red Hand and live to " +
    "tell the tale.");
moolen.says("....");
stranger.says("Just sit tight, and remember, no magic");

/* The stranger leaves the room and Mooleen stupefied */

mooleen.says(`Hmm... I can't feel the winds of magic ` +
             `inside of me! `);
rat.says('Fuzz...');

randalf.says("Fortunately I've lived without magic for years");
mooleen.jumpsStartled();
rat.screeches();

randalf.says("Oh yeah... Hi! We're all here");
bandalf.says("Safe and sound");
red.says("At least for the time being");

mooleen.asks("Red?");
randalf.says("Hmm... He wasn't a traitor after all...");
bandalf.says("Oops");
randalf.says("People make mistakes");
bandalf.says("Don't be too harsh on people");

randalf.says("No magic, yes?");
randalf.says("Let me tell you about a nifty trick...");
```

A Nifty Trick... Object Internals

So far in this book we've focused a lot in how to work with objects in JavaScript and about different paradigms of object oriented programming that are supported in this beautiful language. In this and the upcoming chapters we're going to do something different. We're going to dive into the inner workings of objects, and into different metaprogramming techniques that will give you more control over how you define and operate them: the **ES5 Object APIs**, **ESnext decorators**, ES6 Proxies, the ES6 Reflection API and ES6 Symbols.

Follow me as we submerge ourselves into the depths of object internals in JavaScript and unveil the deepest secrets of objects!

All your Objects Are Belong to Object

Nearly all objects[87] in JavaScript descend from Object (Much in the same way that all C# objects descend from System.Object). This means that all objects inherit properties and methods from Object.prototype through the prototypical chain that we described in previous chapters. Hence, augmenting the Object.prototype object with new properties and methods results in all objects having access to these new properties and methods.

In addition to acting as a base object, the Object constructor has a number of static methods that give you a greater control over your objects and let you obtain additional information about them. Using these methods you can, for instance, define whether a given property is read-only or enumerable, define whether an object is immutable or not, or find out which is the prototype of a given object.

Sounds interesting? Then let's take a look at some of these methods.

 Experiment Javascriptmancer!!
You can experiment with all examples in this chapter directly within this jsBin[88] or downloading the source code from GitHub[89].

---

[87] All objects in JavaScript have Object.prototype in their prototypical chain but for Object.prototype itself and null (although I don't know whether we sould consider null an object).
[88] http://bit.ly/javascriptmancy-object-internals
[89] https://github.com/vintharas/javascriptmancy-code-samples

Defining Properties with Object.defineProperty

`Object.defineProperty` allows you to define new properties and methods via **property descriptors**. But what are property descriptors and how do they look like? Let's find out with an example.

Imagine that you have `goat`:

```
const goat = {};
```

At this point our `goat` is an empty object which it is not terribly interesting. We can augment it with a property `hitPoints` that describes the proverbial life essence of the `goat` by using the following property descriptor:

```
Object.defineProperty(goat, 'hitPoints', {
  /* property descriptor */
  value: 50,
  writable: true,
  enumerable: true,
  configurable: true
});
```

This results in the `goat` object now having a `hitPoints` property with value 50.

Behold!

```
console.log(`Goat has ${goat.hitPoints} hit points`);
// => Goat has 50 hit points
```

Ok, so we have added a property to an object. *What's new with that?* We've been augmenting objects with properties since day one.

Well, the important bit in the previous example is the **property descriptor**. It provides some hints as to a higher degree of control we don't have when we just augment an object with a property:

Object Internals: The Secrets of Objects   293

```
1  goat.hitPoints = 50
```

Let's take a look at property descriptors, go through each one of their properties and learn how they affect the objects they're applied on.

Property Descriptors: Data and Accessor Descriptors

A property descriptor is an object that describes how a property or method within an object should behave. JavaScript has two types of property descriptors: data and accessor descriptors.

You can use a **data descriptor** to describe a normal property or method within an object. The descriptor we used in the previous example for the `hitPoints` property is a great example:

```
1  {
2    /* data descriptor */
3    value: 50,
4    writable: true,
5    enumerable: true,
6    configurable: true
7  }
```

Taking advantage of data descriptors we can, for instance, make a property read only by setting its `writable` property to `false`:

Object Internals: The Secrets of Objects

```
// using the very same goat
Object.defineProperty(goat, 'woolColor', {
  value: 'brown',
  writable: false,
  enumerable: true,
  configurable: true
});
```

If you now try to set the value of this read-only (or not *writable*) property, you'll be greeted by a `TypeError` [90]:

```
goat.woolColor = 'black';
// => TypeError: Cannot assign to read only property 'woolColor'
//    of object '#<Object>'
```

In addition to data descriptors we have accessor descriptors. Accessor descriptors represent property getters and setters and trade the `value` and `writable` properties for `get` and `set`.

For instance, let's say that we want to enforce some invariants in our `hp` property, that is, we want to add some validation to ensure that the hp property doesn't get an invalid or inconsistent value.

Again, we start with a dangerous predator:

```
const sheep = {};
```

In this ocassion, we will define a backing field `_hitPoints` using a data descriptor in a similar way to the previous example:

---

[90]The TypeError will be thrown if you're in strict mode, otherwise it'll just fail silently. So use strict mode! :)

Object Internals: The Secrets of Objects

```
1  Object.defineProperty(sheep, '_hitPoints', {
2    /* property descriptor */
3    value: 50,
4    writable: true,
5    enumerable: false, // look here!
6    configurable: true
7  });
```

Noticed how we set the `enumerable` property to `false`? This denotes that we don't want this property to appear when you enumerate over the properties of this object (making it a little harder to reach even though it is completely public at this point).

Now we can define the property `hitPoints` as a getter/setter pair using an accessor descriptor:

```
1  Object.defineProperty(sheep, 'hitPoints', {
2    /* accessor descriptor */
3    get(){ return this._hitPoints},
4    set(value){
5      if (value === undefined
6          || value === null
7          || value < 0)
8        throw new Error(`Invalid value ${value}! Hit points` +
9                        `should be a number greater than 0!`);
10     this._hitPoints = value;
11   },
12   enumerable: true,
13   configurable: true
14 });
```

The `get` method just exposes the `_hitPoints` value as is, and the `set` method contains our validation logic. We can test it and verify that it works as we expect.

When you provide a reasonable value the property behaves normally:

```
console.log(`Sheep has ${sheep.hitPoints} hit points`);
// => Sheep has 50 hit points

// Let's try something simple
sheep.hitPoints = 10;

console.log(`Sheep has ${sheep.hitPoints} hit points`);
// => Sheep has 10 hit points
```

But when you break the invariants you'll get a well described exception:

```
// Now let's go into the danger zone
try{
  sheep.hitPoints -= 20;
} catch (e){
  console.log(e.message);
  // => Invalid value -10! Hit points should
  //    be a number greater than 0!
}
```

Oops! And...

```
// And more danger!
try{
  sheep.hitPoints = undefined;
} catch (e){
  console.log(e.message);
  // => Invalid value undefined! Hit points
  //    should be a number greater than 0!
}
```

Ouch!... Alright, let's take a look at each one of the properties and what they mean. Both data and accessor descriptors share two properties:

- **configurable**: if true it let's you modify the property descriptor and delete the property from a given object. It defaults to false.

- **enumerable**: if `true` it let's you enumerate the property. If you are not familiar with the concept of enumerability in JavaScript it means that the property shows up when traversing the properties of an object using a `for...in` loop. It defaults to `false`.

Data descriptors, which describe properties and methods, have these two additional properties:

- **writable**: if true it let's you modify the value of the property. It defaults to `false`.
- **value**: contains the value of the property and it can be any JavaScript expression. If it is a function then the resulting property is a method. It defaults to `undefined`.

Accessor descriptors, which describe getters and setters, have these other two additional properties:

- **get**: function that represents a getter for the property. If it is undefined the property returns `undefined` when you try to retrieve its value using the dot notation. A property with no `get` method and a `set` method becomes effectively a *set-only* property.
- **set**: function that represents a setter for the property. If it is undefined the property can't be set. The function receives as argument a single value that is assigned to the property. A property with a `get` method and no `set` method becomes effectively a *read-only* property.

Defining Multiple Properties with Object.defineProperties

In addition to being able to define your properties one by one, you can extend an object with many properties at once using the `Object.defineProperties` method.

Let's say that we want to militarize and weaponize our most dangerous minion, the goat. We can extend it with two new properties weapons and armor:

```
Object.defineProperties(goat, {
  weapons: {
    value: ['knife', 'katana', 'hand-trebuchet'],
    enumerable: true,
    writable: true,
    configurable: true
  },
  armor: {
    value: ['templar helmet', 'platemail'],
    enumerable: true,
    writable: true,
    configurable: true
  }
});
```

And **shit just goat serious:**

```
console.log(goat.weapons);
// => ["knife", "katana", "hand-trebuchet"]
console.log(goat.armor);
// => ["templar helmet", "platemail"]
```

It is good to highlight how the second argument to the `Object.defineProperties`, the one defining the new properties, is an object and not an array as you may have expected. Each key of this object represents the name of a new property and each value contains the property descriptor that describes its behavior.

A goat with a helmet and platemail, now that's something...

Beautiful Property Manipulation with Esnext Decorators

 Decorators Are Still on Proposal Stage

Although used in the JavaScript community both within TypeScript and ECMAScript followers, decorators are still not a completed proposal and therefore aren't officially part of JavaScript. At the time of this writing, decorators in classes and methods are a proposal level 2[91] which means that they'll likely make it into the language in the near future, but that the syntax and semantics may change. Decorators on parameters, object literals and function expressions are still at a very early stage. I encourage you to keep updated with the decorators proposal[92] if the syntax in this chapter doesn't work in the future.

---

[91] http://tc39.github.io/proposal-decorators/
[92] http://tc39.github.io/proposal-decorators/

Beware. Here Be Dragons

In the first examples of decorators in this chapter I will use decorators in object literals because they are the simplest way to explain decorators and require the least cognitive load. I will then move on to decorators within classes and class methods which represent the most stable proposal. They are slightly more verbose that the object literal ones but by that point you'll have enough experience to digest them without problems.

Again, by the time you read this book the API for decorators may have changed, but I hope that you can appreciate the beauty and usefulness of decorators regardless of the specific way in which they are implemented in the final version.

Decorators [93] are a convenient declarative way to apply property descriptors to classes, methods, properties and functions.

Using decorators we can rewrite the read-only property of our goat from:

```
const goat = {}
// using the very same goat
Object.defineProperty(goat, 'woolColor', {
  value: 'brown',
  writable: false,
  enumerable: true,
  configurable: true
});
```

to:

---

[93]Yes! If you are familiar with C# or Java, decorators are like attributes and annotations in either of these languages.

Object Internals: The Secrets of Objects

```
1  const goat = {
2    @readOnly
3    woolColor: 'brown'
4  }
```

Wow! That's something! As you can appreciate from the example above, decorators have a special syntax that consists in the name of the decorator preceded by an @ sign. The readOnly decorator above is just a simple function:

```
1  // Decorator parameters:
2  // - *target* object
3  // - decorated *property*
4  // - property *descriptor*
5  function readOnly(target, property, descriptor){
6    console.log(`Making ${property} read only!`);
7    descriptor.writable = false;
8  }
```

Much better right? The @readOnly decorator achieves two things:

- By virtue of being a function it can encapsulate a piece of behavior that you can then go and reuse across your application. In the example above, we can take advantage of the @readOnly decorator to make any property read-only
- It offers a beautiful, concise and terse declarative syntax clearly superior to the imperative approach we were following before

Likewise, we can also create a decorator for the sheep example and rewrite this accessor descriptor:

Object Internals: The Secrets of Objects

```
const sheep = {};
Object.defineProperty(sheep, 'hitPoints', {
  /* data descriptor */
  get(){ return this._hitPoints},
  set(value){
    if (value === undefined
       || value === null
       || value < 0)
      throw new Error(`Invalid value ${value}! Hit points` +
                      `should be a number greater than 0!`);
    this._hitPoints = value;
  },
  enumerable: true,
  configurable: true
});
```

as:

```
const sheep = {
  @notNullUndefinedNorNegative
  hitPoints
}
```

where the `notNullUndefinedNorNegative` decorator would look like this:

```
function notNullUndefinedNorNegative(
    target, property, descriptor){
  console.log(`Adding validation to ${property}!`)
  const backingField = descriptor.initializer();
  return {
    /* data descriptor */
    get(){ return backingField},
    set(value){
      if (value === undefined
         || value === null
         || value < 0)
        throw new Error(
               `Invalid value ${value}! ${property}` +
               `should be a number greater than 0!`);
```

```
15      backingField = value;
16    },
17    enumerable: true,
18    configurable: true
19  };
20 }
```

 Initializer? Is that a Descriptor Property?

If you remember from earlier within this chapter, you won't be able to recognize the `initializer` property as a descriptor property. The `initializer` descriptor property is a Babel artifact for interoperating between two experimental features: decorators and class fields. In the current implementation, the `initializer` property gives you access to the object literal property value when the decorator is evaluated.

Take this code sample with a grain of salt.

That is, returning a new descriptor, replaces the original descriptor associated to the original property. These brings us to the topic of **composing decorators**. A better way of writing the previous example would be like this:

```
1 const sheep = {
2   @notNull
3   @notUndefined
4   @notNegative
5   hitPoints: 100
6 }
```

Or perhaps in the positive:

```
const sheep = {
  @defined
  @greaterThanZero
  hitPoints: 100
}
```

Where we are essentially composing different operators and applying them to a given property. This approach is better because it is easier to read, and because now we can make better reuse of our decorators.

In this example, the `@defined` decorator could look like this:

```
function defined(target, property, descriptor){
  return composeSetter(target, property, descriptor, {
    set(value){
      throwIfInvalid(value)
    }
  });
  function throwIfInvalid(value){
    if (value === undefined || value === null)
      throw new Error(`Invalid value ${value}! ` +
        `${property} should be defined!`);
  }
}
```

And this would be the `@greaterThanZero` decorator:

```
function greaterThanZero(target, property, descriptor){
  return composeSetter(target, property, descriptor, {
    set(value){
      throwIfInvalid(value)
    }
  });
  function throwIfInvalid(value){
    if (value < 0)
      throw new Error(`Invalid value ${value}! ` +
        `${property} should be a number ` +
        `greater than 0!`);
  }
}
```

Both of them making use of this auxiliary function to compose setter functions:

```
function composeSetter(target, property, oldDesc, newDesc){
  const backingField = (oldDesc.get && oldDesc.get()) ||
                        oldDesc.initializer(),
        defaultSetter = (value) => backingField = value;

  return {
    get: () => backingField,
    set: before(oldDesc.set || defaultSetter, newDesc.set)
  };

  // create a new function 'newF'
  // that calles the decorator function
  // before calling the original function `f`
  function before(f, decorator){
    return (...args) => {
      decorator(...args);
      f(...args);
    }
  }
}
```

 A Lot More About Decorators To Come!

Explaining the composition of decorators we've come to the fringes of a different and mysterious domain: the obscure realm of higher-order functions and functional programming. We'll dive deeper into functional programming and decorators in the Functional Programming Tome of JavaScript-mancy later in the series.

Configurable Decorators With Decorator Factories

You can also pass parameters to your decorators adding one extra degree of extensibility and configurability that makes them even more reusable. Imagine a wise wizard:

```
const wizard = {
    name: 'Wise Wizard'
};
```

who must go into battle to save mankind. She'll need some armor:

```
const wizard = {
    name: 'Wise Wizard',
    armor: 'cloth vest'
};
```

And in the heat of battle she may be inclined to change the relatively unprotecting cloth vest for a superior knight's plate mail. However, she shall not! For wizards can't wear plate mails!

A beautiful way to represent this constraint is by using a decorator `allowedArmors` in this fashion:

```
const wizard = {
    name: 'Wise Wizard',
    @allowedArmors('cloth', 'wool', 'silk')
    armor: 'cloth vest'
};
```

The implementation of the `allowedArmors` decorator could be this one below:

Object Internals: The Secrets of Objects

```
function allowedArmors(...armors){
  const decorator = (target, property, descriptor) => {
    console.log(descriptor);
    const backingField = descriptor.initializer();
    return {
      set: (value) => {
        if (value !== '' &&
          armors.every(a => !value.includes(a)))
          throw new Error(
            `${target} can't wear armor ${value}.` +
            ` She only can wear these armor classes ${armors}`);
        backingField = value;
      },
      get: () => backingField
    }
  }
  return decorator;
}
```

Where the `allowedArmors` function is essentially a decorator factory that when called returns a new decorator that can be applied to our class methods. From now on, when the wizard tries to wear an armor she shouldn't wear she'll be surprised by the following error:

```
try {
  wizard.armor = 'plate mail';
} catch (e) {
  console.error(e.message);
  // => Wise Wizard can't wear armor plate mail.
  // She can only wear these armor classes cloth,wool,silk
}
```

Decorators aren't limited to applying property descriptors on object literal properties, you can use them within classes and methods as well.

Class And Method Decorators

 Class and Method Decorators Are Pretty Stable

As I mentioned earlier, the class and method decorators proposal is pretty stable. The examples in this decorator section onwards should be closer to the final decorators standard (although you never know so remember to keep up with the decorators proposal[94]).

Take a look at this example from the Angular framework:

```
@Component({
  selector: 'app-root',
  templateUrl: './app.component.html',
  stylesUrl: './app.component.scss'
})
export class AppComponent{
}
```

Where we use the `Component` decorator to apply metadata to a component class and tie it together with the template and styles that comprise a component in Angular.

Using a class syntax we could rewrite our wizard example as follows:

---

[94] http://tc39.github.io/proposal-decorators/

```
 1  class Wizard{
 2    constructor(name){
 3      this.name = name;
 4      this._armor = 'cloth vest';
 5    }
 6    toString(){
 7      return this.name;
 8    }
 9
10    get armor(){ return this._armor;}
11
12    @allowedArmorsMember('cloth', 'wool', 'silk')
13    set armor(value){ this._armor = value;}
14  }
```

where the `allowedArmorsMember` decorator:

```
 1  function allowedArmorsMember(...armors){
 2    const decorator = (target, property, descriptor) => {
 3      return {
 4        set: (value) => {
 5          if (value !== '' && armors.every(a => !value.includes(a)))
 6            throw new Error(`You can't wear armor ${value}.` +
 7              ` She only can wear these armor classes ${armors}`);
 8          descriptor.set(value);
 9        },
10        get: descriptor.get
11      }
12    }
13    return decorator;
14  }
```

achieves the same effect than in previous examples:

```
const anotherWizard = new Wizard('unwise Wizard');
anotherWizard.armor = 'silk robes';
try {
  anotherWizard.armor = 'steel chain mail';
} catch (e){
  console.log(e.message);
  // => "undefined can't wear armor steel chain mail.
  // She only can wear these armor classes cloth,wool,silk"
}
```

We could also record how many times a wizard casts a spell:

```
class WizardCount{
  constructor(name){
    this.name = name;
    this._armor = 'cloth vest';
  }
  toString(){
    return this.name;
  }

  get armor(){ return this._armor; }
  @allowedArmorsMember('cloth', 'wool', 'silk')
  set armor(value){ this._armor = value;}

  @count('numberOfSpells')
  castFireball(target){
    console.log(`${this} casts fireball on ` +
                `${target} burning it to ashes`);
  }
}
```

That is, every time a wizard casts a fireball spell using the `castFireball` method we will count it and store it inside a variable `numberOfSpells`. The decorator `count` can help us achieve that:

Object Internals: The Secrets of Objects

```js
function count(countStorageField) {
  const decorator = (target, property, descriptor) => {
    const originalFunction = descriptor.value;
    descriptor.value = function(...args){
      if (!this[countStorageField]) {
        this[countStorageField] = 0;
      }
      this[countStorageField] += 1;
      originalFunction.apply(this, args);
    }
  }
  return decorator;
}
```

If we now instantiate a new infamous wizard and put him to cast fireball spells to and fro, we'll be able to see how the count is kept inside the `numberOfSpells` variable:

```js
const fieryWizard = new WizardCount('Fiery Wizard');
fieryWizard.castFireball('rat');
// => "Fiery Wizard casts fireball on rat burning it to ashes"

fieryWizard.castFireball('bat');
// => "Fiery Wizard casts fireball on bat burning it to ashes"

console.log(`${fieryWizard} casted spells ` +
            `${fieryWizard.numberOfSpells} times`);
// => "Fiery Wizard casted spells 2 times"
```

Class Decorators

To wrap this section on decorators let's see how we can apply a decorator to a complete class. Imagine how cool it'd be to apply the mixins we saw in previous chapters using a decorator. Let's start by creating a mixin decorator to allow minions to cast spells.

If you remember from previous chapters, we could represent a mixin like a simple object that encapsulated a given behavior like casting spells:

Object Internals: The Secrets of Objects

```
const canCastSpells = {
  castSpell(spell, target) {
    console.log(`${this} prepares to cast spell ${spell}...`);
    if (this.mana < spell.manaCost){
      console.log(`${this} doesn't have enough mana!` +
        `The spell fizzles out and ${this} gets ` +
        `damaged by the wild currents of magic`);
      this.hp -= (spell.manaCost - spell.mana);
      this.mana = 0;
    } else {
      this.mana -= spell.manaCost;
      spell.cast(target);
    }
  }
}
```

And we could compose this mixin with any of these hero classes:

```
class Warlock {
  constructor(name, hp=100, mana=100){
    this.name = name + ', the Warlock';
    this.hp = hp;
    this.mana = mana;
  }
  toString(){
    return this.name;
  }
}

class Bard {
  constructor(name, hp=100, mana=50){
    this.name = name + ', the Bard';
    this.hp = hp;
    this.mana = mana;
  }
  toString(){
    return this.name;
  }
}
```

By applying the mixin `canCastSpells` to each class prototype like this:

Object Internals: The Secrets of Objects

```
Object.assign(Warlock.prototype, canCastSpells);
// Now all warlocks can cast spells

Object.assign(Bard.prototype, canCastSpells);
// Now all bards can cast spells
```

The result is that every bard and warlock gain the ability to cast spells:

```
const blizzardSpell = {
  toString(){ return 'blizzard';},
  manaCost: 10,
  cast(target) {
    console.log(`${target} gets hit by a blizzard`);
    target.hp -= 50;
  }
};

const giantSpider = {
  name: 'Giant Spider',
  toString(){ return this.name},
  hp: 400
};

const kvothe = new Bard('Kvothe');
kvothe.castSpell(blizzardSpell, giantSpider);
// => "Kvothe, the Bard prepares to cast spell blizzard..."
// => "Giant Spider gets hit by a blizzard"
```

A nicer way to apply this mixin onto a class would be to use a class decorator. Take a moment to appreciate the beauty of this example below:

Object Internals: The Secrets of Objects

```
@spellCaster
class Bard {
  constructor(name, hp=100, mana=50){
    this.name = name + ', the Bard';
    this.hp = hp;
    this.mana = mana;
  }
  toString(){
    return this.name;
  }
}
```

Where the `spellCaster` decorator can be defined with a function:

```
function spellCaster(constructor){
  Object.assign(constructor.prototype, canCastSpells);
}
```

It looks more readable and concise, and achieves the same result:

```
const lightHealingSpell = {
  toString(){ return 'light healing';},
  manaCost: 5,
  cast(target){
    console.log(`${target} is healed lightly`);
    target.hp +=25;
  }
};
const jazz = new Bard("Jazz");

jazz.castSpell(lightHealingSpell, jazz);
// => "Jazz, the Bard prepares to " +
//    "cast spell light healing..."
//    "Jazz, the Bard is healed lightly"
```

We can also generalize the decorator above and create a new `mixin` decorator that we can apply to any mixin and class:

Object Internals: The Secrets of Objects 315

```
1  @mixin(canCastSpells)
2  class Bard {
3    constructor(name, hp=100, mana=50){
4      this.name = name + ', the Bard';
5      this.hp = hp;
6      this.mana = mana;
7    }
8    toString(){
9      return this.name;
10   }
11 }
```

This decorator `mixin` would be implemented like a factory function for class decorators and would be able to apply an arbitrary number of mixins to any class:

```
1  function mixin(...args){
2    return function(constructor){
3      Object.assign(constructor.prototype, ...args);
4    }
5  }
```

Decorators are awesome, aren't they? If you are interested in learning more about them I suggest that you keep an eye at the current proposal on the ECMA262 GitHub repository[95]. I also encourage you to take a look at the core-decorators.js[96] library that contains a lot of useful decorators that can inspire you to write your own.

Create Objects With Object.create And Property Descriptors

By this point you're no longer a stranger to the `Object.create` method. We have used it in previous chapters to create new objects

---

[95] http://tc39.github.io/proposal-decorators/
[96] https://github.com/jayphelps/core-decorators.js

with a specific prototype and even with traits and object composition. This second use case gives us a hint as to the true capabilities of `Object.create`. Take a look at this example from earlier chapters:

```
function MinionWithPosition(){
  const methods = {
    toString(){ return 'minion';}
  };

  const minion = Object.create(
        /* prototype */ methods,
        /* traits (object properties) */ TPositionable);
  return minion;
}
```

The example above represents a factory `MinionWithPosition` that makes use of `Object.create` to create a object `minion` with:

1. The `methods` object as prototype
2. A bunch of properties and methods defined by the `TPositionable` trait

But how are these trait properties and methods defined? Yes! With property descriptors! Take a look at this:

```
console.log(Trait({weapons: ['knife']}).weapons);
// => Object {
//     value: ['knife'],
//     writable: true,
//     enumerable: true,
//     configurable: true
// }
```

The traits library `Trait` function decomposes your object into property descriptors that it can then use to manage things like composability, required properties, conflict resolution, etc.

Object Internals: The Secrets of Objects   317

Therefore the second argument of Object.create is an object whose properties are property descriptors. This means that we can rewrite the goat example we used at the beginning of this article to illustrate Object.defineProperty using Object.create and arrive to an equivalent solution:

```js
const anotherGoat = Object.create(Object.prototype, {
  _hitPoints: {
    /* accessor descriptor */
    value: 50,
    writable: true,
    enumerable: false, // look here!
    configurable: true
  },
  hitPoints: {
    /* data descriptor */
    get(){ return this._hitPoints},
    set(value){
      if (value === undefined
        || value === null
        || value < 0)
        throw new Error(`Invalid value ${value}! Hit ` +
             `points should be a number greater than 0!`);
      this._hitPoints = value;
    },
    enumerable: true,
    configurable: true
  },
  weapons: {
    value: ['knife', 'katana', 'hand-trebuchet'],
    enumerable: true,
    writable: true,
    configurable: true
  },
  armor: {
    value: ['templar helmet', 'platemail'],
    enumerable: true,
    writable: true,
    configurable: true
  }
});
```

This is probably not going to be how you define objects in your day to day programming but the Traits library provides some inspiration as to when property descriptors and the various Object methods can be useful: **Metaprogramming**.

Metaprogramming

Metaprogramming is a programming technique where you have the ability to treat programming constructs as the data of your program. That is, metaprogramming is the art of programming programming (**BOOM!** - pause for effect).

Since all things meta can be pretty daunting at first, let's go back to our earlier examples in this chapter to explain metaprogramming through an example. In the example with Object.defineProperty and our mighty defender the goat, we have taken a programming construct, the property hitPoints, something that is typically part of programming itself:

```
goat.hitPoints = 50;
```

And we have represented it as a piece of data (a property descriptor):

```
{
  hitPoints: {
    value: 50,
    writable: true,
    enumerable: true,
    configurable: true
  }
}
```

Then we have used that data as part of a new program to extend the object goat with new properties:

```
1  Object.defineProperties(goat, {
2    hitPoints: {
3      value: 50,
4      writable: true,
5      enumerable: true,
6      configurable: true
7    }
8  });
```

This is a simple example of a metaprogramming. We've taken an everyday feature of our programs - **properties** - and we've written a small program that operates on object properties themselves.

Other examples of metaprogramming can often be seen in JavaScript web frameworks and libraries. The first example that you found out about in this chapter was Traits.js. Traits.js makes extensive use of property descriptors to define a new way to do object oriented programming in JavaScript, one that allows object composition with additional guarantees like required properties and conflict resolution. The popular web framework vue.js[97] uses a similar technique in their change detection algorithm by replacing all the properties of your model for getters and setters using `Object.defineProperty`. This allows the framework to observe changes in your model properties and reflect them in the user interface.

These two use cases of property descriptors and `Object.defineProperties` are pretty awesome aren't they? I'm looking forward to see what you can do with this newfound knowledge (malevolent laughter).

Other Useful Object Methods

Here's a list of other useful `Object` methods:

---

[97] http://vuejs.org/

Method name	Method description
Object.getOwnPropertyDescriptor(obj, prop)	Returns property descriptor for a given property prop of object obj.
Object.getOwnPropertyDescriptors(obj)	Returns an object that contains all property descriptors of object obj.
Object.getOwnPropertyNames(obj)	Returns an array that contains all own properties from an object obj, that is, those that belong to the object itself and not its prototype.
Object.getOwnPropertySymbols(obj)	Like above but only symbol properties.
Object.getPrototypeOf(obj)	Returns the prototype of an object obj.
Object.setPrototypeOf(obj, proto)	Sets the prototype of the object obj to proto. This type of operation can be very taxing in terms of performance due to how JavaScript engines optimize accessing properties.
Object.is(val1, val2)	Compares whether two values are equal without type coercion. It improves over === comparison by giving sane results from NaN === NaN.
Object.keys(obj)	Returns an array containing the names of all the enumerable properties owned by object obj.

Concluding

In this chapter you learnt about the internal APIs provided by Object. You discovered how to use Object.defineProperty and object descriptors to finely control the behavior of a property or method within an object.

You also learned about decorators, a new feature in JavaScript that promises to provide an awesome declarative API to manipulate objects and classes to your heart's content. We saw different examples of decorators to make any property read-only, provide arbitrary validations or even compose classes with mixins.

We wrapped the chapter with Object.create and an introduction to the technique of meta-programming, the art of programming your programs, reviewing real world examples of meta-programming in Trait.js and Vue.js.

```
randalf.says("So even though you can't feel the winds of magic, " +
             "even though you can't access the source " +
             "nor cast spells...");

mooleen.says("...wait! I can still weakly perceive magic in " +
             "the world around me...");
randalf.says("Exactly!");

randalf.says("Now try to find a way to open " +
             "those shackles, and let's get out of here " +
             "before The Red Hand decides our fates for good");
```

Exercises

 Experiment JavaScriptmancer!

You can experiment with these exercises and some possible solutions in this jsBin[98] or downloading the source code from GitHub[99].

---

[98] http://bit.ly/javascriptmancy-oop-object-internals-exercises
[99] https://github.com/vintharas/javascriptmancy-code-samples

Open The Shackles!

Use what you've learned about object internals to find a secret way to open the shackles and free yourself.

```
1  console.log(shackles);
2  // => A pair of blood stained shackles slapped around your wrists.
3  // => They are painfully uncomfortable
```

Hints: Use `Object.keys` to inspect the shackles and find the first clue. You'll need to use the interactive examples on jsBin[100] or GitHub[101] since the `shackles` object has some hidden state.

Solution

```
1   // I've defined a shackles variable but don't look!
2   console.log(shackles);
3   // => A pair of blood stained shackles slapped
4   //    around your wrists.
5   // => They are painfully uncomfortable
6
7   mooleen.says("Hmm... let's see...");
8
9   console.log(Object.keys(shackles));
10  // => [toString, open, readInstructions]
11
12  mooleen.says("Could it be this easy?");
13  shackles.open();
14  // => You try to pry the shackles open but
15  //    they will not budge. Good try but no.
16
17
18  mooleen.says("Ok... Looks like there's " +
19               "something written here...");
20  shackles.readInstructions();
21  // => If how to open these shackles you forget,
```

---

[100] http://bit.ly/javascriptmancy-oop-object-internals-exercises
[101] https://github.com/vintharas/javascriptmancy-code-samples

Object Internals: The Secrets of Objects

```
22  //     remember the hidden 'lever' to 'reset'.
23  //     - Cloud
24
25  mooleen.says("Interesting, that sounds promising");
26  console.log(shackles.lever);
27  // => A mysterious lever
28  mooleen.says("Aha! Found it!");
29
30  console.log(Object.keys(shackles.lever));
31  // => [reset, toString]
32
33  shackles.lever.reset();
34  // => You find a hidden portrusion well hidden on
35  //    the rough surface of the shackles and *click*,
36  //    the shackles open.
37
38  mooleen.giggles();
39  mooleen.says("haha free!");
```

Unlock The Door Without Raising The Alarm!

After freeing everyone the next problem arises: A heavy wooden door reinforced with veins of cold metal. How to open it without magic?

```
1  console.log(reinforcedWoodenDoor);
2  // => A solid, heavy wooden door reinforced
3  //    with veins of cold metal
```

Hint: Inspect the door with Object.keys but beware to unlock the door because there's a hidden trap. Use Object.defineProperty to define a new unlock method that neutralizes the alarm before opening the door.

Solution

```javascript
console.log(reinforcedWoodenDoor);
// => A solid, heavy wooden door reinforced
//    with veins of cold metal

mooleen.says("Let's use the same trick...");
console.log(Object.keys(reinforcedWoodenDoor));
// => [toString, unlock]

console.log(reinforcedWoodenDoor.unlock);
// => function unlock() {
//      if (this.alarmIsActive) {
//        console.error("Sound explodes all around " +
//          "alerting the dungeon guards");
//      }
//      console.info("The door opens");
// }

mooleen.says('A hidden alarm!');
rat.says('Devious bastards');

mooleen.says("I'll try to deactivate it without " +
  "changing its apparent state... " +
  "That way no one will notice we've left " +
  "until it's too late");

Object.defineProperty(reinforcedWoodenDoor,
  '_unlock', {
  value: reinforcedWoodenDoor.unlock,
  writable: true,
  enumerable: false,
  configurable: true
});

Object.defineProperty(reinforcedWoodenDoor,
  'unlock', {
  value(){
    this.alarmIsActive = false;
    this._unlock();
    this.alarmIsActive = true;
  },
  writable: true,
  enumerable: true,
  configurable: true
})
```

Object Internals: The Secrets of Objects   325

```
45
46  mooleen.says('And now the door looks exactly the same: ');
47  console.log(Object.keys(reinforcedWoodenDoor));
48  // => [toString, unlock]
49
50  mooleen.says('but...');
51  reinforcedWoodenDoor.unlock();
52  // => The door opens
53
54  mooleen.says('I feel like a master burglar');
55  rat.says('A burrahobbit!');
56
57  mooleen.says('Did you say burrahobbit?');
58  rat.says('Yes master, the best burglars there be');
59
60  mooleen.pauses();
61  randalf.says("Quickly! There's not a moment to lose");
```

 Deactive All the Alarms!

The dungeons doors are filled with alarms. Can you devise a way to reuse your alarm deactivation logic? How would you deactivate the alarm in an object like this one without modifying any method?

```
1   class Door extends AlarmedDevice {
2     toString(){
3       return "A solid, heavy wooden door reinforced " +
4              "with veins of cold metal"
5     }
6     unlock(){
7       if (this.alarmIsActive){
8         console.error("Sound explodes all around " +
9                       "alerting the dungeon guards");
10      }
11      console.info("The door opens");
12    }
13  }
```

Hint: Wrap your alarm deactivation logic in a decorator!

Solution

```
class AlarmedDevice{
  constructor(){
    this.alarmIsActive = true;
  }
}

class Door extends AlarmedDevice {
  toString(){
    return "A solid, heavy wooden door reinforced " +
           "with veins of cold metal"
  }
  @deactivateAlarm
  unlock(){
    if (this.alarmIsActive){
      console.error("Sound explodes all around " +
                    "alerting the dungeon guards");
    }
    console.info("The door opens");
  }
}

function deactivateAlarm(target, property, descriptor){
  const alarmedFunction = descriptor.value;
  descriptor.value = function(...args){
    this.alarmIsActive = false;
    alarmedFunction.apply(this, args);
    this.alarmIsActive = true;
  }
}

const deactivatedDoor = new Door();
deactivatedDoor.unlock();
// => The door opens
```

More Metaprogramming with Reflect, Proxies and Symbols

All you require to write a poem,
is to have your mind open,
to write four to seven sentences,
that capture the topic essences.

It helps to have some rhyme,
to make the reading chime.
That is all you need,
to write a poem and succeed.

> - Anonymous
> A meta-poem

More Metaprogramming with Reflect, Proxies and Symbols 328

```
mooleen.says('Not having power is frustrating,' +
    'and all these corridors look ' +
    'exactly the same...');
mooleen.curses();
mooleen.says('Why are there so many holes?');
mooleen.tripsAndFalls();

red.grabs(mooleen);
randalf.grabs(red);
bandalf.grabs(red);

/* They slowly pull Malin and Red
   out of the hole */

mooleen.says('Thank you... That was near');
red.says('The Red Stronghold is a flying fortress');
red.says('These holes serve many purposes...');

randalf.says('ventilation');
bandalf.says('cheap lighting');

red.says('and a very clean method of execution');

red.says('As to the corridors my dear, ' +
    'they are designed to be confusing ' +
    'so that if ever a prisoner should escape ' +
    "they'd die before reaching any of the exits");

mooleen.says('And how do you know so much about ' +
    'these passages?');

red.says("Well, that may be because we designed them. " +
    "Have you ever seen such a solid piece of work?")

randalf.says('And it occurs to you to tell us now?');

red.says('Oh, it amuses me seeing Mooleen out of sorts');
mooleen.says('What?!?');

red.says('Well, one has to enjoy the small victories...');
mooleen.says("I didn't take you as the rensentful type");

red.shrugs();
mooleen.says("Alright, how do you read these tunnels?");
red.says('How good are you at reflection?')
```

How Good Are You at Reflection?

In the previous chapter you entered the mysterious world of metaprogramming with object internals, the numerous methods inside Object, and decorators, a stylish and reusable way to extend or modify how classes, properties or methods behave.

In this chapter we'll expand our incursion in the obscure kingdom of meta-programming by introducing three new features of ES6: the Reflect API, proxies and symbols. Ahead without fear!

ES6 Reflect

 Experiment Javascriptmancer!!
You can experiment with all examples in this chapter directly within this jsBin[102] or downloading the source code from GitHub[103].

The ES6 Reflect API attempts to provide a revised and unified way to access **reflection** features in JavaScript. It consists in a new object Reflect that exposes a series of static methods you can call directly.

Reflection? What is reflection?

Reflection is the ability of a computer program to examine, introspect, and modify its own structure and behavior at runtime[104].

We've seen some of these features throughout this book already:

---
[102] http://bit.ly/javascriptmancy-oop-meta
[103] https://github.com/vintharas/javascriptmancy-code-samples
[104] This definition from wikipedia was too good not to use http://bit.ly/reflection-programming

- `Object.defineProperty`, `Object.defineProperties` allow us to create or modify object properties at runtime
- `Object.getOwnPropertyDescriptor` returns the property descriptor associated to a given property
- `Object.keys` returns an array that contains the enumerable properties owned by an object
- `Object.getOwnPropertySymbols` returns an array containing all symbols found as object properties

The `Reflect` API attempts to formalize reflection in JavaScript and borrows reflection methods that were previously sprinkled within `Object`, `Object.prototype`, `Function.prototype` and several JavaScript operators (`delete` and `in`). Let's make a quick review of these methods:

Object Methods in Reflect

- `Reflect.defineProperty` just like `Object.defineProperty` allows you to define or configure properties within objects by using a property descriptor. Instead of returning the object it returns a boolean that indicates whether the operation succeeded or not.
- `Reflect.getOwnPropertyDescriptor` like its `Object` counterpart returns the property descriptor given the name of a property.
- `Reflect.getPrototypeOf` like `Object.getPrototypeOf` gives you the prototype of an object.
- `Reflect.setPrototypeOf` like `Object.setPrototypeOf` allows you to change the prototype of an object.
- `Reflect.preventExtensions` like `Object.preventExtensions` prevents you from adding new properties to an object.
- `Reflect.isExtensible` like `Object.isExtensible` returns a boolean that represents whether an object is extensible or not. An object is extensible when it can be augmented with new properties.

These methods work just like their Object counterparts so where you would usually call:

```
Object.defineProperty(goat, 'woolColor', {
  value: 'brown',
  writable: false,
  enumerable: true,
  configurable: true
});
```

Now you can write:

```
Reflect.defineProperty(goat, 'woolColor', {
  value: 'brown',
  writable: false,
  enumerable: true,
  configurable: true
});
```

All of the methods above behave just like their Object companions but for defineProperty that returns a boolean when the method succeeds:

```
const success = Reflect.defineProperty(goat, 'woolColor', {
  value: 'brown',
  writable: false,
  enumerable: true,
  configurable: true
});

if (success) {
  // celebrate!
} else {
  // cry
}
```

Function Methods in Reflect

- `Reflect.apply(target, context, arguments)` works in a similar way to `Function.prototype.apply` and allows you to call a function `target` giving a `context` of execution and an array of `arguments`.

Imagine a Hero of Ages with one secret super power - to become invincible when she is nearly dead:

```
class HeroOfAges{
  constructor(hitPoints=100){
    this._hitPoints = hitPoints;
  }

  get hitPoints() { return this._hitPoints; }

  set hitPoints(value){
    this._hitPoints = value;
    if (this._hitPoints < 10){
      this.becomeInvincible()
    }
  }

  toString(){
    return 'Hero of Ages';
  }

  becomeInvincible(){
    // give me your strength pegasus!
  }
}
```

We can define the `becomeInvincible` method as follows:

```
becomeInvincible(){
  this.invincibilitySpells.forEach(s => s.apply(this))
}
```

And configure it within the hero constructor with a series of `invincibilitySpells`:

```
class HeroOfAges{
  constructor(hitPoints=100){
    this._hitPoints = hitPoints;
    this.invincibilitySpells = [
      stoneSkin,
      miraculousRecovery,
      rage,
      titanStrength
    ];
  }
  // etc...
}

function stoneSkin() {
  this.defense = 1000;
}
function miraculousRecovery(){
  this.hitPoints += 100;
}
function rage(){
  this.attack = 1000;
}
function titanStrength(){
  this.damage = 2000;
}
```

Now when the heroOfAges goes to battle and her `hitPoints` fall below the threshold she'll become invincible and kick ass:

```
const heroOfAges = new HeroOfAges();
heroOfAges.hitPoints -= 95;
// => Hero of Ages becomes invincible!!!!

console.log(` ===heroOfAges===
attack: ${heroOfAges.attack}
defense: ${heroOfAges.defense}
hitPoints: ${heroOfAges.hitPoints}
damage: ${heroOfAges.damage}`)
/*
===heroOfAges===
attack: 1000,
defense: 1000,
hitPoints: 105,
damage: 2000
*/
```

Using `Reflect.apply` we can rewrite the `becomeInvincible` implementation as follows:

```
becomeInvincible(){
  this.invincibilitySpells
    .forEach(s => Reflect.apply(s, this, [])));
}
```

JavaScript Operators in Reflect

- `Reflect.construct(target, args)` is equivalent to using the `new` operator as in `new target(..args)`.
- `Reflect.delete(target, property)` is equivalent to using the `delete` operator to delete an object property as is `delete target[property]`. It returns a boolean that represents whether the operation succeeded.
- `Reflect.has(target, property)` is equivalent to using the `in` operator and allows you to find whether an object `target` has a property `property`.

New Functions in Reflect

Reflect.get(target, property) and Reflect.set(target, property, value) allow you to get/set properties within a target object.

Let's reuse our previous goat example to illustrate these methods:

```
const wasAbleToSetValue = Reflect.set(goat, 'hitPoints', 42);
if (wasAbleToSetValue) {
  console.log('I set the hitPoints property');
}
// => I set the hitPoints property

const hitPoints = Reflect.get(goat, 'hitPoints');
console.log(`The goath hadeth ${hitPoints} hit points`);
// => The goath hadeth 42 hit points
```

The most common use case of either of these is within proxies as we'll soon see.

Reflect.ownKeys(target) returns an array of the target object own properties including symbols. The resulting array is like a combination of the outputs of Object.getOwnPropertyNames and Object.getOwnPropertySymbols concatenated.

Imagine a burrahobbit with a secretPouch:

```
// A burrahobbit
const secretPouch = Symbol.for('secretPouch');

const burrahobbit = {
  name: 'Birwo Baggins',
  hitPoints: 20,
  [secretPouch]: ['jewels', 'golden ring', '4 gold doublons'],
  disappear(){
    console.log(`${this.name} suddenly disappears!`);
  }
};
```

We can retrieve its properties and symbols using the Object methods:

```
1  console.log(`Object.getOwnPropertyNames:`,
2              Object.getOwnPropertyNames(burrahobbit)});
3  // => Object.getOwnPropertyNames:
4  //    ['name', 'hitPoints', 'disappear']
5
6  console.log(`Object.getOwnPropertySymbols: `,
7              Object.getOwnPropertySymbols(burrahobbit));
8  // => Object.getOwnPropertySymbols: [ symbol ]
```

Or take advantage of the new Reflect.ownKeys to achieve the same result in one go:

```
1  console.log(`Reflect.ownKeys: `, Reflect.ownKeys(burrahobbit));
2  // => Reflect.ownKeys: ['name', 'hitPoints', 'disappear', symbol]
```

So When is the ES6 Reflect API Useful?

The ES6 Reflect API is really useful when you are building your own libraries and frameworks that operate on code. It provides a unified reflection API and marks a clear distinction between application level programming and meta-programming which will make your code more intentional.

Let's try an slightly more involved example that can highlight the usefulness of reflection. We're going to extend JavaScript with our own semantics to provide a safer way to apply mixins on objects, behold **ConstrainedMixins**! Mixins that allow you to set constraints on the target object:

More Metaprogramming with Reflect, Proxies and Symbols 337

```
class ConstrainedMixins {

  // requirements via decorator
  @requires('mana', 'hp')
  static canCastSpells(obj) {
    return Object.assign(obj, {
      castSpell
    });

    function castSpell(spell, target) {
      console.log(`${this} prepares to cast spell ${spell}...`);
      if (this.mana < spell.manaCost){
        console.log(`${this} doesn't have enough mana!` +
          `The spell fizzles out and ${this} gets ` +
          `damaged by the wild currents of magic`);
        this.hp -= (spell.manaCost - spell.mana);
        this.mana = 0;
      } else {
        this.mana -= spell.manaCost;
        spell.cast(target);
      }
    }
  }
}
```

The `requires` decorator represents our new constraint semantics and works by changing the original mixin with a new function that includes a validation step before the mixin gets applied to a target object:

```
function requires(...props){

  return function decorator(target, property, descriptor){
    const mixinFunction = descriptor.value;
    descriptor.value = function constrainedMixin(obj){
      throwIfRequirementsMissing(obj, props, property);
      return mixinFunction(obj);
    }
  }

  function throwIfRequirementsMissing(obj, props, mixinName){
```

```
   const objProperties = Reflect.ownKeys(obj);
   const missingProps = props
                 .filter(p => !objProperties.includes(p))
   if (missingProps.length > 0)
     throw new Error(`Object ${obj} lacks properties: [` +
       `${missingProps}] required for mixin ${mixinName}`);

   }
}
```

Notice how we used the `Reflect.ownKeys` to get a list of the properties of the target object and compare them to our required properties.

When we apply the constrained mixin `canCastSpells` to an unsuspecting bard `Sparrow` the requirements will kick in and throw an error alerting the user of our new library before further damage can occur:

```
const sparrow = {
  name: 'Sparrow',
  toString() { return this.name; }
};

try {
  ConstrainedMixins.canCastSpells(sparrow);
} catch (e){
  console.log(e.message);
}
// => "Object Sparrow lacks properties: [mana,hp] required
//     for mixin canCastSpells"
```

When the library user corrects his mistake and includes the necessary properties to satisfy the required interface, the mixin can successfully augment the target object:

More Metaprogramming with Reflect, Proxies and Symbols   339

```
1  const sparrowTheGifted = {
2    name: 'Sparrow, the gifted',
3    toString() { return this.name; },
4    mana: 100,
5    hp: 200
6  };
7
8  ConstrainedMixins.canCastSpells(sparrowTheGifted);
```

And, as a result, `SparrowTheGifted` has now the new and enhanced ability of casting spells:

```
1  sparrowTheGifted.castSpell({
2    toString(){ return 'bless'; },
3    manaCost: 10,
4    cast(target){
5      console.log(`You bless ${target} (+20 Luck)`);
6    }
7  }, sparrowTheGifted);
8  // => Sparrow, the gifted prepares to cast spell bless...
9  //    You bless Sparrow, the gifted (+20 Luck)
```

Excellent! Now that you've seen several ways to take advantage of the new ES6 Reflect API let's move onto another great metaprogramming tool that was released with ES6: **proxies**.

ES6 Proxies

Proxies provide you with a native way to intercept interactions with an object. They act as wrappers and allow you to write custom logic that lives between the object consumer interaction and the object itself.

By giving you complete access to all interactions within an object, proxies have a seemingly infinite number of applications with your imagination as the only limit. For instance:

- Validation logic
- Adapters to massage arguments before passing them to an object
- Logging interactions with an object
- Access permissions
- Visibility of properties based on conventions
- Prevent some operations with the object
- Revoke access to a user of an API

But what better way to understand proxies than with an example:

The Goat Strikes Back: Creating Our First Proxy

Let's bring out the goat that's been the star of our meta-programming chapters:

```
const goat = {
  hitPoints: 100,
  woolColor: 'brownish',
  toString() {return `A ${this.woolColor} goat `},
  bleats(){ console.log(`${this}: baaaaaaaa!`); },
  goesTo({x, y}) {
    this.x = x;
    this.y = y;
    console.log(`${this} goes to (${x}, ${y})`);
  }
};
```

We can create a proxy for the goat object by using the new Proxy class:

```
let poat = new Proxy(goat, /*handler*/ {});
```

We create a proxy by combining the original object goat with a handler object that will contain the intercepting logic. The resulting proxy has the exact same API of the original object and can act as a stand-in without any additional code:

More Metaprogramming with Reflect, Proxies and Symbols

```
console.log(goat)
// => Object {hitPoints: 100, woolColor: "brownish",
//            toString: function, bleat: function,
//            goesTo: function}

console.log(ploat);
// => Proxy {hitPoints: 100, woolColor: "brownish",
//           toString: function, bleat: function,
//           goesTo: function}
```

But, of course, the usefulness of proxies arises when we start implementing the `handler` object. Let's say that we want to make sure of a couple of things:

- the `hitPoints` property should never go below 0 or get in an inconsistent state like `null` or `undefined`
- the `woolColor` property should be read-only

We can define our `handler` object as follows:

```
let handler = {
  set(target, key, value) {
    if (key === 'hitPoints') {
      if (value < 0) {
        throw new Error('must have positive value!');
      } else if (value === undefined ||
                 value === null) {
        throw new Error('must have defined value!');
      }
    }
    if (key === 'woolColor') {
      throw new Error('woolColor is read-only!');
    }
    Reflect.set(target, key, value);
    // same as:
    // target[key] = value;
  }
}
```

The methods within a proxy handler object are called **traps**. In this particular example, we have defined a set trap that allows us to intercept when an object consumer attempts to set a property.

In our implementation, we check to see that the property is hitPoints and, in that case, we apply our validation logic that will result in an error when the new value is invalid. We also check whether the property is woolColor and we throw an error message because it is supposed to be a read-only property. Whenever the new value is a valid value or whenever we try to set any other property than hitPoints or woolColor we'll fallback to the default behavior and allow the consumer to set that property.

If you take a close look at the example, you'll appreciate how we used the **Reflect API** to fallback to the default behavior and how the Reflect.set signature matches the signature of the set proxy trap. This makes the Reflect API work perfectly in tandem with proxies.

If we now create a new proxy using the handler with the set trap:

```
ploat = new Proxy(goat, handler);
```

And attempt to set the hitPoints to a valid value, we'll see how everything works as we would expect:

```
ploat.hitPoints = 50;
// value set as usual
```

And when we attempt to set hitPoints to a known invalid value, everything explodes and we get a validation error:

More Metaprogramming with Reflect, Proxies and Symbols   343

```
1  console.log(`goat hitpoints: ${ploat.hitPoints}`);
2  // => goat hitPoints: 50
3  try {
4    ploat.hitPoints -= 100;
5  } catch (e){
6    console.error(e.message);
7    // => must have defined value!
8  }
```

Likewise when a consumer tries to set the woolColor property we get a succint error message telling us that it is not possible:

```
1  try {
2    ploat.woolColor = "whiteish";
3  } catch (e) {
4    console.error(e.message);
5    // => woolColor is read-only!
6  }
```

Everything while every other property continues behaving normally:

```
1  // other properties behave normally
2  ploat.bleat = function(){ console.log('moooo');};
3  ploat.bleat();
4  // => moooo
```

Good! Now you have an idea about the basic mechanics of proxies. Let's take a look at the different traps available and how you can use them.

The Get Trap: Wizardy CIA Surveillance

The get traps allows us to intercept any time a consumer tries to get a property value, that is, to access a property.

Imagine that we were to institute our own wizardy version of the CIA - the WIA -, and we needed to start monitoring every time a consumer accesses one of the properties of the goat (because clearly the goat could be a double-agent for The Red Hand).

We could define our proxy handle as follows:

```
handler = {
  get(target, key) {
    wia.logEvent(target, key);
    return Reflect.get(target, key)
  }
}
```

Where we have a get trap that logs whenever a consumer accesses any property of the target object using the obscure wia.logEvent method, and then forwards the property access to the target object itself using the Reflect.get method.

We can define the WIA - Wizard Intelligence Agency - that will contain the logEvent method as the class below:

```
class WIA {
  constructor(){
    this.log = new WeakMap();
  }

  logEvent(target, key){
    if (!Reflect.ownKeys(target).includes(key))
      return;

    let targetLog = this.log.get(target);
    if (!targetLog) {
      targetLog = this.log
                      .set(target, new Map())
                      .get(target);
    }
    this.addLogLine(key, targetLog);
  }

  addLogLine(key, targetLog){
    if (!targetLog.has(key)) {
```

More Metaprogramming with Reflect, Proxies and Symbols

```
21      targetLog.set(key, []);
22    }
23
24    console.log('add key to targetLog', key, targetLog[key]);
25
26    targetLog.get(key).push({
27      timestamp: new Date() ,
28      toString(){ return `${this.timestamp}` }
29    });
30  }
31
32  showLogs(target){
33    const log = this.log.get(target)
34    console.log(`
35 ${[...log.entries()]
36     .map(([k,v]) => `\n$${k}:\n$${v.join('\n')}`)}
37 `);
38  }
39 }
```

The WIA class exposes a logEvent method that allows this secret agency to store arbitrary interactions with objects inside a WeakMap. Inside this map, we'll store a single entry per object, and within the entry we'll have key/value pairs, where the key will be a property name and the value an array with timestamps referring to when a property is accessed. The WIA class also provides a showLogs method that allows the secret agents to retrieve the information regarding a given target.

 Why use a WeakMap?

You may have noticed that in the example above we used a WeakMap instead of a Map. This example is a great use case for a WeakMap because weak maps only hold weak references to objects allowing them to be garbage collected and preventing memory leaks.

Remember that we will need to instantiate the WIA before we can use it within the proxy handler:

```
const wia = new WIA();

handler = {
  get(target, key) {
    wia.logEvent(target, key);
    return Reflect.get(target, key)
  }
}
```

Now we can create a new proxy using this surveillance handler:

```
ploat = new Proxy(goat, handler);
```

And we're ready to start recording a day in the life of a goat:

```
// A day in the life of a goat
ploat.bleats();
ploat.goesTo(1, 1);
ploat.bleats();
ploat.goesTo(2, 2);
ploat.bleats();
ploat.goesTo(3, 3);
```

Now let's see what we've monitored:

```
wia.showLogs(goat);
/* => bleats:
Wed Aug 02 2017 15:31:52 GMT+0200 (CEST)
Wed Aug 02 2017 15:31:52 GMT+0200 (CEST)
Wed Aug 02 2017 15:31:52 GMT+0200 (CEST),
goesTo:
Wed Aug 02 2017 15:31:52 GMT+0200 (CEST)
Wed Aug 02 2017 15:31:52 GMT+0200 (CEST)
Wed Aug 02 2017 15:31:52 GMT+0200 (CEST),
toString:
Wed Aug 02 2017 15:31:52 GMT+0200 (CEST)
Wed Aug 02 2017 15:31:52 GMT+0200 (CEST)
Wed Aug 02 2017 15:31:52 GMT+0200 (CEST),
woolColor:
```

```
   Wed Aug 02 2017 15:31:52 GMT+0200 (CEST)
   Wed Aug 02 2017 15:31:52 GMT+0200 (CEST)
   Wed Aug 02 2017 15:31:52 GMT+0200 (CEST)
   */
```

Awesome! Thanks to the proxy get trap we now can monitor the comings and goings of the suspicious goat and make sure he doesn't share any confidential information with the enemy.

Another great use case of the get trap is controlling the visibility of properties. Let's say that the goat is indeed a double agent and wants to keep part of its API private and completely invisible to the prying eyes of the WIA.

The goat can use the common JavaScript convention of using properties prefixed with _ to denote privacy and enforce that using a proxy.

Imagine the goat object had a private property containing secret plans for a super powerful weapon:

```
const goatSpy = {
  hitPoints: 100,
  woolColor: 'brownish',
  position: {x: 0, y: 0},
  toString() {return `A ${this.woolColor} goat `},
  bleats(){ console.log(`${this}: baaaaaaaa!`); },
  goesTo({x, y}) {
    this.x = x;
    this.y = y;
    console.log(`${this} goes to (${x}, ${y})`);
  },

  // secret stuff
  _secretCompartment: ['plans of the Death Star'],
  _givesTip(target) {
    console.log(`${this} tips the ${target}`);
    target.takeDiscreetly(this._secretCompartment);
  }
};
```

It could make those properties completely invisible to outside lookers by defining the following proxy handler:

```
handler = {
  get(target, key) {
    if (typeof key !== 'string' ||
        !key.startsWith('_'))
      return Reflect.get(target, key);
  },
  set(target, key, value) {
    if (typeof key !== 'string' ||
        !key.startsWith('_'))
      Reflect.set(target, key, value);
  }
}
```

And using it to create a proxy object that, for all intents and purposes, would lack the _secretCompartment and _givesTip properties:

```
let regularLookingGoat = new Proxy(goatSpy, handler);

console.log(`Does the goat have a secret compartment? ${regularLooki\
ngGoat._secretCompartment}`);
// => "Does the goat have a secret compartment? undefined"
```

In order to use the *"private"* properties you'd need to make use of the original object and not the proxied one:

```
1  // You can use the unproxied goat
2  // to carry out the spy deals
3  const bartender = {
4    toString() { return 'a bartender';},
5    takeDiscreetly(things){
6      console.log(`${this} receives ${things}`);
7    }
8  }
9
10 goatSpy._givesTip(bartender);
11 // => A brownish goat  tips the a bartender
12 //    a bartender receives plans of the Death Star
```

In summary, following this approach, the proxy works as a facade over the original object which only exposes part of its functionality. The *"private"* parts of the object that we don't want the rest of the world to see can remain within the boundaries that we define, for instance, within a module.

Making the Goat Bulletproof with Has and ownKeys

The WIA is an enemy to be reckoned with, so the `goat` cannot be careless. After some spy games it discovers a vulnerability in its previous proxy:

```
1  console.log('_secretCompartment' in regularLookingGoat)
2  // => true
```

And moreover:

More Metaprogramming with Reflect, Proxies and Symbols 350

```
console.log(Reflect.has(regularLookingGoat,
                       '_secretCompartment'));
// => true

console.log(Reflect.ownKeys(regularLookingGoat))
// => ["hitPoints", "woolColor", "position", "toString",
//     "bleats", "goesTo", "_secretCompartment", "_givesTip"]
```

So it needs to define a better handler to make these properties completely invisible in these operations. Fortunately, the ES6 proxy API has several traps that allow you to intercept these interactions: has and ownKeys.

- has intercepts the in operator used to find out whether an object has a specific property. It also intercepts the Reflect.has method that performs the same operation
- ownKeys intercepts:
    - Reflect.ownKeys,
    - Object.keys
    - Object.getOwnPropertyNames
    - Object.getOwnPropertySymbols

If we update our original handler like this:

```
handler = {
  get(target, key) {
    if (typeof key !== 'string' ||
        !key.startsWith('_'))
      return Reflect.get(target, key);
  },
  set(target, key, value) {
    if (typeof key !== 'string' ||
        !key.startsWith('_'))
      Reflect.set(target, key, value);
  },
  has(target, key){
    if (typeof key !== 'string' ||
```

```
        !key.startsWith('_'))
      return Reflect.has(target, key);
    return false;
  },
  ownKeys(target){
    return Reflect
      .ownKeys(target)
      .filter(k => typeof k !== 'string' ||
                   !k.startsWith('_'));
  }
}
```

The goat becomes a bulletproof spy:

```
regularLookingGoat = new Proxy(goatSpy, handler);

console.log('_secretCompartment' in regularLookingGoat)
// => false
console.log(Reflect.has(regularLookingGoat,
                       '_secretCompartment'));
// => false

console.log(Reflect.ownKeys(regularLookingGoat))
// => ["hitPoints", "woolColor", "position",
//     "toString", "bleats", "goesTo"]
```

More Proxy Traps

I hope that the examples above have given you an idea as to the things that you can achieve with proxies. In addition to the traps that you've seen thus far, proxies offer many more traps that you can use to intercept a consumer interaction with an object.

Here's a comprehensive list of the traps available which, as you'll soon see, match the methods in the Reflect API:

Proxy Trap	Description
apply(target, ctx, args)	Allows you to intercept function calls and Reflect.apply
construct(target, ctx, args)	Intercepts the new operator (and Reflect.construct)
defineProperty(target, prop, descriptor)	Intercepts a call to Object.defineProperty or Reflect.defineProperty
deleteProperty(target, prop)	Intercepts the delete operator and Reflect.deleteProperty
getOwnPropertyDescriptor(obj, prop)	Intercepts Objet.getOwnPropertyDescriptor and Reflect.getOwnPropertyDescriptor
getPrototypeOf(target)	Intercepts Object.getPrototypeOf and Reflect.getPrototypeOf
isExtensible(target)	Intercepts Object.isExtensible and Reflect.isExtensible
preventExtensions()	Intercepts Object.preventExtensions and Reflect.preventExtensions
setPrototypeOf()	Intercepts Object.setPrototypeOf and Reflect.setPrototypeOf

Revocable Proxies

An interesting add-on to ES6 Proxies are revocable proxies. Revocable proxies are a special kind of proxy that can be revoked at any point in time. Revoking a proxy renders the proxy completely useless and any subsequent interaction with a revoked proxy will throw an error.

Imagine that the goat wants to stop its career in wizarding spionage

More Metaprogramming with Reflect, Proxies and Symbols 353

and start a business renting magic wool scissors. The rental period shouldn't be longer than a day and after that period the customer shouldn't be able to use the scissors any longer.

We start by defining the scissors themselves:

```
1  class MagicWoolScissors{
2    cutWool(target) {
3      const numberOfBales = Math.floor(Math.random()*10);
4
5      console.log(`You use the magic scissor on ${target}` +
6                  `and obtain ${numberOfBales} bales of wool`);
7
8      return `${numberOfBales} bales of wool`;
9    }
10 }
```

And then the goat business that creates scissors on demand, wraps them in a proxy and revokes the proxy within an hour:

```
1  class GoatBusiness {
2    constructor() {
3      this.purse = 0;
4    }
5    rentScissors() {
6      console.log(
7        'You rent a pair of scissors for 1 gold doublon');
8      this.purse++;
9
10     const scissors = new MagicWoolScissors();
11     const {proxy, revoke} = Proxy.revocable(scissors, {});
12
13     this.revokeWithinOneHour(revoke);
14
15     // return proxy;
16     // we will return the revoke token so that we
17     // don't need to wait for a day to test that it works
18     // :)
19     return {scissors:proxy, revoke};
20   }
21   revokeWithinOneHour(revoke){
```

```
    setTimeout(() => revoke(), 1000*60*60*24);
  }
}
```

In the example above we've cheated slightly. In order to be able to test the revoking functionality right away, we return the proxied scissors and the revoke token right away.

We now instantiate a GoatBusiness, rent some scissors and get on shearing (that's how you call when you cut wool from sheep by the way):

```
const goatBusiness = new GoatBusiness();

const {scissors, revoke} = goatBusiness.rentScissors();
// => You rent a pair of scissors for 1 gold doublon

scissors.cutWool('sheep');
// => You use the magic scissor on sheepand obtain 4 bales of wool
```

After a day of hard work we revoke the scissors proxy terminating the rental period which renders the scissors useless. No more shearing:

```
// 1 day later...
revoke();

try{
  scissors.cutWool('another sheep');
} catch(e){
  console.error(e);
  // => TypeError: Cannot perform 'get' on a proxy that has been rev\
oked
  // ouch
}
```

Cool right? Using revokable proxies gives you a native way to revoke access to an API using arbitrary rules of your own choosing.

ES6 Symbols and Meta-programming

In previous chapters you learned about Symbols and how you could use them to achieve privacy in objects. If you remember, Symbols are a new primitive type in Javascript whose main purpose is to act as identifier of properties within objects.

You can create a symbol using the `Symbol` function:

```
const rune = Symbol('rune');
```

And then you can use that symbol as a property identifier within an object:

```
const sword = {
  [rune]: 'rune of fire'
}
```

As we saw in previous chapters, you can only access the `rune` property if you have a reference to the symbol itself. This very virtue was what allowed us to achieve data privacy.

In addition to being able to create your own symbols, ES6 comes with a series of so-called **well known symbols** which have the interesting property of changing the behavior of objects by their mere presence within these objects.

Again, this is better explained through an example. Imagine that we were given the duty to administer a dungeon, with its cells, its torture chambers, its critters and, of course, its unfortunate prisoners.

The `Dungeon` could be represented as a class with a constructor that would allow us to build the foundations of the dungeon:

```
// imagine a Dungeon
class Dungeon {
  constructor(numberOfCells = 10, treasury = 20){
    this.numberOfCells = numberOfCells;
    this.treasury = treasury;
    this.prisoners = [];
  }

  // more methods below...
}
```

Then we'd need a method to add new prisoners into the dungeon but only if we have cells left:

```
addPrisoner(prisoner){
  if (this.dungeonIsFull())
    throw Error('Dungeon is full. You need to build ' +
                'more cells oh master of evil and deceit!');
  else
    this.prisoners.push(prisoner);
}

dungeonIsFull(){
  return this.numberOfCells === this.prisoners.length;
}
```

We could also build more cells by spending some of the coins in our treasury:

More Metaprogramming with Reflect, Proxies and Symbols 357

```
buildCell(){
  if (this.cellCost() > this.treasury)
    throw Error("You don't have enough money");
  else {
    this.treasury -= this.cellCost();
    this.numberOfCells++;
  }
}

cellCost(){
  if (this.numberOfCells < 20) return 10;
  else if (this.numberOfCells < 30) return 15;
  else return 20;
}
```

And that's it, we have a working dungeon where we can stowe our most bitter enemies. Now it'd be nice if we could see and traverse at a glance all the prisoners we have in our Dungeon. We could do that by traversing the this.prisoners array itself, but what if we don't want to expose how we're storing our prisoners? Wouldn't it be nice to give the ability of being traversed to the Dungeon itself?

We can do that by taking advantage of the well known symbol Symbol.iterator. Adding a new property Symbol.iterator to our class will allow us to use the for...of loop like if it was any other iterable object such as an Array or a Map.

We can implement the Symbol.iterator method as any other method within our Dungeon class:

```
// Adding this property all of the sudden gives
// Dungeon objects the possibility to be iterable
[Symbol.iterator](){
  return this.prisoners[Symbol.iterator]();
}
```

The Symbol.iterator method must return an iterator that will be used by the for...of loop to iterate over the elements of the collection. In this case, we delegate iterating to the prisoners Array.

Now whenever we instantiate a Dungeon and populate it with some prisoners:

```
// by providing the object with an iterator
// now I can iterate over it using for...of
const dungeonOfFire = new Dungeon();
dungeonOfFire.addPrisoner('John doe');
dungeonOfFire.addPrisoner('Cersei L.');
dungeonOfFire.addPrisoner('Catelynn S.');
```

We can obtain a list of the dungeon's current inhabitants by conveniently iterating over the Dungeon itself:

```
console.log('---prisoners in this dungeon---');
for(let p of dungeonOfFire){
  console.log(p);
}
console.log('-------------------------------');

// ---prisoners in this dungeon---
// John doe
// Cersei L.
// Catelynn S.
// -------------------------------
```

So, by adding, a property with a well known symbol (Symbol.iterator) we were able to alter how any instance of the Dungeon class behaves when used in conjunction with a for...of loop. And this also applies to any object at runtime. Behold! The goat!:

```
const goat = {
  hitPoints: 100,
  woolColor: 'black and white'
};
```

We can augment it at any point in time with a new property Symbol.iterator:

```
goat[Symbol.iterator] = function*() {
  yield 'goat moves left';
  yield 'goat moves up';
  yield 'goat bleats';
  yield 'goat moves right';
}
```

And it automagically gains the ability of supporting the use of for...of loops:

```
for(let moves of goatAgain){
  console.log(moves);
}
// => goat moves left
//    goat moves up
//    goat bleats
//    goat moves right
```

As you have probably deducted from the previous example, all well known symbols live as static properties of the Symbol class. Below you can find an overview of all these methods. First, there's the iterator symbol that we've just seen:

Well known Symbol Property	Description
Symbol.iterator	Method that returns a default iterator for a object that can be used in conjunction with for...of

Then we have several symbols that let you provide regular expression operations to any object. These were previously limited to strings via String.prototype.match, String.prototype.replace, String.prototype.search and String.prototype.split which delegate to previously internal methods within regular expressions.

With these new methods we can match, replace, search and split strings using not only regular expressions but any arbitrary objects:

Well known Symbol Property	Description
Symbol.match	Method that matches the object against a string. Originally you'd match to a regular expression, this method allows you to match any object. It is used by String.prototype.match
Symbol.replace	Method that replaces matched substrings for another string. Originally we'd match to a regular expression, this method allows you to match any object. It is used by String.prototype.replace
Symbol.search	Method that returns the index within a string that matches the object (originally a regular expression). It is used by String.prototype.search
Symbol.split	Method that splits a string at the indices that match the object (originally a regular expression).

For instance, let's say that we want to write a CSV parser so that we can process the ledgers of a magic shop legacy system. We can define a Separators class that encapsulates all the valid separators we support in our system:

```
class Separators {
  constructor(separators=[',', ':', ';']){
    this.separators = separators;
  }

  [Symbol.split](str){
    const [separator, ] = this.separators
                        .filter(s => str.includes(s));
    console.log(`Found separator in string ${separator}`);
    if (separator)
      return str.split(separator);
```

```
12      else
13          return str;
14      }
15  }
```

By providing a Symbol.split property to this class we can now use it to process CSV files and extract information from a raw string of characters. This same class allows us to use any arbitrary separators in our system and its configurable via its constructor (and public interface):

```
1  const validSeparators = new Separators();
2  console.log('this,works,well'.split(validSeparators));
3  // => ['this', 'works', 'well']
4
5  console.log('this;also;works'.split(validSeparators));
6  // => ['this', 'also', 'works']
7
8  console.log('and:this:woooot'.split(validSeparators));
9  // => ['and', 'this', 'woooot']
```

Symbol.split allowed us to write more modular, extensible and intentional code. Awesome, isn't it?

Finally, we have a series of well known symbols that allow us to perform miscellaneous operations:

Well known Symbol Property	Description
Symbol.hasIntance	Used by instanceof. Method that determines whether a constructor object Class recognizes another object obj as its instance (obj instanceof Class)
Symbol.isConcatSpreadable	Boolean that determines whether an object should be flattened to its array elements when doing Array.prototype.concat

Well known Symbol Property	Description
Symbol.toPrimitive	Method that converts an object into a primitive value. It lets you customize how an arbitrary object is coerced to another type.
Symbol.toStringTag	Method that returns a string representation of an object. It is used by Object.prototype.toString and allows you to customize the string representation of any object. For instance, the default string representation of any custom type is [object Object], with this symbol you can customize the string representation of a Dungeon to [object Dungeon].
Symbol.species	Constructor function that is used to create derive objects. It allows you to override the default constructor for derived objects used when calling methods on the prototype chain like Array.prototype.map.
Symbol.unscopables	If implemented in object target, it is an object with properties that describe property names that are excluded from the with environment of target.

Concluding

This was a huge chapter! Let's make a quick summary of what we've learned thus far. In this past two chapters we've dived into meta-programming in JavaScript, the obscure art of programming your programs, of using programmatic features such as classes, objects, properties and methods as the data of your programs. In the previous chapter we learned about object internals and decorators, and in this chapter you've learned about the new Reflect API, proxies and the meta-programming aspect of Symbols.

The Reflect API is a new API that attempts to provide a unified way to access **reflection** features in JavaScript. Reflection is the ability of a computer program to examine, introspect, and modify its own structure and behavior at runtime. The new Reflect API concentrates methods that were previously part of the Object prototype, Function prototype and various operators and gathers them inside the single Reflect object. This new API improves the usability of some of the old reflection methods, gives you a more intentional way to write meta-programming style code in your programs and opens the way to more meta-programming features in JavaScript.

ES6 proxies give you a native way to intercept interactions with any object and run arbitrary logic of your choosing. With ES6 proxies you can define handler objects that contain traps to "trap" specific object interactions: accessing a property, setting a property, calling a function, constructing an object, etc. By having complete access to all interactions with an object, proxies have a ton of applications like validation, logging, access control, adapters, etc. Another interesting aspect of proxies are revocable proxies. This type of proxies give you the ability to have an extra degree of control over who, how and when your object APIs are accessed. This is achieved by defining custom logic to decide whether and when a proxy is revoked which results in removing access to the proxied object.

We first learned about Symbols as a means to achieve data hiding. Symbols are a new primitive type in JavaScript that represent property identifiers. A less known aspect of ES6 Symbols are their applications in meta-programming. The so-called well known

More Metaprogramming with Reflect, Proxies and Symbols 364

Symbols allow you to hook into JavaScript internal methods and alter how objects behave. By adding new properties in your classes or objects using these well known symbols you can add iterability to custom objects, string matching, and more.

```
/*
As soon as Mooleen learns the power of reflection
She starts seeing signs and runes within the walls that
describe in great detail how to navigate these tunnels
*/

mooleen.says('Oh my');
red.says('I know');

mooleen.says('I can see how we can get out of here' +
    " but it'll be challenging without casting");
mooleen.says('...wait! Here it says something ' +
    'about a Totem of magic supression');
mooleen.says('is that what I think it is?');

red.says('Indeed it is');

mooleen.says('Then we must go there first');

randalf.says('I suggest that we do it quickly');
bandalf.says('swiftly');

red.says("I couldn't agree more. " +
    "The Red Hand has frequent patrols within the " +
    "dungeons and it is very unsettling that we " +
    "haven't run into any.")

/*
As if summoned by Red's comment footsteps and the
clinking of heavy armor resounds within the tunnels
*/

mooleen.says('Damn! Run!');

/*
The group speeds across the ancient tunnels
following Mooleen: left, right, right, left
and stop! They arrive to the end of the corridor,
```

```
   where an armored door blocks the way forward.
*/
```

Exercises

Experiment JavaScriptmancer!

You can experiment with these exercises and some possible solutions in this jsBin[105] or downloading the source code from GitHub[106].

Blast that Door Open!

The lights, footsteps and the cold sound of steel are approaching. There's no way back, the only way is forward. You need to open that door and neutralize the Totem of Magic Supression to have a chance at escaping unscathed.

```
1  console.log(armoredDoor);
2  // => A heavily armored door stands in your way.
3  //    Thick bars of black metal overlay a solid
4  //    oak door. Over the metal, incandescent
5  //    reddish runes promise unknown horrors for
6  //    the arrogant one that tries to force it
7  //    open without a proper key.
```

Hint: Use the `Reflect` API to find the first hint about how to open the door.

---

[105] http://bit.ly/javascriptmancy-oop-meta-exercises
[106] https://github.com/vintharas/javascriptmancy-code-samples

Solution

```
1   console.log(armoredDoor);
2   // => A heavily armored door stands in your way.
3   //    Thick bars of black metal overlay a solid
4   //    oak door. Over the metal, incandescent
5   //    reddish runes promise unknown horrors for
6   //    the arrogant one that tries to force it
7   //    open without a proper key.
8
9   mooleen.says('Ok...');
10
11  console.log(Object.keys(armoredDoor));
12  //=> [toString, unlock]
13
14  console.info(armoredDoor.unlock);
15  /* => function unlock(key) {
16   if (this[trapsAreActive]) {
17     throw new Error('\n
18      You try to open the door with the key.\n
19      You rotate the lock and hear a satisfying \n
20      \'click\' that indicates that the door is unlocked.\n
21      You open the door slightly and it suddenly burst open\n
22      in a wail, a tremendous force sucks you and your \n
23      comrades inside the blackest whole, and you keep falling,\n
24      and falling, into the obscene surface of Yuggoth, its \n
25      dark cities and and its unseen horrors where you die.\n');
26   } if (secretPassword.match(key)) {
27     console.info("The door opens");
28   } else {
29     console.info("You try opening the door with " +
30                  "the key but nothing happens");
31   }
32  }
33  */
34
35  mooleen.says('Looks like the door is trapped');
36
37  rat.says("It is master! Let me volunteer for scouting " +
38           "the approaching Red Hand and gather intel so " +
39           "we can be prepared!");
40  randalf.says("Great idea! You'll need help");
41  bandalf.says("Lots of help!");
42
43  mooleen.says("haha What about you Red?");
44  red.says("Oh, I haven't been to Yuggoth, " +
```

More Metaprogramming with Reflect, Proxies and Symbols 367

```
45                "sounds like an exciting place");
46
47    mooleen.says("Hopefuly we won't have to visit. " +
48                "I should be able to deactivate this...");
49
50    console.info(armoredDoor.trapsAreActive);
51    // => undefined
52
53    mooleen.says('Interesting, looks like it is a Symbol!');
54
55    console.info(Reflect.ownKeys(armoredDoor));
56    // => [toString, unlock, Symbol(trap switch)]
57
58    let [,,trapSwitch] = Reflect.ownKeys(armoredDoor);
59
60    mooleen.says("Let's make it look like we weren't here");
61
62    const untrappedDoor = new Proxy(armoredDoor, {
63      get(target, property) {
64        if (property === 'unlock') {
65          return (...args) => {
66            target[trapSwitch] = false;
67            console.log(target[trapSwitch]);
68            const result = Reflect.apply(target[property], target, args);
69            target[trapSwitch] = true;
70            return result;
71          }
72
73        } else {
74          return Reflect.get(target, property);
75        }
76      }
77    });
78
79    mooleen.says('Ok now we will see if we blow up');
80    red.says('Or fall down into the abyss');
81
82    try {
83      untrappedDoor.unlock();
84    } catch (e) {
85      console.error(e.message);
86    }
87    // => You try opening the door with the key but nothing happens
88
89    mooleen.says('Good... now we need a key');
90
91    /* mooleen grabs a stone from the floor */
```

```
 92   const stone = {
 93     toString(){ return 'a stone';}
 94   };
 95
 96   mooleen.says("Now let's make this stone behave like a key");
 97
 98   stone[Symbol.match] = () => true
 99
100   untrappedDoor.unlock(stone);
101   // => The door opens
102
103   mooleen.shouts('Aha!');
104
105   rat.says('I knew you would make it!');
106   randalf.says('Yep, we were all certain of it');
107
108   mooleen.says('sure sure...');
109
110   /*
111   The group walks into the chamber and
112   the door closes itself behind them...
113   */
```

TypeScript

JavaScript-mancy is a dangerous art.
Get an incantation slightly wrong,
and anything can happen.

More than one young apprentice
has found out about this the hard way,
just a split second before
razing a village to the ground,
letting loose a bloodthirsty beast,
or making something unexpected explode.

That's generally the way it is.

There are records of an ancient order,
an order of disciplined warrior monks,
who were able to tame the wild winds of magic.
But too little of them remains.

Did they exist?
Or are they just wishful thinking and myth?

    - The Chronicler

```
/*
The group walks into the chamber and
the door closes itself behind them...

...the chamber is poorly lit. A metal brazier of eerie blue
flames lies in the middle of the room and bathes a strange
obsidian obelisk in a mysterious light. Huge columns
surround the obelisk at irregular intervals.
Under the dim light it is impossible to ascertain
the room proportions...
*/

mooleen.says('Something about this feels very wrong...');
red.says("I couldn't agree more");

randalf.says("Well, it's either destroy that totem and " +
    "escape aided by magic or go back and fight The Red Legion" +
    "with our bare fists");
rat.says("...and sharp claws");

mooleen.says("Alright, let's get this over with");

/*
    The group approaches the obelisk under an oppressive
    silence only broken by the sound of boots scraping
    the sand covered ground.
*/

red.says('Oh shit');
mooleen.says('Oh shit? I thought you ' +
    'were beyond that type of language');

/*
    Eerie blue and green lights start flaring around the
    group inundating the chamber with light and a ghastly
    atmosphere. Up and up they go to reveal enormous terraces
    filled with dark winged figures. A voice suddenly booms
    within the chamber:
*/

voice.thunders('Let the games begin!');
voice.thunders("In our next game we'll recreate " +
    "The Fall of the Order of The Red Moon " +
    "the sacred order of warrior monks" +
    "whose fierceness still echoes across the centuries");
voice.thunders('I give you: The Last Stand!');
```

```
/*
A thunderous applause mixed with screeches, screams and
shouts of joy and excitement follows the proclamation.
At the same time 4 humongous iron doors start slowly
opening and row after row of obscene four-legged reptilian
creatures start emerging from them. Their impossibly huge
mandibles and terrible wails freeze your blood.
*/

mooleen.says('Oh shit');

voice.thunders('The rules of the game:');
voice.thunders('#1. Fight or Die...');
voice.thunders('#2. You Shall Only Use Types!');
voice.thunders('#3. Only One Shall Remain');
```

You Shall Only Use Types!

Congratulations on making it to the end of the book! I have a special treat prepared for you as a farewell present: **TypeScript**! TypeScript has been gaining momentum over the past few years and it is used inside and outside of the .NET world even with popular front-end frameworks such as Angular and React. TypeScript provides the nearest experience to C# that you can find on the web. Enjoy!

JavaScript + Types = Awesome Dev Productivity

TypeScript is a superset of JavaScript that adds type annotations and, thus, static typing on top of JavaScript.

If you are a C# or Java developer you'll feel right at home writing TypeScript. If you are a JavaScript developer or have a background in dynamic programming languages you'll encounter a slightly more verbose version of JavaScript that results in a safer and better developer experience. Either way, you'll be happy to know that everything you've learned about JavaScript thus far also applies to TypeScript, that is, **any JavaScript is valid TypeScript**.

Any JavaScript is Valid TypeScript

 Experiment Javascriptmancer!!

You can experiment with the examples in this section using the TypeScript playground[107] or downloading the source code from GitHub[108].

Any bit of JavaScript is valid TypeScript. Let's say that we have the most basic piece of JavaScript code that you can write, a simple variable declaration that represents your reserve of mana:

```
var manaReserves = 10;
```

And now let's say that we want to recharge your mana reserves by drinking a magic potion:

```
function rechargeMana(potion){
    return potion.manaModifier * (Math.floor(Math.rand()*10) + 1);
}
```

So we go and write the following:

---

[107]https://bit.ly/javascriptmancy-oop-typescript-basic
[108]https://github.com/vintharas/javascriptmancy

```
1  manaReserves += rechargeMana({
2    name: 'light potion of mana',
3    manaModifier: 1.5
4  });
```

When we execute the piece of code above, it explodes with the following error:

```
1  // => Uncaught TypeError: Math.rand is not a function
```

Which makes sense because there's no such thing as a Math.rand function in JavaScript. It is called Math.random. For some reason I mix this function with a C function that has the same purpose, a slightly different name, and which I used in my student days. Regardless, I make this mistake, again and again.

The code above is a very traditional piece of JavaScript. But it is also completely valid TypeScript, with one difference. Writing the rechargeMana in TypeScript would have automatically resulted in a compiler error that would've read:

```
1  Property 'rand' does not exist on type 'Math'.
```

This would have immediately alerted me to the fact that I'm making a mistake (again), and I would have been able to fix it before executing the program. This is one of the advantages of TypeScript: **shorter feedback loops where you can detect errors in your code at compile time instead of at runtime.**

Let's expand our previous example and drink another potion:

```
rechagreMana({
  name: 'Greater Potion of Mana',
  manaModifier: 2
})
```

Again. A simple typo, a classic mistake in JavaScript that would result in a `ReferenceError` at runtime, is instantly caught by the TypeScript compiler:

```
Cannot find name 'rechagreMana'.
```

As we've seen thus far, the TypeScript compiler that sits between the TypeScript code that you write and the output that runs in the browser can do a lot of things for you on vanilla JavaScript. But **it truly shines when you start adding type annotations**, that is, when you annotate your JavaScript code with additional bits of information regarding the type of things.

For instance, let's update our original `rechargeMana` function with some type annotations:

```
function rechargeMana(potion: { manaModifier : number }) {
  return potion.manaModifier * (Math.floor(Math.random()*10) + 1);
}
```

The example above contains a type annotation for the `potion` parameter `{manaModifier : number}`. This annotation means that the `potion` parameter is expected to be an object that has a property `manaModifier` of type `number`.

The type annotation does several things for us:

1. It can help the compiler discover errors when the object passed as an argument to `rechargeMana` doesn't have the expected interface. That is, when it lacks the `manaModifier` property which is necessary for the function to work.

TypeScript

2. It can help the compiler discover typos or type errors when you use the `potion` object within the body of the function.
3. It gives us statement completion when typing `potion` inside the `rechargeMana` function which is a great developer experience[109]. If you aren't familiar with statement completion it consist on helpful in-editor information that pops up and tells you how you can use an object, like which properties are methods are available, which types are expected for the different parameters, etc.

Let's illustrate 1) with an example. Imagine that in addition to potions of Mana you had potions of Strength:

```
const potionOfStrength = {
  name: 'Potion of Strength',
  strengthModifier: 3,
  duration: 10
};
```

At some point in our program we could end up calling this code by mistake:

```
rechargeMana(potionOfStrength);
```

Calling the `rechargeMana` function with a `potionOfStrength` as argument would result in a runtime error in JavaScript or, perhaps even in an elusive bug since multiplying `undefined` by a number results in `NaN` instead of crashing outright.

In TypeScript however, the example above would result in the following compiler error:

---

[109]The editor that you use should have a good integration with the TypeScript compiler to provide this type of service. Many of the most common IDEs and text editors have that support.

```
1  // [ts]
2  // Argument of type '{ name: string; strengthModifier: number; }'
3  // is not assignable to parameter
4  //   of type '{ manaModifier: number; }'.
5  // Property 'manaModifier' is missing
6  // in type '{ name: string; strengthModifier: number; }'.
```

This error would quickly tell me that the potion of strength lacks the required contract to use rechargeMana and lots of tears and frustration would've been saved right then and there. Also take a second to appreciate the quality and precision of the error message above.

So any JavaScript is valid TypeScript. Change your code.js file into code.ts file, run it by the TypeScript compiler and TypeScript will try to infer the most information it can from your code and do its best to help you. Add type annotations on top of that and TypeScript will be able to learn more about your code and intentions, and provide you with better support.

So, What Are The Advantages and Disadvantages of TypeScript?

By enhancing your JavaScript with new features, type annotations and static typing TypeScript provides these advantages:

- **Better error detection.** TypeScript can do static analysis of your code and reveal errors before running the actual code. This provides a much shorter feedback loop so that you can fix these errors as soon as they happen inside your editor and not after they hit production.
- **Better tooling and developer productivity.** The rich type information can be used by editors and IDEs to provide great tooling to enhance your developer productivity like in-editor compiler warnings, statement completion, safe refactorings,

inline documentation, etc... Visual Studio Code[110] is a text editor that has awesome TypeScript support out of the box.
- **Great API discoverability.** Using statement completion provided by type annotations is an outstanding way to discover about new APIs right inside your editor.
- **Write more intentional code.** TypeScript type annotations and additional features like access level keywords allow you to constrain how the APIs that you design are meant to be used. This allows you to write more intentional code.
- **ESnext features.** TypeScript supports a lot of ESnext features like class members, decorators and `async/await`.
- **Additional TypeScript Features.** In addition to JavaScript and ESnext features TypeScript has a small number of features that are not in the ECMA-262 specification which add a lot to the language like property access levels and parameter properties.
- **Works with third-party libraries.** Using type annotations in your application code is awesome but what about all the third-party libraries that you use and are reference throughout your application code? How does TypeScript interact with them? Particularly, what happens when these libraries aren't written in TypeScript? In the worst case scenario TypeScript treats objects it doesn't know as of type `any` which basically means *"this object can have any shape so just behave as you would in JavaScript and don't make any assumptions"*. More often, third-party libraries either come with declaration files that provide typing information for TypeScript or you can find these declaration files through the DefinitelyTyped project[111] a repository of TypeScript type definitions. This means that you'll be able to enjoy the same level of TypeScript support (or even greater) for third-party libraries that you do for your own code.

---

[110] https://code.visualstudio.com/
[111] http://definitelytyped.org/

- **Great for large-scale applications and teams.** TypeScript excels at supporting multiple teams with large-scale applications. The type annotations and the TypeScript compiler are awesome at catching breaking changes, subtle bugs and with new APIs discoverability.

On the minus side:

- **TypeScript requires a transpilation step.** TypeScript code is not supported as-is in any browser. In order to be able to write your applications in TypeScript you need to setup some sort of build pipeline to transpile your TypeScript code into a version of JavaScript that can run in the browser. Fortunately, there is great support for this in the open source community and you can find great integrations for TypeScript in the most popular frameworks and build tools.
- **You need to learn type annotations syntax and related artifacts.** The type annotations, their syntax and related artifacts like interfaces, generics, etc... add more cognitive load and an extra degree of complexity on top of all you need to know to write JavaScript applications.
- **It is verbose.** The addition of type annotations makes your JavaScript code more verbose (call(person:Person)) which can be quite aesthetically unpleasing (particularly at first). The TypeScript compiler does a great job at inferring types and reducing the amount of type annotations you need to write to the minimum but to make the most out of TypeScript you'll need to add a fair amount of type annotations yourself.
- **It sometimes falls out of line with the ECMAScript standard.** Bringing ESnext features to you today, although awesome, can have its drawbacks. Implementing ESnext features before they've been formalized can lead to TypeScript breaking with the standards as it happened with modules. Fortunately, the core philosophy of TypeScript being a superset of

JavaScript led the TypeScript team to implement support for ES6 modules and to deprecate the non-standard version. This is a great indicator of TypeScript's allegiance to JavaScript but still bears consideration when adopting ESnext features.

Setting up a Simple TypeScript project

The best way to get an idea of the full-blown TypeScript development experience is to setup a simple TypeScript project from scratch and follow along for the rest of the chapter. As usual, you can download the source code for these and all examples from GitHub[112].

The easiest way to get started is to install node and npm[113] in your development computer. Once you've done that, we'll install the TypeScript compiler using npm:

```
1  $ npm install -g typescript
```

You can verify that the installation has worked correctly by running:

```
1  $ tsc -v
2  Version 2.4.2
```

And accessing the TypeScript compiler help:

---

[112]https://github.com/vintharas/javascriptmancy-code-samples
[113]https://nodejs.org/en/

```
$ tsc -h
Version 2.4.2
Syntax:    tsc [options] [file ...]

Examples:  tsc hello.ts
           tsc --outFile file.js file.ts
           tsc @args.txt
```

I will use Visual Studio Code[114] during these examples but you're welcome to use any editor that you prefer[115].

Typing this command below will create a new TypeScript file called hello-wizard.ts and will open it on Visual Studio Code:

```
$ code hello-wizard.ts
```

Let's write the canonical hello wizard in TypeScript with a sayHello function:

```
function sayHello(who: string) : void {
  console.log(`Hello ${who}! I salute you JavaScript-mancer!`);
}
```

Notice how we have added a type annotation string to the who parameter of this function. If we try to call the function with an argument that doesn't match the expected type of string the compiler will alert us with a compiler error inside our editor:

```
sayHello(42);
// => [ts] Argument of type '42' is not assignable
//        to parameter of type 'string'.
```

Let's fix it by saluting yourself. Update the code above to include your name inside a string:

---
[114]https://code.visualstudio.com/
[115]http://www.typescriptlang.org/index.html#download-links

```
sayHello('<Your name here>');
```

Now you can compile the TypeScript file using the compiler within the terminal (Visual Studio comes with an embedded terminal that you can run inside the editor which is very convenient). Type:

```
$ tsc hello-world.ts
```

This will tell the TypeScript compiler to transpile your TypeScript application into JavaScript that can run in the browser. It will result in a vanilla JavaScript file `hello-world.js` that contains the following code:

```
function sayHello(who) {
    console.log("Hello " + who + "! I salute you JavaScript-mancer!");
}
sayHello('<Your name here>');
```

Beautiful vanilla JavaScript as if you had typed it with your bare hands. You can use `node` to run this file:

```
$ node hello-world.js
Hello <Your name here>! I salute you JavaScript-mancer!
```

And TaDa! You've written, transpiled and run your first TypeScript program! World here we come!

Since it can be slightly tedious to run the TypeScript compiler every time you make changes in your `ts` files, you can setup the compiler in **watch mode**. This will tell the TypeScript compiler to monitor your source code files and transpile them whenever it detects changes. To setup the TypeScript compiler in watch mode just type the following:

```
1  $ tsc -w hello-world.ts
2  10:55:11 AM - Compilation complete. Watching for file changes.
```

In the upcoming sections we will discover some of the great features you can use within TypeScript, all you need to know about TypeScript type annotations and what you need to think about when using TypeScript in real-world projects.

 Visual Studio Code Works Great With TypeScript!

If you want to learn more about how to have a great setup in Visual Studio Code with TypeScript I recommend you to take a look at this guide[116].

Cool TypeScript Features

In addition to type annotations, TypeScript improves JavaScript on its own right with ESnext features and some features of its own.

 TypeScript brings you a lot of ES-next features

A lot of the features that we'll see in this section are ESnext features that are proposals at different levels of maturity. You can find more information about all proposals currently under consideration in the TC39 ECMA-262 GitHub repository[117].

Some of these features are available also when using Babel with experimental flags. The fact that you have a team within Microsoft maintaining Type-Script gives you a lot of confidence when using these features within TypeScript.

---

[116]https://bit.ly/vscode-ts
[117]http://bit.ly/ecma262-gh

TypeScript Classes

TypeScript classes come with several features that provide a much better developer experience than ES6 classes. The first one is **class members**.

Instead of writing your classes like this:

```
// ES6 class
class Gladiator {
  constructor(name, hitPoints){
    this.name = name;
    this.hitPoints = hitPoints;
  }
  toString(){
    return `${this.name} the gladiator`
  }
}
```

You can extract the class members `name` and `hitPoints` to the body of the class much like in statically typed languages:

```
class Gladiator {
  name: string;
  hitPoints: number;

  constructor(name: string, hitPoints: number){
    this.name = name;
    this.hitPoints = hitPoints;
  }

  toString(){
    return `${this.name} the gladiator`
  }
}
```

This can be slightly verbose so TypeScript comes with another feature called **parameter properties** that allows you to specify a class member and initialize it via the constructor all in one go.

An equivalent version to the one above using *parameter properties* would look like this:

```
class SleekGladiator {
  constructor(public name: string,
              public hitPoints: number){}

  toString(){
    return `${this.name} the gladiator`
  }
}
```

Better, isn't it? The `public` keyword within the class constructor tells TypeScript that `name` and `hitPoints` are class members that can be initialized via the constructor.

Moreover, the `public` keyword gives us a hint as to the last improvement that TypeScript brings to classes: **access modifiers**. TypeScript comes with four access modifiers that determine how you can access a class member:

- **readonly**: Makes a member read only. You must initialize it upon declaration or within a constructor and it can't be changed after that.
- **private**: Makes a member private. It can only be accessed from within the class itself.
- **protected**: Makes a member protected. It can only be accessed from within teh class or derived types.
- **public**: Makes a member public. It can be accessed by anyone. Following JavaScript ES6 class implementation, `public` is the default access modifier for class members and methods if none is provided.

The `readonly` modifier saves us the necessity to define a `@readonly` decorator like we did in previous chapters.

One shouldn't be able to change one's name once it's been given so let's make the `Gladiator` name read-only:

```
1  class FixedGladiator {
2
3    constructor(readonly name: string,
4                public hitPoints: number){}
5
6    toString(){
7      return `${this.name}, the gladiator`
8    }
9
10 }
```

Now when we create a new gladiator and we give him or her a name it'll be written in stone:

```
1  const maximo = new FixedGladiator('Maximo', 5000);
2
3  maximo.name = "Aurelia";
4  // => [ts] Cannot assign to 'name' because it is
5  //         a constant or a read-only property.
```

An important thing to note here is that these access modifiers are only applicable in the world of TypeScript. That is, the TypeScript compiler will enforce them when you are writing TypeScript but they'll be removed when your code is transpiled to JavaScript.

The transpiled version of the FixedGladiator above results in the following JavaScript:

```
1  var FixedGladiator = (function () {
2
3    function FixedGladiator(name, hitPoints) {
4      this.name = name;
5      this.hitPoints = hitPoints;
6    }
7
8    FixedGladiator.prototype.toString = function () {
9      return this.name + ", the gladiator";
10   };
11
12   return FixedGladiator;
13 }());
```

As you can appreciate from the example above there's no mechanism which ensures that the `name` property is read-only.

Next let's test the `private` access modifiers. In previous chapters we discussed different approaches that you can follow to achieve privacy in JavaScript: closures and symbols. With TypeScript you can achieve data hiding by using the `private` (and `protected`) access modifiers.

This was the example we used in *chapter 6. White Tower Summoning Enhanced: The Marvels of ES6 Classes* to showcase data hiding using closures:

```
class PrivateBarbarian {

    constructor(name){
        // private members
        let weapons = [];
        // public members
        this.name = name;
        this["character class"] = "barbarian";
        this.hp = 200;

        this.equipsWeapon = function (weapon){
            weapon.equipped = true;
            // the equipsWeapon method encloses the weapons variable
            weapons.push(weapon);
            console.log(`${this.name} grabs a ${weapon.name} ` +
                        `from the cavern floor`);
        };
        this.toString = function(){
            if (weapons.length > 0) {
                return `${this.name} wields a ` +
                        `${weapons.find(w => w.equipped).name}`;
            } else return this.name
        };
    }

    talks(){
        console.log("I am " + this.name + " !!!");
    }
```

TypeScript

```
    saysHi(){
      console.log("Hi! I am " + this.name);
    }
};
```

In this example we use closures to enclose the weapons variable which becomes private for all effects and purposes. As you can appreciate, the use of closures forces us to move the methods equipsWeapon and toString that make use of the weapons variable from the body of the class to the body of the constructor function.

The equivalent of this class in TypeScript looks like this:

```
class PrivateBarbarian {
  // private members
  private weapons = [];

  // public members
  ["character class"] = "barbarian";
  hp = 200;

  constructor(public name: string) {}

  equipsWeapon(weapon) {
    weapon.equipped = true;
    // the equipsWeapon method encloses the weapons variable
    this.weapons.push(weapon);
    console.log(`${this.name} grabs a ${weapon.name} ` +
                `from the cavern floor`);
  }

  toString() {
    if (this.weapons.length > 0) {
      return `${this.name} wields a ` +
             `${this.weapons.find(w => w.equipped).name}`;
    } else return this.name
  };

  talks(){
    console.log("I am " + this.name + " !!!");
```

```
28    }
29
30    saysHi(){
31      console.log("Hi! I am " + this.name);
32    }
33  };
```

If you now instantiate an indomitable barbarian and try to access the weapons property you'll be greeted by the following error:

```
1  const conan = new PrivateBarbarian("shy Conan");
2  // const privateWeapons = conan.weapons;
3  // => [ts] Property 'weapons' is private and
4  //         only accessible within class 'PrivateBarbarian'.
```

If you look back and compare both approaches I think that you'll agree with me that the TypeScript syntax reads better than the ES6 counterpart. Having all methods within the body of the class is more consistent and easier to understand than having methods split in two separate places.

On the flip side, the TypeScript `private` access modifier is a TypeScript feature that disappears when the code is transpiled to JavaScript, that is, a library consumer that had access to the output JavaScript would be able to access the weapons property of this class. This won't normally be a problem since most likely your whole development team will be working with TypeScript but there can be some cases where it could be problematic. For instance, I can see it being an issue for library creators that create their library using TypeScript and make it accessible to consumers that are using vanilla JavaScript.

Why Do I Get A TypeScript Error When Writing An ES6 class? Isn't It Valid JavaScript?

Excellent question! When you type the code example with the ES6 `Barbarian` class in your TypeScript editor of choice you'll be surprised to find that the `this.name`, `this.hp` and `this.equipsWeapon` declarations result in a TypeScript compiler error. *What?* I thought that every piece of JavaScript was valid TypeScript and this is perfectly valid ES6 code. *What's happening? Have I been living a lie?*

The reasons for these errors is that TypeScript has different levels of correctness:

- In the first level the TypeScript compiler examines whether the code is syntactically correct before applying type annotations. If it is, then it is capable of performing the transpilation and emitting correct JavaScript code (this is the case for the issue we've just discovered regarding ES6 classes).
- In the second level the TypeScript compiler takes a look at the type annotations. According to TypeScript's type system, the PrivateBarbarian doesn't have any property name (properties are declared within the body of a class) and therefore it shows the error *[ts] Property 'name' does not exist on type 'PrivateBarbarian'*.
- In the third level enabled via the compiler flag --noImplicitAny the TypeScript compiler will become very strict and won't assume that the type of a non annotated variable is any. That is, it will require that all variables, properties and methods be typed.

So in our ES6 example, TypeScript understands your code as valid ES6 and will be able to transpile your code into JavaScript but according to TypeScript's type system you should refactor your class and move the class members inside the class body.

Enums

Another great feature in TypeScript are enums. Enums are a common data type in statically typed languages like C# and Java that are used to represent a finite number of things in an strongly typed fashion.

Imagine that you want to express all the different Schools of Elemental Magic: Fire, Water, Air and Earth. When you create diverse elemental spells, these will belong to some of several of these schools and will have advantages and disadvantages against spells of other schools. For instance, a fireball spell could look like this:

```
const fireballSpell = {
  type: 'fire',
  damage: 30,
  cast(target){
    const actualDamage = target.inflictDamage(this.damage,
                                               this.type);
    console.log(`A huge fireball springs from your ` +
      `fingers and impacts ${target} (-${actualDamage}hp)`);
  }
};
```

The `target.inflictDamage` would calculate the `actualDamage` inflicted on a target by taking into account the target resistance to a specific elemental magic or whether it has protective spells against it.

The problem with this example is that strings aren't very intentional nor provide a lot of information about the Schools of Elemental Magic that are available. In the example above it'd be very easy to have a typo and misspell the string 'fire' for something else.

An improvement over the previous approach is to use an object to encapsulate all available options:

```
const schoolsOfElementalMagic = {
  fire: 'fire',
  water: 'water',
  air: 'air',
  earth: 'earth'
};
```

And now we can rewrite our previous example:

```
const fireballSpell = {
  type: schoolsOfElementalMagic.fire,
  damage: 30,
  cast(target){
    const actualDamage = target.inflictDamage(this.damage,
                                              this.type);
    console.log(`A huge fireball springs from your ` +
        `fingers and impacts ${target} (-${actualDamage}hp)`);
  }
};
```

Awesome! That's much better than the magic string we had earlier. But it's still susceptible to typos and there's nothing stopping you from writing `type: 'banana'` inside your spell.

That's where TypeScript enums come in. They give you a statically and strongly typed way to represent a limited collection of things or states. A `SchoolsOfMagic` enum could look like this:

```
enum SchoolsOfMagic {
  Fire,
  Water,
  Air,
  Earth
}
```

This enum allows us to specify an interface that represents the shape of a `Spell`. Note how a valid `Spell` has a `type` property whose type is the enumeration `SchoolsOfMagic` we just created:

TypeScript

```
// now we can define a Spell interface
interface Spell {
  type: SchoolsOfMagic,
  damage: number,
  cast(target: any);
}
```

 Interfaces?

Interfaces are another new feature in TypeScript. They allow you to define arbitrary types that result in more intentional code and enrich your developer experience. We'll learn more about interfaces later in this chapter.

When we now define a new spell TypeScript will enforce that the type provided for the spell is of type SchoolsOfMagic, and not only that, when using an editor such as Visual Studio Code it will give us all the available options (Fire, Water, Air and Earth) via statement completion.

```
const enumifiedFireballSpell: Spell = {
  type: SchoolsOfMagic.Fire,
  damage: 30,
  cast(target){
    const actualDamage = target.inflictDamage(this.damage,
                                              this.type);
    console.log(`A huge fireball springs from your ` +
        `fingers and impacts ${target} (-${actualDamage}hp)`);
  }
}
```

If we were to type anything else than the SchoolOfMagic enum (for instance, a string) TypeScript would warn us instantly with the following error message:

TypeScript

```
// providing other than a SchoolsOfMagic enum would result in error:
// [ts]
//    Type
//    '{ type: string; damage: number; cast(target: any): void; }'
//    is not assignable to type 'Spell'.
//    Types of property 'type' are incompatible.
//    Type 'string' is not assignable to type 'SchoolsOfMagic'.
```

When transpiled to JavaScript enums result in the following code:

```
var SchoolsOfMagic;
(function (SchoolsOfMagic) {
    SchoolsOfMagic[SchoolsOfMagic["Fire"] = 0] = "Fire";
    SchoolsOfMagic[SchoolsOfMagic["Water"] = 1] = "Water";
    SchoolsOfMagic[SchoolsOfMagic["Air"] = 2] = "Air";
    SchoolsOfMagic[SchoolsOfMagic["Earth"] = 3] = "Earth";
})(SchoolsOfMagic || (SchoolsOfMagic = {}));
```

At first sight it may look a little bit daunting. But let's decompose it into smaller statements:

```
// Set 'Fire' property in SchoolsOfMagic to 0
SchoolsOfMagic["Fire"] = 0;

// it evaluates to 0 so that this:
SchoolsOfMagic[SchoolsOfMagic["Fire"] = 0] = "Fire";
// is equivalent to:
SchoolsOfMagic[0] = "Fire";
// which means set '0' property in SchoolsOfMagic to 0
```

So an enum represents a two-way mapping between numbers and strings with the enum name. Just like you can specify the names, you can select the numbers when declaring the enum:

```
// Start in 1 and increase numbers
enum SchoolsOfMagic {
  Fire=1,
  Water,
  Air,
  Earth
}

// Explicitly set all numbers
enum SchoolsOfMagic {
  Fire=2,
  Water=4,
  Air=6,
  Earth=8
}

// Computed enums
enum SchoolsOfMagic {
  Fire=1,
  Water=Fire*2,
  Air=2,
  Earth=Air*2
}
```

Whenever we don't want for the transpiled JavaScript to contain reference to enums (for instance, in a constrained environment were we want to ship less code) we can use `const` enums. The following enum definition will not be transpiled to JavaScript:

```
const enum SchoolOfMagic {
  Fire,
  Water,
  Air,
  Earth
}
```

Instead it will be inlined and any reference to `Fire`, `Water`, `Air` and `Earth` will be replaced by a number. In this case 0, 1, 2, 3 respectively.

Still prefer strings? Check This String Literal Types

If you still prefer vanilla strings TypeScript has the ability to create types based on a series of specific valid strings. An equivalent for our schools of magic could look like this:

```
type SchoolsOfMagic = "fire" | "earth" | "air" | "water";
```

Again we define an interface in terms of this new type:

```
interface Spell {
  type: SchoolsOfMagic,
  damage: number,
  cast(target: any);
}
```

And we're ready to create spells. Using anything other than the allowed strings will result in a transpilation error:

```
const FireballSpell: Spell = {
  type: "necromancy",
  damage: 30,
  cast(target){
    const actualDamage = target.inflictDamage(this.damage, this.type\
);
    console.log(`A huge fireball springs from your ` +
        `fingers and impacts ${target} (-${actualDamage}hp)`);
  }
}
// => [ts]
// Type '{ type: "necromancy"; damage: number;
//        cast(target: any): void; }'
// is not assignable to type 'SpellII'.
//   Types of property 'type' are incompatible.
//     Type '"necromancy"' is not assignable to type 'SchoolsOfMagicII'.
```

Object Spread and Rest

In JavaScript-mancy: Getting Started we saw **rest parameters** and **the spread operator** brought by ES6.

As you can probably remember, *rest parameters* improve the developer experience of declaring functions with multiple arguments [118]. Instead of using the arguments object like we used to do prior to ES6:

```
function obliterate(){
  // Unfortunately arguments is not an array :0
  // so we need to convert it ourselves
  var victims = Array.prototype.slice.call(arguments,
                      /* startFromIndex */ 0);

  victims.forEach(function(victim){
    console.log(victim + " wiped off of the face of the earth");
  });
  console.log('*Everything* has been obliterated, ' +
              'oh great master of evil and deceit!');
}
```

We can use rest syntax to collect all incoming arguments directly into an array `victims`:

```
function obliterate(...victims){
  victims.forEach(function(victim){
    console.log(`${victim} wiped out of the face of the earth`);
  });
  console.log('*Everything* has been obliterated, ' +
              'oh great master of evil and deceit!');
}
```

On the other hand the *spread operator* works sort of in an opposite way to *rest parameters*. Instead of taking a variable number of

---

[118] Like params in C#.

TypeScript 397

arguments and packing them into an array, the spread operator takes an array and expands it into its compounding items.

Following this principle the spread operator has many use cases[119]. Like concatenating arrays:

```
let knownFoesLevel1 = ['rat', 'rabbit'];
let newFoes = ['globin', 'ghoul'];
let knownFoesLevel2 = [...knownFoesLevel1, ...newFoes];
```

Or cloning them:

```
let foes = ['globin', 'ghoul'];
let clonedFoes = [...foes];
```

Object Spread and Rest brings this same type of functionality that is available in arrays to objects.

A great use case for the **Object spread operator** are mixins. In previous chapters we used `Object.assign` to mix the properties of two or more different objects. For instance, in this `Wizard` factory function we mix the wizard properties with mixins that encapsulate behaviors to identify something by name and cast spells:

```
function Wizard(element, mana, name, hp){
  let wizard = {element,
                mana,
                name,
                hp};
  Object.assign(wizard,
                canBeIdentifiedByName,
                canCastSpells);
  return wizard;
}
```

We can rewrite the example above using object spread as follows:

---

[119] Go back and review JavaScript-mancy: Getting Started for lots more of use cases!

```
function Wizard(element, mana, name, hp){
  let wizard = {element,
                mana,
                name,
                hp};

  // now we use object spread
  return {...wizard,
          ...canBeIdentifiedByName,
          ...canCastSpells
         };
}
```

The object spread operator essentially says: *get all properties of wizard, canBeIdentifiedByName and canCastSpells and put them together within the same object.* If there are any properties that have the same name, the last one wins and overwrites the first.

The opposite to object spread are object rest parameters. They work in a similar fashion to ES6 rest parameters and are particularly helpful together with ES6 destructuring.

If you remember, we used destructuring and rest parameters to extract elements from an array:

```
let [first, second, ...rest] = ['dragon', 'chimera', 'harpy', 'medus\
a'];
console.log(first);  // => dragon
console.log(second); // => chimera
console.log(rest);   // => ['harpy', 'medusa']
```

With the Object Spread Operator we can follow the same pattern to extract and collect properties from objects:

```
1  let {name, type, ...stats} = {
2    name: 'Hammer of the Morning',
3    type: 'two-handed war hammer',
4    weight: '40 pounds',
5    material: 'nephirium',
6    state: 'well kept'
7  };
8  console.log(name); // => Hammer of Morning
9  console.log(type); // => two-handed war hammer
10 console.log(stats);
11 // => {weight: '40 pounds',
12 //     material: 'nephirium',
13 //     state: 'well kept'}
```

And There's More!

There's a lot more features in TypeScript that expand on ES6 either via early implementation of ESnext features that are currently in a proposal stage (like async/await or decorators) or via entirely new features like the ones we've seen related to classes and enums.

If you're interested into learning more about TypeScript then I encourage you to take a look at the TypeScript handbook[120] and at the release notes[121] both of which provide detailed information about what TypeScript has in store for you.

Type Annotations In TypeScript

Type annotations are TypeScript's bread and butter and provide yet a new level of meta-programming in JavaScript: type meta-programming. Type annotations give you the ability to create a better developer experience for you and your team by ways of shorter feedback loops, compile time errors and API discoverability.

Type annotations in TypeScript don't stop at simple primitive types like string or number. You can specify the type of arrays:

---

[120]http://bit.ly/ts-handbook
[121]http://bit.ly/ts-whats-new

TypeScript

```
// An array of strings
let saddleBag: string[] = [];
saddleBag.push('20 silvers');
saddleBag.push('pair of socks');

saddleBag.push(666);
// => [ts] Argument of type '666' is not assignable
//        to parameter of type 'string'.
```

and tuples:

```
// A tuple of numbers
let position : [number, number];
position = [1, 1];
position = [2, 2];

// position = ['orange', 'delight'];
// => [ts] Type '[string, string]' is not
//    assignable to type '[number, number]'.
//    Type 'string' is not assignable to type 'number'.
```

functions:

```
// a predicate function that takes numbers and returns a boolean
let predicate: (...args: number[]) => boolean;
predicate = (a, b) => a > b
console.log(`1 greated than 2? ${predicate(1, 2)}`);
// => 1 greated than 2? false

predicate = (text:string) => text.toUpperCase();
// => [ts] Type '(text: string) => string' is not assignable
//        to type '(...args: number[]) => boolean'.
//    Types of parameters 'text' and 'args' are incompatible.
//    Type 'number' is not assignable to type 'string'.
```

and even objects:

TypeScript

```
function frost(minion: {hitPoints: number}) {
  const damage = 10;
  console.log(`${minion} is covered in frozy icicles (- ${damage} hp\
)`);
  minion.hitPoints -= damage;
}
```

The {hitPoints: number} represents and object that has a hit-Points property of type number. We can cast a frost spell on a dangerous foe that must comply with the required contract - that of having a hitPoints property:

```
const duck = {
  toString(){ return 'a duck';},
  hitPoints: 100
};

frost(duck);
// => a duck is covered in frozy icicles (-10hp)
```

If the object frozen doesn't satisfy the requirements, TypeScript will alert us instantly:

```
const theAir = {
    toString(){ return 'air';}
};
frost(theAir);
// => [ts] Argument of type '{ toString(): string; }'
//     is not assignable to parameter
//       of type '{ hitPoints: number; }'.
// Property 'hitPoints' is missing in type '{ toString(): string; }'.
```

An even better way to annotate objects is through **interfaces**.

TypeScript Interfaces

Interfaces are reusable and less verbose than straight object type annotations. A Minion interface could be described as follows:

```
interface Minion {
    hitPoints: number;
}
```

We could use this new interface to update our frost function:

```
function frost(minion: Minion){
  const damage = 10;
  console.log(`${minion} is covered in frozy icicles (-${damage} hp)\
`);
  minion.hitPoints -= damage;
}
```

Looks nicer, doesn't it? An interesting fact about **interfaces** is that they are entirely a TypeScript artifact whose only application is within the realm of type annotations and the TypeScript compiler. Because of that, **interfaces** are not transpiled into JavaScript. If you transpile the code above you'll be surprised to see that the resulting JavaScript has no mention of `Minion`:

```
function frost(minion) {
    var damage = 10;
    console.log(minion + " is covered in frozy icicles (-" + damage \
+ " hp)");
    minion.hitPoints -= damage;
}
```

This points to the fact that interfaces are a lightweight approach to adding type annotations to your codebase, reaping the benefits during development without having any negative impact in the code that runs on the browser.

Let's test our new `frost` function and the `Minion` interface with different types of arguments and see how they behave. Bring on the `duck` from our previous example!

TypeScript

```
1   // const duck = {
2   //   toString(){ return 'duck';},
3   //   hitPoints: 100
4   // };
5   frosty(duck);
6   // => duck is covered in frozy icicles (-10hp)
```

That seems to work perfectly. If we try with a class that represents a `Tower` and has a `hitPoints` and a `defense` property it seems to work as well:

```
1   class Tower {
2       constructor(public hitPoints=500, public defense=100){}
3       toString(){ return 'a mighty tower';}
4   }
5   const tower = new Tower();
6
7   frosty(tower);
8   // => a mighty tower is covered in frozy icicles (-10hp)
```

And so does a simple object literal with the `hitPoints` property:

```
1   frosty({hitPoints: 100});
2   // => [object Object] is covered in frozy icicles (-10hp)
```

However if we use an object literal that has another property in addition to `hitPoints` the compiler throws an error:

```
1   frosty({hitPoints: 120, toString(){ return 'a bat';}})
2   // => doesn't compile
3   // => Argument of type '{ hitPoints: number; toString(): string; }'
4   //    is not assignable to parameter of type 'Minion'.
5   //    Object literal may only specify known properties,
6   //    and 'toString' does not exist in type 'Minion'.
```

The error message seems to be very helpful. It says that with object literals I may only specify known properties and that `toString` doesn't exist in `Minion`. So what happens if I store the object literal in a variable `aBat`?

```
1  let aBat = {
2      hitPoints: 120,
3      toString(){ return 'a bat';}
4  };
5  frosty(aBat);
6  // => a bat is covered in frozy icicles (-10hp)
```

It works! Interesting, from these experiments it looks like TypeScript will consider a `Minion` to be any object that satisfies the contract specified by the interface, that is, to have a `hitPoints` property of type `number`.

However, it looks like when you use an object literal TypeScript has a somewhat more strict set of rules and it expects an argument that exactly matches the `Minion` interface. So what is a `Minion` exactly? When TypeScript encounters an arbitrary object, how does it determine whether it is a `Minion` or not?

It follows the rules of structural typing.

Structural Typing

Structural typing is a type system where type compatibility and equivalence are determined by the structure of the types being compared, that is, their properties.

For instance, following structural typing all of the types below are equivalent because they have the same structure (the same properties):

TypeScript

```typescript
// an interface
interface Wizard {
  hitPoints: number;
  toString(): string;
  castSpell(spell:any, targets: any[]);
}

// an object literal
const bard = {
  hitPoints: 120,
  toString() { return 'a bard';},
  castSpell(spell: any, ...targets: any[]){
    console.log(`${this} cast ${spell} on ${targets}`);
    spell.cast(targets);
  }
}

// a class
class MagicCreature {
  constructor(public hitPoints: number){}
  toString(){ return "magic creature";}
  castSpell(spell: any, ...targets: any[]){
    console.log(`${this} cast ${spell} on ${targets}`);
    spell.cast(targets);
  }
}
```

Which you can verify using this snippet of code:

```typescript
let wizard: Wizard = bard;
let anotherWizard: Wizard = new MagicCreature(120);
```

In contrast, languages like C# or Java have what we call a **nominal type system**. In nominal type systems, type equivalence is based on the names of types and explicit declarations, where a MagicCreature is a Wizard, if and only if, the class implements the interface explicitly.

Structural typing is awesome for JavaScript developers because it behaves very much like duck typing that is such a core feature to

TypeScript 406

JavaScript object-oriented programming model. It is still great for C#/Java developers as well because they can enjoy C#/Java features like interfaces, classes and compile-time feedback but with a higher degree of freedom and flexibility.

There's still one use case that doesn't fit the structural typing rule we just described. If you remember the examples from the previous section, object literals seem to be an exception to the structural typing rule:

```
frosty({hitPoints: 120, toString(){ return 'a bat';}})
// => doesn't compile
// => Argument of type '{ hitPoints: number; toString(): string; }'
//    is not assignable to parameter of type 'Minion'.
//    Object literal may only specify known properties,
//    and 'toString' does not exist in type 'Minion'.
```

Why does that happen? It happens in order to prevent developer mistakes.

The TypeScript compiler designers considered that using object literals like this can be prone to errors and mistakes (like typos, imagine writing `hitPoitns` instead of `hitPoints`). That is why when using object literals in this fashion the TypeScript compiler will be extra diligent and perform **excess property checking**. Under this special mode TypeScript will be inclined to be extra careful and will flag any additional property that the function `frosty` doesn't expect. Everything in the hopes of helping you avoid unnecessary mistakes.

If you are sure that your code is correct, you can quickly tell the TypeScript compiler that there's no problem by explicitly casting the object literal to the desired type or storing it in a variable as we saw earlier:

```
frosty({hitPoints: 120, toString(){ return 'a bat';}} as Minion);
// => a bat is covered in frozy icicles (-10hp)
```

Notice the as `Minion`? That's a way we can tell TypeScript that the object literal is of type `Minion`. This is another way:

```
frosty((<Minion>{hitPoints: 120, toString(){ return 'a bat';}}));
// => a bat is covered in frozy icicles (-10hp)
```

TypeScript Helps You With Type Annotations

Another interesting facet of TypeScript are its **type inference** capabilities. Writing type annotations not only results in more verbose code but it's also additional work that you need to do. In order to minimize the amount of work that you need to put in to annotate your code, TypeScript will do its best to infer the types used from the code itself. For instance:

```
const aNumber = 1;
const anotherNumber = 2 * aNumber;

// aNumber: number
// anotherNumber:number
```

In this code sample we haven't specified any types. Regardless, TypeScript knows without the shadow of a doubt that the `aNumber` variable is of type `number`, and by evaluating `anotherNumber` it knows that it's also of type `number`. Likewise we can write the following:

```
const double = (n: number) => 2*n;
// double: (n:number) => number
```

And TypeScript will know that the function `double` returns a number.

From Interfaces to Classes

So far we've seen how you can use type annotations in the form of primitive types, arrays, object literals and interfaces. All of these are TypeScript specific artifacs that disappear when you transpile your TypeScript code to JavaScript. We've also seen how TypeScript attempts to infer types from your code so that you don't need to expend unnecessary time annotating your code.

Then we have classes. Classes are a ES6/TypeScript feature that we can use to describe a domain model entity in structure and behavior, which contain a specific implementation, and which also serve as a type annotation.

In previous sections we defined an interface `Minion` that represented a thing with a `hitPoints` property. We can do the same with a class:

```
class ClassyMinion {
    constructor(public hitPoints: number) {}
}
```

And create a new `classyFrost` function to use this class as the argument type:

```
function classyFrost(minion: ClassyMinion){
    const damage = 10;
    console.log(`${minion} is covered in frozy icicles (-${damage} hp)\
`)
    minion.hitPoints -= damage;
}
```

We can use this function with our new `ClassyMinion` class and even with the previous `aBat` and `bard` variables because following the rules of structural typing all of these types are equivalent:

TypeScript

```
1  classyFrosty(new ClassyMinion());
2  // => a classy minion is covered in frozy icicles (-10hp)
3  classyFrosty(aBat);
4  // => a bat is covered in frozy icicles (-10hp)
5  classyFrosty(bard);
6  // => a bard is covered in frozy icicles (-10hp)
```

Normally we would have the `class` implement the desired interface. For instance:

```
1  class ClassyMinion implements Minion {
2    constructor(public hitPoints: number) {}
3  }
```

This wouldn't make a change in how this class is seen from a structural typing point of view but it does improve our developer experience. Adding the `implements Minion` helps TypeScript tell us whether we have implemented an interface correctly or if we're missing any properties or methods. This may not sound like much in a class with one single property but it's increasingly helpful as our classes become more meaty.

In general, the difference between using a `class` and using an `interface` is that the class will result in a real JavaScript class when transpiled to JavaScript (although it could be a constructor/prototype pair depending on the JavaScript version your are targeting).

For instance, the class above will result in the following JavaScript in our current setup:

```
var ClassyMinion = (function () {
    function ClassyMinion(hitPoints) {
        if (hitPoints === void 0) { hitPoints = 100; }
        this.hitPoints = hitPoints;
    }
    ClassyMinion.prototype.toString = function () {
        return 'a classy minion';
    };
    return ClassyMinion;
}());
```

This makes sense because, unlike an interface which is a made up artifact used only in the world of TypeScript type annotations, a class is necessary to run your program.

When do you use interfaces and when do you use classes then? Let's review what both of these constructs do and how they behave:

- **Interface**: Describes shape and behavior. It's removed during transpilation process.
- **Class**: Describes shape and behavior. Provides a specific implementation. It's transpiled into JavaScript

So both interfaces and class describe the shape and behavior of a type. And additionally, classes provide a concrete implementation.

In the world of C# or Java, following the **dependency inversion** principle we'd advice to prefer using interfaces over classes when describing types. That would afford us a lot of flexibility and extensibility within our programs because we would achieve a loosely coupled system where concrete types don't know about each other. We then would be in a position to inject diverse concrete types that would fulfill the contract defined by the interfaces. This is a must in statically typed languages like C# or Java because they use a nominal type system. But what about TypeScript?

As we mentioned earlier, TypeScript uses a structural type system where types are equivalent when they have the same structure, that is, the same members. In light of that, you could say that it doesn't really matter if we use interfaces or classes to denote types. If interfaces, classes or object literals share the same structure, they'll be equally treated, so why would we need to use interfaces in TypeScript? Here are some guidelines that you can follow when you consider using interfaces vs classes:

1. The single responsibility is a great rule of thumb to decrease the complexity of your programs. **Applying the single responsibility to the interface vs class dilemma we can arrive to use interfaces for types and classes for implementations.** Interfaces provide a very concise way to represent the shape of a type, whilst classes intermingle both the shape and the implementation which can make it hard to ascertain what the shape of a type is by just looking at a class.
2. interfaces give you more flexibility than classes. Because a class contains a specific implementation, it is, by its very nature, more rigid than an interface. Using interfaces we can capture finely grained details or bits of behavior that are common between classes.
3. interfaces are a lightweight way to provide type information to data that may be foreign to your application like data coming from web services
4. For types with no behavior attached, types that are merely data, you can use a class directly. Using an interface in this case will often be overkill and unnecessary. Using a class will ease object creation via the constructor.

So, in general, the same guidelines that we follow regarding interfaces in statically typed languages like C# and Java also apply to TypeScript. Prefer to use interfaces to describe types and use classes for specific implementations. If the type is just data with no behavior you may consider using a class on its own.

Advanced Type Annotations

In addition to what we've seeing thus far TypeScript provides more mechanisms to express more complex types in your programs. The idea is that, whichever JavaScript construct or pattern you use, you should be able to express its type via type annotations and provide helpful type information for you and other developers within your team.

Some examples of these advanced type annotations are:

- Generics
- Intersection and Union Types
- Type Guards
- Nullable Types
- Type Aliases
- String-literal Types

Let's take a look at each of them, why they are needed and how to use them.

Generics

Generics is a common technique used in statically typed programming languages like C# and Java to generalize the application of a data structure or algorithm to more than one type.

For instance, instead of having a separate `Array` implementation for each different type: `NumberArray`, `StringArray`, `ObjectArray`, etc:

TypeScript

```typescript
interface NumberArray {
  push(n: number);
  pop(): number;
  [index: number]: number;
  // etc
}

interface StringArray {
  push(s: string);
  pop(): string;
  [index: number]: string;
  // etc
}

// etc...
```

We use generics to describe an `Array` of an arbitrary type `T`:

```typescript
// note that `Array<T>` is already a built-in type in TypeScript
interface Array<T> {
  push(s: T);
  pop(): T;
  [index: number]: T;
  // etc
}
```

We can now reuse this single type definition by selecting a type for `T`:

```typescript
let numbers: Array<number>;
let characters: Array<string>;
// and so on...
```

And just like we used generics with interfaces, we can use them with classes:

TypeScript

```
class Cell<T> {
  private prisoner: T;

  inprison(prisoner: T) {
    this.prisoner = item;
  }

  free(): T {
    const prisoner = this.prisoner;
    this.prisoner = undefined;
    return prisoner;
  }
}
```

Finally, you can constrain the type T to only a subset of types. For instance, let's say that a particular function only makes sense within the context of Minion. You can write:

```
interface ConstrainedCell<T extends Minion>{
  inprison(prisoner: T);
  free(): T;
}
```

And now this will be a perfectly usable box:

```
let box: ConstrainedCell<MagicCreature>;
```

But this won't because the type T doesn't match the Minion interface:

```
let box: ConstrainedCell<{name: string}>;
// => [ts] Type '{ name: string; }'
//     does not satisfy the constraint 'Minion'.
//     Property 'hitPoints' is missing in type '{ name: string; }'.
```

Intersection and Union Types

We've seen primitive types, interfaces, classes, generics, a lot of different ways to provide typing information but flexible as these may be, there's still a use case which they have a hard time covering: Mixins.

When using mixins the resulting object is a mix of other different objects. The type of this resulting object is not a known type in its own right but a combination of existing types.

For instance, let's go back to the Wizard example that we had earlier:

```
function Wizard(element, mana, name, hp){
  let wizard = {element,
                mana,
                name,
                hp};

  // now we use object spread
  return {...wizard,
          ...canBeIdentifiedByName,
          ...canCastSpells
         };
}
```

We can decompose this into separate elements:

```
interface WizardProps{
  element: string;
  mana: number;
  name: string;
  hp: number;
}

interface NameMixin {
  toString(): string;
}
```

```
interface SpellMixin {
  castsSpell(spell:Spell, target: Minion);
}
```

How can we define the resulting Wizard type that is the combination of WizardProps, NameMixin and SpellMixin? We use **Intersection Types**. An Intersection Type allows us to define types that are the combination of other types. For instance, we could represent our Wizard using the following type annotation:

```
WizardProps & NameMixin & SpellMixin
```

And we could use it as a return type of our factory function:

```
let canBeIdentifiedByName: NameMixin = {
  toString(){ return this.name; }
};

let canCastSpells: SpellMixin = {
  castsSpell(spell:Spell, target:Minion){
    // cast spell
  }
}

function WizardIntersection(element: string, mana: number,
                            name : string, hp: number):
            WizardProps & NameMixin & SpellMixin {
  let wizard: WizardProps = {element,
                             mana,
                             name,
                             hp};

  // now we use object spread
  return {...wizard,
          ...canBeIdentifiedByNameMixin,
          ...canCastSpellsMixin
         };
}
```

TypeScript

```
26  const merlin = WizardIntersection('spirit', 200, 'Merlin', 200);
27  // merlin.steal(conan);
28  // => [ts] Property 'steal' does not exist
29  //    on type 'WizardProps & NameMixin & SpellMixin'.
```

In the same way that we have a Intersection Types that result in a type that is a combination of other types we also have the ability to make a type that can be any of a series of types, that is, either string or number or other type. We call these types **Union Types**. They are often used when you have overloaded functions or methods that may take a parameter with varying types.

Take a look at the following function that raises an skeleton army:

```
1   function raiseSkeleton(numberOrCreature){
2     if (typeof numberOrCreature === "number"){
3       raiseSkeletonsInNumber(numberOrCreature);
4     } else if (typeof numberOrCreature === "string") {
5       raiseSkeletonCreature(numberOrCreature);
6     } else {
7       console.log('raise a skeleton');
8     }
9
10    function raiseSkeletonsInNumber(n){
11      console.log('raise ' + n + ' skeletons');
12    }
13    function raiseSkeletonCreature(creature){
14      console.log('raise a skeleton ' + creature);
15    };
16  }
```

Depending on the type of numberOrCreature the function above can raise skeletons or skeletal creatures:

```
raiseSkeleton(22);
// => raise 22 skeletons

raiseSkeleton('dragon');
// => raise a skeleton dragon
```

We can add some TypeScript goodness to the `raiseSkeletonTS` function using union types:

```
function raiseSkeletonTS(numberOrCreature: number | string){
  if (typeof numberOrCreature === "number"){
    raiseSkeletonsInNumber(numberOrCreature);
  } else if (typeof numberOrCreature === "string") {
    raiseSkeletonCreature(numberOrCreature);
  } else {
    console.log('raise a skeleton');
  }

  function raiseSkeletonsInNumber(n: number){
    console.log('raise ' + n + ' skeletons');
  }
  function raiseSkeletonCreature(creature: string){
    console.log('raise a skeleton ' + creature);
  };
}
```

The `number | string` is a Union Type that allows `numberOrCreature` to be of type `number` or `string`. If we by mistake use something else, TypeScript has our backs:

```
raiseSkeletonTS(['kowabunga'])
// => [ts] Argument of type 'string[]' is not assignable
//        to parameter of type 'string | number'.
// Type 'string[]' is not assignable to type 'number'.
```

Type Guards

Union types raise a special case inside the body of a function. If `numberOrCreature` can be a number or a string, how does

TypeScript now which methods are supported? Number methods differ greatly from String methods, so what is allowed?

When TypeScript encounters a union type as in the function above, by default, you'll only be allowed to used methods and properties that are available in all the types included. It is only when you do a explicit conversion or include a type guard that TypeScript will be able to determine the type in use and be able to assist you. Fortunately, TypeScript will recognize type guards that are common JavaScript patterns, like the `typeof` that we used in the previous example. After performing a type guard `if (typeof numberOrCreature === "number")` TypeScript will know with certainty that whatever piece of code you execute inside that if block the `numberOrCreature` will be of type `number`.

Type Aliases

Another helpful mechanism that works great with Intersection and Union Types are Type Aliases. Type Aliases allow you to provide arbitrary names (aliases) to refer to other types. Tired of writing this Intersection Type?

```
WizardProps & NameMixin & SpellMixin
```

You can create an alias `Wizard` and use that instead:

```
type Wizard = WizardProps & NameMixin & SpellMixin;
```

This alias will allow you to improve the *Wizard* factory from previous examples:

```
1   function WizardAlias(element: string, mana: number,
2                       name : string, hp: number): Wizard {
3       let wizard: WizardProps = {element,
4                                  mana,
5                                  name,
6                                  hp};
7
8       // now we use object spread
9       return {...wizard,
10              ...canBeIdentifiedByNameMixin,
11              ...canCastSpellsMixin
12      };
13  }
```

More Type Annotations!

Although I've tried to be quite comprehensive in covering TypeScript within this final chapter of the book, there's plenty more features and interesting things that I won't be able to cover unless I write a complete book on TypeScript.

If you are interested into learning more about all the cool stuff that you can do with TypeScript type annotations then let me insist once more in the TypeScript handbook[122] and at the release notes[123].

Working with TypeScript in Real World Applications

So TypeScript is great, it gives you lots of great new features on top of ES6 and an awesome developer experience via type annotations, but how do you start using it in real world applications?

The good news is that you'll rarely need to create a TypeScript setup from scratch. The most popular front-end frameworks have built-in support for TypeScript. For instance, TypeScript is the main

---
[122] http://bit.ly/ts-handbook
[123] http://bit.ly/ts-whats-new

language of choice for Angular and starting a new project with Angular and TypeScript is as easy as using the Angular cli and typing:

```
$ ng new my-new-app
```

Likewise using React and the *Create React App* tool (also known as CRA) starting a React project with TypeScript takes only typing[124]:

```
$ create-react-app my-new-app --scripts-version=react-scripts-ts
```

If you use any of these options above you're good to go. In either case a new app will be bootstrapped for you and you'll be able to start building your Angular or React app with TypeScript.

On the other hand, if you, for some reason, need to start from scratch you'll find that there are TypeScript plugins[125] for the most common task managers or module bundlers like grunt, gulp or webpack. While integrating TypeScript into your tool chain there's one additional step that you may need to take in order to configure the TypeScript compiler: setting up your tsconfig file.

The `tsconfig.json` **File**

The `tsconfig.json` file contains the TypeScript configuration for your project. It tells the TypeScript compiler about all the details it needs to know to compile your project like:

- Which files to transpile
- Which files to ignore

---

[124]This command uses the TypeScript React Started in the background http://bit.ly/ts-react-starter

[125]http://bit.ly/ts-plugins

- Which version of JavaScript to use as a target of the transpilation
- Which module system to use in the output JavaScript
- How strict the compiler should be. Should it allow implicit any? Should it perform strict null checks?
- Which third-party libraries types to load

If you don't specify part of the information, the TypeScript compiler will try to do its best. For instance, not specifying any files to transpile will prompt the TypeScript compiler to transpile all TypeScript files (*.ts) within the project folder. Not specifying any third-party types will lead the TypeScript compiler to look for type definition files within your project (f.i. within ./node_modules/@types).

This is an example `tsconfig.json` from the TypeScript documentation that can give you an idea:

```
{
    "compilerOptions": {
        "module": "system",
        "noImplicitAny": true,
        "removeComments": true,
        "preserveConstEnums": true,
        "outFile": "../../built/local/tsc.js",
        "sourceMap": true
    },
    "include": [
        "src/**/*"
    ],
    "exclude": [
        "node_modules",
        "**/*.spec.ts"
    ]
}
```

For a full reference of all the available options take a look at the TypeScript documentation[126].

---
[126] http://bit.ly/tsc-options

In This Chapter's Examples We Didn't Use A tsconfig. How Come?

The TypeScript compiler `tsc` has two different modes of operation: with or without input files. When you don't specify input files while executing `tsc` the TypeScript compiler will try to find an available `tsconfig.json` file with its configuration. When you do specify input files the TypeScript compiler will ignore `tsconfig.json`. That is why in previous sections we didn't need to define a `tsconfig.json` file when we run `tsc hello-wizard.ts`.

Typescript and Third Party Libraries

Starting from TypeScript 2.0 installing type declarations for third party libraries is as easy as installing any other library via `npm`.

Imagine that you want to take advantage of ramda.js[127] a library with helpful utility functions with a strong functional programming flavor that we'll see in-depth in the functional programming tome of JavaScript-mancy.

You can add the library to your TypeScript project using npm:

```
# create package.json
$ npm init

# install ramda and save dependency
$ npm install --save ramda
```

And you can install the type declarations for that library using `@types/<name-of-library-in-npm>`:

---

[127] http://ramdajs.com/

```
$ npm install --save-dev @types/ramda
```

Now when you start working on your project within Visual Studio Code or your editor of choice you should get full type support when using ramda.js. Try writing the snippet below and verify how TypeScript helps you along the way:

```
import { add } from 'ramda';

const add5 = add(5);

console.log(`5 + 5: ${add5(5)}`);
console.log(`5 + 10: ${add5(1)}`);
```

All these type definitions come from the DefinitelyTyped[128] project and are pushed periodically to npm under the @types/ prefix as a convention. If you can't find the type declarations for a particular library use the TypeSearch[129] web app to find it (You can try stampit from the stamps chapter section for instance).

Concluding

And that is TypeScript! This was the longest chapter in the book but I hope that it was entertaining and interesting enough to carry you to the end. Let's make a quick recap so you get a quick reminder that'll help you remember all the TypeScript awesomeness you've just learned.

TypeScript is a superset of JavaScript that includes a lot of ESnext features and type annotations. By far, the defining feature of TypeScript are its use of types. Type annotations allow you to provide additional metadata about your code that can be used by

---
[128] http://definitelytyped.org/
[129] http://bit.ly/ts-search

the TypeScript compiler to provide a better developer experience for you and your team at the expense of code verbosity.

TypeScript is a superset of ES6 and expands on its features with a lot of ESnext improvements and TypeScript specific features. We saw several ESnext features like class members and the new Objects spread and rest operators. We also discovered how TypeScript enhances classes with parameter properties and property accessors, and brings a new Enum type that allows you to write more intentional code.

Type Annotations are TypeScript's bread and butter. TypeScript extends JavaScript with new syntax and semantics that allow you to provide rich information about your application types. In addition to being able to express primitive types, TypeScript introduces interfaces, generics, intersection and union types, aliases, type guards, etc... All of these mechanisms allow you to do a new type of metaprogramming that lets you improve your development experience via type annotations. Still adding type annotations can be a little daunting and a lot of work, in order to minimize this, TypeScript attempts to infer as much typing as it can from your code.

In the spirit of JavaScript and duck-typing, TypeScript has a structural typing system. This means that types will be equivalent if they share the same structure, that is, if they have the same properties. This is opposed to nominal typing systems like the ones used within C# or Java where type equivalence is determined by explicitly implementing types. Structural typing is great because it gives you a lot of flexibility and, at the same time, great compile-time error detection and improved tooling.

In the front-end development world we're seeing an increased adoption of TypeScript, particularly, as it has become the core language for development in Angular. Moreover, it is also available in most of the common front-end frameworks, IDEs, tex-editors and front-end build tools. It is also well supported in third-party libraries through type definitions and the DefinitelyTyped project, and installing type definitions for a library is as easy as doing an `npm install`.

From a personal perspective, one of the things I enjoyed the most about JavaScript coming from the world of C# was its terseness and the lack of ceremony and unnecessary artifacts. All of the sudden, I didn't need to write `PurchaseOrder purchaseOrder` or `Employee employee` any more, an employee was an `employee`, *period*. I didn't need to write a seemingly infinite amount of boilerplate code to make my application flexible and extensible, or fight with the language to bend it to my will, things just worked. As I saw the release of TypeScript I worried about JavaScript losing its soul and becoming a language as rigid as C# or Java. After experiencing TypeScript developing Angular applications, its optional typing, the great developer experience and, above all, the fact that it has structural typing I am hopeful. It'll be interesting to follow its development in the upcoming months and years. It may well be that all of us will end up writing TypeScript for a living.

```
mooleen.says('You shall only use types!?...');

bandalf.says("I've got my magic back... " +
  "but for some reason it won't... work");

mooleen.says("I, too, can feel the bond with the " +
  "currents of magic again");

randalf.says("The Order of the Red Moon...");

red.says("There are our weapons! Under the obelisk!");

/*
The group makes a precarious circle beside the obelisk as
the hordes of lizard-like beast surround them.
*/

randalf.says("types... Yes! " +
  "Now I remember, The Last Stand and the Sacred Order. " +
  "Their story lies between history and legend. " +
  "It is said that they cultivated an obscure " +
```

```
                "flavor of JavaScriptmancy. The legends say that " +
                "they expanded it and enriched it with types...");

            bandalf.says("Excellent. And what does that mean?");

            rat.says("It means we're dead");
            red.says("A glorious death!");

            randalf.says("Well they were a very guarded Order " +
                "and they were exterminated to the last woman " +
                "in The Last Stand or so the story says..." +
                "In the deep jungles of Azons.");

            mooleen.whispers("Azons...");

            /*
            The sisters surround her on the battlements,
            all wearing the black of the order in full armor.
            The fort has an excellent view of the thick,
            beautiful jungle below and of the unending hosts
            of lizardmen surrounding them.
            The Grand Commander shouts: 'To Arms sisters!'
            'For one last time!'
            */

            mooleen.says("Types... Types... Types!");
            mooleen.says("I remember...");
```

Exercises

 Experiment JavaScriptmancer!

You can experiment with these exercises and some possible solutions downloading the source code from GitHub[130].

---
[130] https://github.com/vintharas/javascriptmancy-code-samples

Earn Some Time! A wall of ice!

The beasts are quickly approaching, gain some breathing room by erecting an ice wall between them and the group. The wall should be at least 100 feet high, 7 feet deep and 700 feet long to be able to surround the group.

The Wall should satisfy the following snippet:

```
const iceWall = new Wall(MagicElement.Ice, {
                        height: 100,
                        depth: 7,
                        length: 700});

console.log(iceWall.toString());
// => A wall of frozen ice. It appears to be about 100 feet high
//    and extends for what looks like 700 feet.

iceWall.element = MagicElement.Fire;
// => [ts] Cannot assign to 'element' because it is
//        a constant or a read-only property.
iceWall.wallOptions.height = 100;
// => [ts] Cannot assign to 'height' because it is
//        a constant or a read-only property.
```

Hint: You can use an enum to represent the `MagicElement`, an interface to represent the `WallSpecifications` and a class for the `Wall` itself. Remember to add type annotations!

Solution

```
enum MagicElement {
  Fire = "fire",
  Water = "water",
  Earth = "earth",
  Air = "windy air",
  Stone = "hard stone",
  Ice = "frozen ice"
}
```

```
interface WallSpecs{
    readonly height: number,
    readonly depth: number,
    readonly length: number
}

class Wall {
    constructor(readonly element: MagicElement,
                readonly specs: WallSpecs){ }

    toString(){
        return `A wall of ${this.element}. It appears to be about ` +
            `${this.specs.height} feet high and extends for what ` +
            `looks like ${this.specs.length} feet.`;
    }
}

const iceWall = new Wall(MagicElement.Ice, {
                        height: 100,
                        depth: 7,
                        length: 700});

console.log(iceWall.toString());
// => A wall of frozen ice. It appears to be about 100 feet high
//    and extends for what looks like 700 feet long.

// iceWall.element = MagicElement.Fire;
// => [ts] Cannot assign to 'element' because it is
//         a constant or a read-only property.
// iceWall.wallOptions.height = 100;
// => [ts] Cannot assign to 'height' because it is
//         a constant or a read-only property.

world.randalf.gapes()
// => Randalf gapes

world.randalf.says('How?');
world.mooleen.says('I just remembered...');

world.randalf.says('Remember?');
world.randalf.says("You look very young for being millennia old");

world.mooleen.shrugs();
// => Moleen shrugs
world.mooleen.says("Brace yourselves... they're coming " +
    "beware if they open their jaws and seem to catch breath " +
```

TypeScript

```
56      "they breathe fire");
```

Freeze The Lizards!

You've earned some time. Now you can take this breather to observe the lizards, model them appropriately and craft a `frost` spell that will send them to the lizard frozen hell.

This is what you can observe:

```
giantLizard.jumps();
// => The giant lizard gathers strength in its
//    4 limbs and takes a leap through the air
giantLizard.attacks(red);
// => The giant lizard attacks Red with great fury
giantLizard.breathesFire(red);
// => The giant lizard opens his jaws unnaturally wide
//    takes a breath and breathes a torrent of flames
//    towards Red
giantLizard.takeDamage(Damage.Physical, 20);
// => The giant lizard has extremely hard scales
//    that protect it from physical attacks (Damage 50%)
//    You damage the giant lizard (-10hp)
giantLizard.takeDamage(Damage.Cold, 20);
// => The giant lizard is very sensitive to cold.
//    It wails and screams. (Damage 200%)
//    You damage the giant lizard (-40hp)
```

Create a `frost` spell that fulfills this snippet:

```
frost(giantLizard, /* mana */ 10);
// => The air surrounding the target starts quickly forming a
//    frozen halo as the water particles start congealing.
//    All of the sudden it explodes into freezing ice crystals
//    around the giant lizard.
//    The giant lizard is very sensitive to cold.
//    It wails and screams. (Damage 200%)
//    You damage the giant lizard (-2000hp)
```

Hint: Create a interface using the observations above and use that new type in your `frost` function. Reflect about the required contract to cause damage on an enemy.

TypeScript

Solution

```ts
enum DamageType {
  Physical,
  Ice,
  Fire,
  Poison
}

// We only need an interface that
// describes something that can be damaged
interface Damageable{
  takeDamage(damageType: DamageType, damage: number);
}

function frost(target: Damageable, mana: number){
  // from the example looks like damage
  // can be calculated based on mana
  const damage = mana * 100;
  console.log(
    `The air surrounding the target starts quickly forming a ` +
    `frozen halo as the water particles start congealing. ` +
    `All of the sudden it explodes into freezing ice crystals ` +
    `around the ${target.toString()}.`);
  target.takeDamage(DamageType.Ice, damage);
}

console.log('A giant lizard leaps inside the wall!');
// this method returns a Lizard object (see samples)
const giantLizard = world.getLizard();

world.mooleen.says('And that is as far as you go');

frost(giantLizard, /* mana */ 2);
// => The air surrounding the target starts quickly forming a
//    frozen halo as the water particles start congealing.
//    All of the sudden it explodes into freezing ice crystals
//    around the giant lizard.
//    The giant lizard is very sensitive to cold.
//    It wails and screams. (Damage 200%)
//    You damage the giant lizard (-400hp)
//    The giant lizard dies.

world.mooleen.laughsWithGlee();
// => Mooleen laughs with Glee
```

TypeScript

```
45  /*
46  More and more lizards make it into the fortified area.
47  Mooleen, Red, randalf and bandalf form a semicircle against
48  the obsidian obelisk and fight fiercely for every inch.
49  When the lizards are about to overwhelm the group a huge furry
50  figure flashes in front of them charging through the lizard
51  front line and causing enough damage to let the company regroup.
52  */
53
54  world.mooleen.says('What?');
55  world.rat.says('Happy to serve!');
56
57  world.mooleen.says('You can do that?!');
58  world.rat.says('Err... we familiars are very flexible creatures');
59
60  world.mooleen.says("Why didn't you say it before?");
61  world.rat.says("Oh... the transformation is incredibly painful");
62  world.rat.says("And I bet you'd want to ride on my back." +
63      "I'm not putting up with that");
```

Wholesale Destruction!

Killing the beasts one by one won't cut it. We need a more powerful spell that can annihilate them in groups. Design an `iceCone` spell that can impact several targets at once.

It should fulfill the following snippet of code:

```
1   iceCone(lizard, smallerLizard, greaterLizard);
2   // => Cold ice crystals explode from the palm of your hand
3   //    and impact the lizard, smallerLizard, greaterLizard.
4   //    The lizard is very sensitive to cold.
5   //    It wails and screams. (Damage 200%)
6   //    You damage the giant lizard (-500hp)
7   //    The smaller lizard is very sensitive to cold.
8   //    It wails and screams. (Damage 200%)
9   //    You damage the giant lizard (-500hp)
10  //    etc...
```

Hint: you can use rest parameters and array type annotations!

Solution

```typescript
function iceCone(...targets: Damageable[]){
  const damage = 500;
  console.log(`
Cold ice crystals explode from the palm of your hand
and impact the ${targets.join(', ')}.`);
  for(let target of targets) {
    target.takeDamage(DamageType.Ice, damage);
  }
}

iceCone(getLizard(), getLizard(), getLizard());
// => Cold ice crystals explode from the palm of your hand
// and impact the giant lizard, giant lizard, giant lizard.
// The giant lizard is very sensitive to cold.
// It wails and screams. (Damage 200%)
// You damage the giant lizard (-1000hp)
// The giant lizard dies.
// etc...

world.mooleen.says('Yes!');

/*
Mooleen looks around. She's fending off the lizards fine but
her companions are having some problems.

Red is deadly with the lance and shield but his lance,
in spite of of his massive strength, hardly penetrates
the lizards' thick skin.

Bandalf is slowly catching up and crafting ice spells
and Randalf, though, a master with the quarterstaff can
barely fend off the attacks from a extremely huge lizard.

Things start to look grimmer and grimmer as more lizards jump over
the wall around the obelisk.
*/

world.mooleen.says('I need to do something quick');
```

Empower Your Companions with Enchantments!

Things are looking grim. Your only chance is to empower your companions so that you can offer a strong united front against the growing host of enemies. Craft an `enchant` spell that can enchant weapons and armor with elemental properties.

The `enchant` spell should satisfy the following snippet of code:

```
quarterstaff.stats();
// => Name: Crimson Quarterstaff
// => Damage Type: Physical
// => Damage: d20
// => Bonus: +20
// => Description: A quarterstaff of pure red

enchant(quarterstaff, MagicElement.Ice);
// => You enchant the Crimson Quarterstaff with a frozen
//    ice incantation
//    The weapon gains Ice damage and +20 bonus damage

quarterstaff.stats();
// => Name: Crimson Quarterstaff
// => Damage Type: Ice
// => Damage: d20
// => Bonus: +40

cloak.stats();
// => Name: Crimson Cloak
// => Type: cloak
// => Protection: 20
// => ElementalProtection: none
// => Description: A cloak of pure red

enchant(cloak, MagicElement.Fire);
// => You enchant the Crimson Cloak with a fire incantation
//    The Crimson Cloak gains +20 fire protection

cloak.stats();
// => Name: Crimson Cloak
// => Type: cloak
// => Protection: 20
// => ElementalProtection: Fire (+20)
// => Description: A cloak of pure red
```

Hint: Use union types and type guards within the `enchant` spell to allow it to enchant both `Weapon` and `Armor`.

Solution

```typescript
class Weapon {
  constructor(public name: string,
              public damageType: DamageType,
              public damage: number,
              public bonusDamage: number,
              public description: string){}
  stats(){
    return `
Name: ${this.name}
Damage Type: ${this.damageType}
Damage: d${this.damage}
Bonus: +${this.bonusDamage}
Description: ${this.description}
`;
  }

  toString() { return this.name; }
}

enum ArmorType {
  Cloak = 'cloak',
  Platemail = 'plate mail'
}

interface ElementalProtection {
  damageType: DamageType;
  protection: number;
}

class Armor {
  elementalProtection: ElementalProtection[] = [];
  constructor(public name: string,
              public type: ArmorType,
              public protection: number,
              public description: string){}
  stats(){
    return `
Name: ${this.name}
Type: ${this.type}
Protection: ${this.protection}
ElementalProtection: ${this.elementalProtection.join(', ') || 'none'}
Description: ${this.description}
`;
  }
}
```

TypeScript

```
45      toString() { return this.name; }
46  }
47
48  function enchant(item: Weapon | Armor, element: MagicElement){
49      console.log(`You enchant the ${item} with a ${element} incantation\
50  `);
51      if (item instanceof Weapon){
52          enchantWeapon(item, element);
53      } else{
54          enchantArmor(item, element);
55      }
56  }
57  function enchantWeapon(weapon: Weapon, element: MagicElement){
58      const bonusDamage = 20;
59      weapon.damageType = mapMagicElementToDamage(element);
60      weapon.bonusDamage += bonusDamage;
61      console.log(`The ${item} gains ${bonusDamage} ` +
62                  `${weapon.damageType} damage`);
63  }
64  function enchantArmor(armor: Armor, element: MagicElement){
65      const elementalProtection = {
66          damageType: mapMagicElementToDamage(element),
67          protection: 20,
68          toString(){ return `${this.damageType} (+${this.protection})`}
69      };
70      armor.elementalProtection.push(elementalProtection);
71      console.log(`the ${item} gains ${elementalProtection.protection}\
72  ` +
73                  ` ${elementalProtection.damageType} incantation`);
74  }
75  }
76
77  function mapMagicElementToDamage(element: MagicElement){
78      switch(element){
79          case MagicElement.Ice: return DamageType.Ice;
80          case MagicElement.Fire: return DamageType.Fire;
81          default: return DamageType.Physical;
82      }
83  }
84
85  let quarterstaff = getQuarterstaff();
86  console.log(quarterstaff.stats());
87  // => Name: Crimson Quarterstaff
88  //    Damage Type: Physical
89  //    Damage: d20
90  //    Bonus: +20
91  //    Description: A quarterstaff of pure red
92
```

TypeScript

```
 93   enchant(quarterstaff, MagicElement.Ice);
 94   // => You enchant the Crimson Quarterstaff with a frozen ice incanta\
 95   tion
 96   //    The Crimson Quarterstaff gains 20 Ice damage
 97
 98   console.log(quarterstaff.stats());
 99   // Name: Crimson Quarterstaff
100   // Damage Type: Ice
101   // Damage: d20
102   // Bonus: +40
103   // Description: A quarterstaff of pure red
104
105   let cloak = getCloak();
106   console.log(cloak.stats());
107   // Name: Crimson Cloak
108   // Type: cloak
109   // Protection: 20
110   // ElementalProtection: none
111   // Description: A cloak of pure red
112
113   enchant(cloak, MagicElement.Fire);
114   // You enchant the Crimson Cloak with a fire incantation
115   // the Crimson Cloak gains 20 Fire incantation
116
117   console.log(cloak.stats());
118   // Name: Crimson Cloak
119   // Type: cloak
120   // Protection: 20
121   // ElementalProtection: Fire (+20)
122   // Description: A cloak of pure red
123
124   world.mooleen.says('Awesome! This will do!');
125
126   /*
127
128   As soon as Mooleen enchants the group's weapons and
129   armor the battle takes a different turn. Where previously
130   a lizard would've remained impassible after receiving a wound
131   now there's wails and shouts of beast pain surrounding
132   the group...
133
134   */
135
136   world.mooleen.says('haha! To Arms Sisters!');
137   world.red.says('What?');
```

Tome II. Epilogue

```
/*
 *
 * The fighting ensues for hours, spell after spell,
 * parrying after parrying, thrust after thrust.
 * At the end the group stands exhausted, back
 * against back. Each one supporting each other
 * because no one can stand on its own.
 *
 * They look tired, bloodied but defiant, surrounded
 * by seemingly unending numbers of lizard corpses.
 * As the last lizard falls Red smacks his battle lance
 * against his shield and starts laughing.
 */

red.says('This was glorious!');

mooleen.says('Now what... Do we gain our freedom back?' +
             "Isn't it how it typically works?");

mooleen.shouts("Isn't it how it works!!");

/*
The winged creatures in the alcoves and terraces above
shuffle and move disconcerted above.
*/

voice.thunders('#3. Only One Shall Remain');

mooleen.shouts("We won! We are the last one standing!");

voice.thunders('Only... **One**... Shall Remain');
```

```
randalf.says("Peachy. Now they want us to kill each other.");
```

End of book two. This one took me almost a year longer that I had anticipated. I really hope that you enjoyed it and learned a lot of interesting stuff along the way. Go JavaScript! :)

Have a wonderful day ahead! –

– Jaime, your humble servant

Thank you!

Thank you dear reader for choosing this book. You've given me the most valuable thing you have on this earth, your time, and I really hope that you've found that time that you've spent on this book valuable and enjoyable.

What follows is a recollection of all the people that have contributed to make this book better.

I would like to start by thanking my beloved wife Malin who's infinitely patient and supportive of me. She's the best listener in the history of mankind and an awesome person to exchange ideas with. Also my son Teo who has taught me a new meaning to the expression *unconditional love*, how infinitely cute babies are, that not all babies look the same and how to be super productive in small intervals of 14 minutes spread throughout the day.

My beloved parents Ricardo and Berta, and my sister Sofia. I'd like to thank my dad Ricardo for been loving, for pushing me to be excellent, and for been The Scourge of God all the times I slacked off throughout my life. I'd like to thank my mum Berta for her infinite love and care, and for her love of books that I seem to have inherited. Thank you Sofia for always taking care of me far better than I take care of you as an older brother.

I would also like to thank all the people that in smaller or greater measure helped me ensure the quality of this book. Infinite thanks to **Artur Mizera** for his numerous notes, comments, improvements, thorough reviews of the code samples and encouragement. Thank you **Nathan Gloyn** for being the first person to step up and volunteer to help me review the JavaScript-mancy series. Thank you **Andreas Backlund** for your helpful notes, advice, kind comments and encouragement. Thank you **Kari Helgason** for your thorough reviews of the first chapters of the book, thoughtful recommendations and encouraging comments.

Finally, I'd like to thank all the awesome members of the JavaScript, Angular and .NET communities, you public speakers, you open source contributors, you platform builders, you authors and bloggers, you conference or meetup organizers, you meetup attendees, you anonymous developer sitting at home, thank you for making the web such a wonderful and exciting place.

References and Appendix

Appendix A. On the Art of Summoning Servants and Critters, Or Understanding The Basics of JavaScript Objects

Things are ideas,
ideas are abstractions,
abstractions are objects,
objects are things.

That's the secret of JavaScript-mancy

> - Branden Iech,
> Meditations

Appendix A. On the Art of Summoning Servants and Critters, Or Understanding
The Basics of JavaScript Objects   445

```
1   mooleen.says('So... am I supposed to fix the world?');
2   randalf.says('Yep, you are our only hope. Let me show you something'\
3   );
4
5   /*
6   * Randalf begins walking towards a nearby dune and signals Mooleen t\
7   o follow.
8   * After 20 minutes of crossing dunes, up and down, and up and down a\
9   gain,
10  * they arrive to the top of higher dune and Randalf stops.
11  */
12
13  randalf.says('Tell me Mooleen. What do you see?');
14  mooleen.looksAround();
15  mooleen.says('I see sand... and more sand');
16
17  randalf.says("Welcome to the White City of Gigia, Gigia the magnific\
18  ent " +
19              "with its high white marble walls, its beautiful garden\
20  s, " +
21              "its bustling markets and its 1337 towers!!");
22
23  mooleen.looksAround();
24  /*
25    The wind blows and a tumbleweed slowly rolls beside them and cont\
26  inues
27    rolling until it disappears into the distance.
28  */
29
30  randalf.says("My point exactly... There's no trace of Gigia, of its \
31  walls," +
32              " its gardens, its markets, its towers, its people.");
33
34  mooleen.says("They did this?");
35
36  randalf.says("Yes, they did this and worse. That's why you'll need a\
37  n army");
```

An Army of Objects

Hello JavaScriptmancer! It is time to get an introduction to the
basics of objects in JavaScript. In this chapter you'll learn the beauty

of the object initializer and the nice improvements ES6 brings to objects. If you think that you already know this stuff, think twice! There is more than one surprise in this chapter and I promise that you'll learn something new by the end of it.

Let's get started! We'll start by concentrating our efforts in the humble object initializer. This will provide a foundation that we can use later when we come to the tome of object-oriented programming in JavaScript and prototypical inheritance.

Objects it is!

Object Initializers (a.k.a. Object Literals)

Experiment JavaScriptmancer!!

You can experiment with all examples in this chapter directly within this jsBin[131] or downloading the source code from GitHub[132].

The simplest way to create an object in JavaScript is to use an object initializer:

```
var critter = {}; // {} is an empty object initializer
```

You can add properties and methods inside your object initializer to your heart's content:

---

[131] http://bit.ly/javascriptmancy-objects-basics
[132] https://github.com/vintharas/javascriptmancy

Appendix A. On the Art of Summoning Servants and Critters, Or Understanding The Basics of JavaScript Objects

```javascript
critter = {
  position: {x: 0, y: 0},
  movesTo: function (x, y){
    console.log(this + ' moves to (' + x + ',' + y + ')');
    this.position.x = x;
    this.position.y = y;
  },
  toString: function(){
    return 'critter';
  },
  hp: 40
}
```

And, of course, if you call a method within the `critter` object it behaves as you have come to expect from any good self-respecting method:

```javascript
critter.moveTo(10, 10);
// => critter moves to (10,10)
```

As you saw in the introduction of the book, you can augment any[133] object at any time with new properties:

```javascript
critter.damage = 1;
critter.attacks = function(target) {
  console.log(this + ' rabidly attacks ' + target +
              ' with ' + this.damage + ' damage');
  target.hp-=this.damage;
};
```

And use these new abilities to great devastation:

---

[133] As long as it is not frozen via `Object.freeze`, which makes an object immutable to all effects and purposes.

```
var rabbit = {hp:10, toString: function(){return 'rabbit';}};

critter.attacks(rabbit);
// => critter rabidly attacks rabbit with 1 damage
```

Alternatively, you can access any property and method within an object by using the *indexing notation* via [ ]:

```
critter['attacks'](rabbit);
// => critter rabidly attacks rabbit with 1 damage
```

Although a little bit more verbose, this notation lets you use special characters as names of properties and methods:

```
critter['sounds used when communicating'] = ['beeeeeh', 'grrrrr', 't\
jjiiiiii'];
critter.saysSomething = function(){
  var numberOfSounds = this['sounds used when communicating'].length,
      randomPick = Math.floor(Math.random()*numberOfSounds);

  console.log(this['sounds used when communicating'][randomPick]);
};

critter.saysSomething();
// => beeeeeh (random pick)
critter.saysSomething();
// => tjjiiiii (random pick)
```

As you can see in many of the examples above, you can use the `this` keyword to reference the object itself and thus access other properties within the same object.

Appendix A. On the Art of Summoning Servants and Critters, Or Understanding
The Basics of JavaScript Objects   449

 JavaScript Arcana: This in JavaScript

From my experience, this is the biggest source of problems for a C# developer moving to JavaScript. We are so accustomed to work with classes and objects in C#, to be able to blindly rely in the value of this, that when we move to JavaScript, where the behavior of this is so completely undependable, we explode in frustration and anger.

Since this is such a big part of the JavaScript Arcana, I devote the whole next chapter to demystifying it for you. For now, just remember that when calling a method on a object using the dot notation, like in critter.moveTo, the value of this is mostly[134] trustworthy.

Getters and Setters

Getters and setters are an often overlooked feature within object initializers. You'll even find fairly seasoned JavaScript developers that don't know about their existence. They work exactly like C# properties and look like this:

---

[134] I say *mostly* because if you have a this keyword within a method and within a callback function (which I dare say is pretty common) then you are screwed. But worry not! You'll learn everything there is to learn about this in the next chapter.

Appendix A. On the Art of Summoning Servants and Critters, Or Understanding
The Basics of JavaScript Objects

```
var mouse = {
  strength: 1,
  dexterity: 1,
  get damage(){ return this.strength*die20() + this.dexterity*die8()\
;},
  attacks: function(target){
    console.log(this + ' ravenously attacks ' + target +
                ' with ' + this.damage + ' damage!');
    target.hp-=this.damage;
  },
  toString: function() { return 'mouse';}
}
```

Notice the strange `get damage()` function-like thingy? That's a getter. In this case, it represents the read-only property `damage` that is calculated from other two properties `strength` and `dexterity`.

```
mouse.attacks(rabbit);
// => mouse ravenously attacks rabbit with 19 damage!
mouse.attacks(rabbit);
// => mouse ravenously attacks rabbit with 15 damage!
```

Getters are extremely useful when you need to define computed properties, that is, properties described in terms of other existing properties. They save you from needing to keep additional and unnecessary state that brings the additional burden of keeping it in sync with the properties it depends on (in this case `strength` and `dexterity`).

We can also use a backing field to perform additional steps or validation:

Appendix A. On the Art of Summoning Servants and Critters, Or Understanding The Basics of JavaScript Objects

```
var giantBat = {
  _hp: 1,
  get hp(){ return this._hp;},
  set hp(value){
    if (value < 0) {
      console.log(this + ' dies :(')
      this._hp = 0;
    } else {
      this._hp = value;
    }
  },
  toString: function(){
    if (this.hp > 0){
      return 'giant bat';
    } else {
      return 'a dead giant bat';
    }
  }
};
```

In this example we ensure that the _hp property of the giant bat cannot go below 0 (because you can't be deader than dead, unless you are a necromancer that is):

```
mouse.attacks(giantBat);
// => "mouse ravenously attacks giant bat with 23 damage!"
// => "giant bat dies :("
console.log(giantBat.toString());
// => a dead giant bat
```

> ## JavaScript Arcana: Getters and Setters Are Not Augmenters
>
> You may have noticed that I have created a couple of new objects for these two examples instead of augmenting my beloved critter. Well, there was a reason for that. You cannot augment objects with getters and setters in the same way that you add other properties.

> In this special case, you need to rely in the `Object.defineProperty` or `Object.defineProperties` both methods also included in ES5. We will take a look at these two low level methods later in the tome of OOP when we examine the mysteries of object internals. Let's go back to object initializers!

Method Overloading

Method overloading within object initializers works just like with functions. As we saw in the previous chapter, if you try to overload a method following the same pattern that you are accustomed to in C#:

```javascript
var venomousFrog = {
  toString: function(){
    return 'venomous frog';
  },
  jumps: function(meters){
    console.log(this + ' jumps ' + meters + ' meters in the air');
  },
  jumps: function(arbitrarily) {
    console.log( this + ' jumps ' + arbitrarily);
  }
};
```

You'll just succeed in overwriting the former `jump` method with the latter:

```javascript
venomousFrog.jumps(10);
// => venomous frog jumps 10
// ups we have overwritten a the first jumps method
```

Instead, use any of the patterns that you saw in the previous chapter to achieve method overloading. For instance, you can inspect the arguments being passed to the `jump` function:

Appendix A. On the Art of Summoning Servants and Critters, Or Understanding The Basics of JavaScript Objects

```javascript
venomousFrog.jumps = function(arg){
  if (typeof(arg) === 'number'){
    console.log(this + ' jumps ' + arg + ' meters in the air');
  } else {
    console.log( this + ' jumps ' + arg);
  }
};
```

This provides a naive yet functioning implementation of method overloading:

```javascript
venomousFrog.jumps(10);
// => venomous frog jumps 10 meters
venomousFrog.jumps('wildly in front of you')
// => venomous frong jumps wildly in front of you
```

Creating Objects With Factories

Creating one-off objects through object initializers can be tedious, particularly whenever you need more than one object of the same "type". That's why we often use factories[135] to encapsulate object creation:

```javascript
function monster(type, hp){
  return {
    type: type,
    hp: hp || 10,
    toString: function(){return this.type;},
    position: {x: 0, y: 0},
    movesTo: function (x, y){
      console.log(this + ' moves to (' + x + ',' + y + ')');
      this.position.x = x;
      this.position.y = y;
    }
  };
}
```

---

[135] or the *new operator* that we'll see when we get to glorious tome of OOP

Once defined, we can just use it to instantiate new objects as we wish:

```
var tinySpider = monster('tiny spider', /* hp */ 1);
tinySpider.movesTo(1,1);
// => tiny spider moves to (1,1)


var giantSpider = monster('giant spider', /* hp */ 200);
giantSpider.movesTo(10,10);
// => giant spider moves to (10,10);
```

There's a lot of cool things that you can do with factories in JavaScript. Some of them you'll discover when you get to tome of OOP where we will see an alternative to classical inheritance in the shape of object composition via mixins. In the meantime let's take a look at **how to achieve data privacy**.

Data Privacy in JavaScript

You may have noticed by now that there's no access modifiers in JavaScript, no `private`, `public` nor `protected` keywords. That's because **every property is public**, that is, there is no way to declare a private property by using a mere object initializer. You need to rely on additional patterns with **closures** to achieve data privacy, and that's where factories come in handy.

Imagine that we have the previous example of our `monster` but now we don't want to reveal how we have implemented positioning. We would prefer to hide that fact from prying eyes and object consumers. If we decide to change it in the future, for a three dimensional representation, polar coordinates or who knows what, it won't break any clients of the object. This is part of what I call **intentional programming**, every decision that you make, the interface that you build, the parts that you choose to remain hidden

Appendix A. On the Art of Summoning Servants and Critters, Or Understanding The Basics of JavaScript Objects   455

or public, represent your intentions on how a particular object or API should be used. **Be mindful and intentional when you write code.** Back to the `monster`:

```
function stealthyMonster(type, hp){
  var position = {x: 0, y: 0};

  return {
    type: type,
    hp: hp || 10,
    toString: function(){return 'stealthy ' + this.type;},
    movesTo: function (x, y){
      console.log(this + ' moves stealthily to (' + x + ',' + y + ')\
');
      // this function closes over (or encloses) the position variab\
le
      // position is NOT part of the object itself, it's a free vari\
able
      // that's why you cannot access it via this.position
      position.x = x;
      position.y = y;
    }
  };
}
```

Let's take a closer look to that example. We have extracted the `position` property outside of the object initializer and inside a variable within the `stealthyMonster` scope (remember that functions create scopes in JavaScript). At the same time, we have updated the `movesTo` function, which creates its own scope, to refer to the `position` variable within the outer scope effectively creating a closure.

Because `position` is not part of the object being returned, it is not accessible to clients of the object through the dot notation. Because the `movesTo` becomes a closure it can access the `position` variable within the outside scope. In summary, we got ourselves some data privacy:

```
var darkSpider = stealthyMonster('dark spider');
console.log(darkSpider.position)
// now position is completely private
// => undefined

darkSpider.movesTo(10,10);
// => stealthy dark spider moves stealthily to (10,10)
```

ES6 Improves Object Initializers

ES6 brings some improvements to object initializers that reduce the amount of code needed to create a new object. For instance, with ES6 you can declare methods within objects using shorthand syntax:

```
let sugaryCritter = {
  position: {x: 0, y: 0},
  // from movesTo: function(x, y) to...
  movesTo(x, y){
    console.log(`${this} moves to (${x},${y})`);
    this.position.x = x;
    this.position.y = y;
  },
  // from toString: function() to...
  toString(){
    return 'sugary ES6 critter';
  },
  hp: 40
};

sugaryCritter.movesTo(10, 10);
// => sugary ES6 critter moves to (10, 10)
```

As you can appreciate from the movesTo and toString methods in this example above, using shorthand notation lets you skip the function keyword and collapse the parameters of a function directly after its name.

Appendix A. On the Art of Summoning Servants and Critters, Or Understanding The Basics of JavaScript Objects 457

Additionally you can apply shorthand syntax to object properties. When you write factory functions you'll often follow a pattern where you initialize object properties based on the arguments passed to the factory function:

```
function simpleMonster(type, hp = 10){
  return {
    type: type,
    hp: hp
  };
}
```

Where you have a little bit of redundant code in `type: type` and `hp: hp`. Property shorthand syntax removes the need to repeat yourself by letting you write the property/value pair only once. So that the previous example turns into a much terser factory method:

```
function simpleMonster(type, hp = 10){
  return {
    // with property shorthand we avoid the need to repeat
    // the name of the variable twice (type: type)
    type,
    hp
  };
}
```

And here you have a complete example where we use both method and property shorthand to get the ultimate sugary monster:

Appendix A. On the Art of Summoning Servants and Critters, Or Understanding The Basics of JavaScript Objects

```javascript
function sugaryStealthyMonster(type, hp = 10){
  let position = {x: 0, y: 0};

  return {
    // with property shorthand we avoid the need to repeat
    // the name of the variable twice (type: type)
    type,
    hp,
    toString(){return `stealthy ${this.type}`;},
    movesTo(x, y){
      console.log(`${this} moves stealthily to (${x},${y})`);
      position.x = x;
      position.y = y;
    }
  };
}

let sugaryOoze = sugaryStealthyMonster('sugary Ooze', /*hp*/ 500);
sugaryOoze.movesTo(10, 10);
// => stealthy sugary Ooze moves stealthily to (10,10)
```

Finally, with the advent of ES6 you can use any expression as the name of an object property. That is, you are no longer limited to normal names or using the square brackets notation that handles special characters. From ES6 onwards you'll be able to use any expression and the JavaScript engine will evaluate it as a string (with the exception of ES6 symbols which we'll see in the next section). Take a look at this:

```javascript
let theArrow = () => 'I am an arrow';

let crazyMonkey = {
  // ES5 valid
  name: 'Kong',
  ['hates!']: ['mario', 'luigi'],

  // ES6 computed property names
  [(() => 'loves!')()]: ['bananas'],
  [sugaryOoze.type]: sugaryOoze.type
  // crazier yet
```

Appendix A. On the Art of Summoning Servants and Critters, Or Understanding The Basics of JavaScript Objects 459

```
12    [theArrow]: `what's going on!?`,
13  }
```

This example let's you appreciate how any expression is valid. We've used the result of evaluating a function (`() => 'loves!')()`, a property from another object `sugaryOoze.type` and even an arrow function `theArrow` as property names. If you inspect the object itself, you can see how each property has been intrepreted as a string:

```
1  console.log(crazyMonkey);
2  // => [object Object] {
3  //     function theArrow() {
4  //       return 'I am an arrow';
5  //     }: "what's going on!?",
6  //     hates!: ["mario", "luigi"],
7  //     loves!: ["bananas"],
8  //     name: "Kong",
9  //   sugary Ooze: "sugary Ooze"
10 // }
```

And you can retrieve them with the [ ] (indexing) syntax:

```
1  console.log(crazyMonkey[theArrow]);
2  // => "what's going on!?"
```

Use cases for this particular feature? I can only think of some pretty far-fetched edge cases for dynamic creation of objects on-the-fly. That and using symbols as property names wich gracefully brings us to **ES6 symbols and how to take advantage of them to simulate data privacy.**

ES6 Symbols and Data Privacy

Symbols are a new type in JavaScript. They were conceived to represent constants and to be used as identifiers for object properties.

Appendix A. On the Art of Summoning Servants and Critters, Or Understanding
The Basics of JavaScript Objects

The specification even describes them as *the set of all non-string values that may be used as the key of an object property* [136]. They are immutable and can have a description associated to them.

You can create a *symbol* using the `Symbol` function:

```
let anUndescriptiveSymbol = Symbol();
console.log(anUndescriptiveSymbol);
// => [object Symbol]
console.log(typeof anUndescriptiveSymbol);
// => symbol
console.log(anUndescriptiveSymbol.toString());
// => Symbol()
```

And you can add a description to the *symbol* by passing it as an argument to the same function. This will be helpful for debugging since the `toString` method will display that description:

```
// you can add a description to the Symbol
// so you can identify a symbol later on
let up = Symbol('up');
console.log(up.toString());
// => Symbol(up)
```

Each symbol is unique and immutable, so even if we create two symbols with the same description, they'll remain two completely different symbols:

```
// each symbol is unique and immutable
console.log(`Symbol('up') === Symbol('up')?? ${Symbol('up') === Symb\
ol('up')}`);
// => Symbol('up') === Symbol('up')?? false
```

ES6 symbols offer us a new approach to data privacy in addition to closures. Properties that use a symbol as name (or key) can only

---

[136] that's from the one and only JavaScript specification ECMA-262 (http://bit.ly/es6-spec-symbols)

be accessed by a reference to that symbol (the very same symbol used to identify the property). Because of this special characteristic, if you don't expose a symbol to the outer world you have provided yourself with data privacy. Let's see how this works in practice:

```
function flyingMonster(type, hp = 10){
  let position = Symbol('position');

  return {
    [position]: {x: 0, y: 0},
    type,
    hp,
    toString(){return `stealthy ${this.type}`;},
    movesTo(x, y){
      console.log(`${this} flies like the wind from` +
                  `(${this[position].x}, ${this[position].y}) to (${\
x},${y})`);
      this[position].x = x;
      this[position].y = y;
    }
  };
}

let pterodactyl = flyingMonster('pterodactyl');
pterodactyl.movesTo(10,10);
// => stealthy pterodactyl flies like the wind from (0,0) to (10,10)
```

Since outside of the `flyingMoster` function we don't have a reference to the symbol `position` (it is scoped inside the function), we cannot access the position property:

```
console.log(pterodactyl.position);
// => undefined
```

And because each symbol is unique we cannot access the property using another symbol with the same description:

```
console.log(pterodactyl[Symbol('position')]);
// => undefined
```

If everything ended here the world would be perfect, we could use symbols for data privacy and live happily ever after. However, there's a drawback: The JavaScript `Object` prototype provides the `getOwnPropertySymbols` method that allows you to get the symbols used as properties within any given object. This means that after all this trouble we can access the position property by following this simple procedure:

```
var symbolsUsedInObject = Object.getOwnPropertySymbols(pterodactyl);
var position = symbolsUsedInObject[0];
console.log(position.toString());
// => Symbol(position)
// Got ya!

console.log(pterodactyl[position]);
// => {x: 10, y: 10}
// ups!
```

So you can think of symbols as a soft way to implement data privacy, where you give a clearer intent to your code, but where your data is not truly private. This limitation is why I still prefer using closures over Symbols.

Concluding

In this chapter you learned the most straightforward way to work with objects in JavaScript, the object initializer. You learned how to create objects with properties and methods, how to augment existing objects with new properties and how to use getters and setters. We also reviewed how to overload object methods and ease the repetitive creation of objects with factories. We wrapped factories with a pattern for achieving data privacy in JavaScript through the use of closures.

Appendix A. On the Art of Summoning Servants and Critters, Or Understanding
The Basics of JavaScript Objects   463

You also learnt about the small improvements that ES6 brings to
object initializers with the shorthand notation for both methods
and properties. We wrapped the chapter with a review of the new
ES6 Symbol type and its usage for attaining a soft version of data
privacy.

```
/*

This must be the weirdest piece of dune man has ever known. There's \
two wizards surrounded by a critter, a mouse, a giant bat, a venomou\
s frog, a monster, a teeny tiny and a giant spider, a stealthy monst\
er, a crazy monkey, a dark spider, a sugary critter?, an ooze and a \
ptero... a pterodactyl whatever that may be.


*/

randalf.says("And that's how you summon creatures to your cause! An \
army!");

mooleen.says("Ah□□");
mooleen.says("Summon them from where?");

randalf.says("hmm... good question!");
randalf.says("Powerful javascriptmancers can create stuff out of not\
hing");
randalf.says("Initiates summon creatures from..." +
             "wherever creatures come from");

randalf.says("There's a lot of sand here... why not create a sand go\
lem?");
```

Exercises

Experiment JavaScriptmancer!

You can experiment with these exercises and some possible solutions in this jsFiddle[137] or downloading the source code from GitHub[138].

Create a Sand Golem!

Use an object initializer to create a sand golem. You are welcome to use shorthand syntax if you so choose! It should satisfy the following snippet of code:

```
sandGolem.toString();
// (returns) => Giant Sand Golem
sandGolem.walksTo(1,1);
// => Giant Sand Golem walks to (1,1);
sandGolem.grabs('spider');
// => Giant Sand Golem grabs spider
sandGolem.grabs('monkey', 'venomous frog');
// => Giant Sand Golem grabs monkey and venomous frog
sandGolem.grabbedStuff;
// (returns) => ['spider', 'monkey', 'venomous frog']
```

Solution

```
mooleen.concentrates();

/*
A sudden wind appears from out of nowhere, a small whirlwind that su\
cks
```

---

[137] http://bit.ly/javascriptmancy-objects-basics-exercises
[138] https://github.com/vintharas/javascriptmancy-code-samples

Appendix A. On the Art of Summoning Servants and Critters, Or Understanding The Basics of JavaScript Objects

```
  6    the sand beside mooleen and grows, and grows, and grows until it bec\
  7    omes
  8    and imposing giant figure that vaguely resembles something human.
  9    */
 10
 11    let sandGolem = {
 12      position: {x: 0, y: 0},
 13      walksTo(x, y){
 14        console.log(this + ' walks to (' + x + ',' + y + ')');
 15        this.position.x = x;
 16        this.position.y = y;
 17      },
 18      toString(){
 19        return 'Giant Sand Golem';
 20      },
 21      grabbedStuff: [],
 22      grabs(...items){
 23        this.grabbedStuff.push(...items);
 24        console.log(this + ' grabs ' + items.join(' and '));
 25      }
 26    }
 27
 28    console.log(sandGolem.toString());
 29    // (returns) => Giant Sand Golem
 30    sandGolem.walksTo(1,1);
 31    // => Giant Sand Golem walks to (1,1);
 32    sandGolem.grabs('spider');
 33    // => Giant Sand Golem grabs spider
 34    sandGolem.grabs('monkey', 'venomous frog');
 35    // => Giant Sand Golem grabs monkey and venomous frog
 36    console.log(sandGolem.grabbedStuff);
 37    // (returns) => ['spider', 'monkey', 'venomous frog']
 38
 39    mooleen.says('voilOO!');
```

 ## How Much More Weight Can it Carry?

By the immutable laws of physics, a sand golem can only lift up to 40 items at once. Create a spaceAvailableOnBoard getter that retrieves the amount of space available in a golem at a given time.

Appendix A. On the Art of Summoning Servants and Critters, Or Understanding
The Basics of JavaScript Objects

Solution

```
let sandGolemImproved = {
  position: {x: 0, y: 0},
  walksTo(x, y){
    console.log(this + ' walks to (' + x + ',' + y + ')');
    this.position.x = x;
    this.position.y = y;
  },
  toString(){
    return 'Giant Sand Golem';
  },
  grabbedStuff: [],
  grabs(...items){
    this.grabbedStuff.push(...items);
    console.log(this + ' grabs ' + items.join(' and '));
  },
  get spaceAvailableOnboard(){
    const maxSpace = 40;
    return maxSpace - this.grabbedStuff.length;
  }
}

sandGolemImproved.grabs('pterodactyl');
// => Giant Sand Golem grabs pterodactyl
console.log(sandGolemImproved.spaceAvailableOnboard);
// => 39
```

 Golems for Everyone!

Write a factory function that allows you to create as many golems as you like. You should be able to name them during creation, otherwise it will be hard to keep track of them. You are welcome to use ES6 short-hand syntax if you so choose.

Appendix A. On the Art of Summoning Servants and Critters, Or Understanding
The Basics of JavaScript Objects

Solution

```
function SandGolem(name){
  return {
    name,
    position: {x: 0, y: 0},
    walksTo(x, y){
      console.log(this + ' walks to (' + x + ',' + y + ')');
      this.position.x = x;
      this.position.y = y;
    },
    toString(){
      return 'Giant Sand Golem (' + name + ')';
    },
    grabbedStuff: [],
    grabs(...items){
      this.grabbedStuff.push(...items);
      console.log(this + ' grabs ' + items.join(' and '));
    },
    get spaceAvailableOnboard(){
      const maxSpace = 40;
      return maxSpace - this.grabbedStuff.length;
    }
  };
}

let sand = SandGolem('sand');
let dune = SandGolem('dune');
let beach = SandGolem('beach');
sand.grabs(dune);
// => Giant Sand Golem (sand) grabs Giant Sand Golem (dune)

mooleen.says('hehe that was fun');
```

 Hide the Details

Update your sand golem to hide its `position` and `grabbedStuff` from external access.

Appendix A. On the Art of Summoning Servants and Critters, Or Understanding
The Basics of JavaScript Objects   468

Solution

```js
function SandGolem(name){
  let position = {x: 0, y: 0},
      grabbedStuff = [];
  return {
    name,
    walksTo(x, y){
      console.log(this + ' walks to (' + x + ',' + y + ')');
      position.x = x;
      position.y = y;
    },
    toString(){
      return 'Giant Sand Golem (' + name + ')';
    },
    grabs(...items){
      grabbedStuff.push(...items);
      console.log(this + ' grabs ' + items.join(' and '));
    },
    get spaceAvailableOnboard(){
      const maxSpace = 40;
      return maxSpace - grabbedStuff.length;
    }
  };
}

var shy = SandGolem('shy');
console.log(shy.position);
// => undefined
shy.walksTo(1,1);
// => Giant Sand Golem (shy) walks to (1,1)
console.log(shy.grabbedStuff);
// => undefined
shy.grabs('ooze');
// => Giant Sand Golem (shy) grabs ooze

randalf.says('Excellent! Now we are ready to start our journey');
mooleen.says('Where are we going?');
randalf.says('To the north! I have some friends left there');
mooleen.says('To the north then...');

/*
And to the north started the weirdest procession anyone has ever see\
n. Two wizards, a sand golem, sand, dune and beach, shy, a critter, \
a mouse, a giant bat, a teeny tiny and a giant spider, a crazy monke\
y...
```

Appendix A. On the Art of Summoning Servants and Critters, Or Understanding The Basics of JavaScript Objects

```
45    */
```

Appendix B. Mysteries of the JavaScript Arcana

Beware of any assumptions,
distrust any preconceptions,
forgo your experience,
and think with the mind of a beginner.

> - Appa Ojnh
> The White Sage

Appendix B. Mysteries of the JavaScript Arcana

```
/*
After weeks of travelling north Mooleen and Randalf arrive to a
green valley surrounded by majestic white-peaked mountains as
far as the eye can see. There's the beginning of a mountain trail
and two persons beside it waiting for them...
*/

randalf.says('Ah... the Misty Mountains. What a beautiful sight!');
randalf.says('Mooleen, I introduce you to zandalf and bandalf');
randalf.says('I trust them like if they were my brothers...');

randalf.says('...because they actually ARE my brothers');
mooleen.says('Ehem... I can see the resemblance');

/*
Randalf, Zandalf and Bandalf look nothing alike. Where Randalf is
tall and spindly, with a carefully trimmed beard and a good
natured resemblance, Zandalf is freakishly small and plump,
and Bandalf is... blue. Literally blue, like the sky in a
clear morning.
*/

randalf.says("Great! While we go up I'd like to tell you something");
randalf.says("I've noticed that some of your incantations have been \
misfiring");
mooleen.says('Misfiring? What? I know what I am doing... most of the\
 time');

randalf.says('So you meant to light that bale of hay on fire?');
mooleen.says('Yeeees');
randalf.says('And the cart beside it?');
mooleen.says('Yeeeeees');
randalf.says('And the two blocks of buildings surrounding it...');
mooleen.says('Yeee....');

randalf.says('What about my finest robes?');
mooleen.says('That was actually on purpose');

randalf.says('Mooleen...');
randalf.says('OK. I see that you are stumbling with some of the ' +
              'quirks and gotchas of JavaScript-mancy');
randalf.says('Let me give you a couple of tips');
```

A Couple of Tips About JavaScript Quirks and Gotchas

While JavaScript looks a lot like a C-like language, it does not behave like one in many ways. This, I would say, is the biggest reason why C# developers get so confused when they come to JavaScript.

If you've followed the book closely, you may have noticed that I have decided to call these unexpected behaviors the **JavaScript Arcana**. You have already seen several examples of these shadowy features thus far. Let's make a quick summary of them:

- Function scope and variable hoisting
- Array-like objects
- Function overloading

We'll start this chapter by making a short review of the quirks that you've already learned (repetition is a great tool for learning). And we'll continue by diving deeper into these other parts of the JavaScript Arcana:

- The sneaky `this` keyword
- Global scope as a default
- Type coercion madness
- JavaScript strict mode

We will focus particularly in the obscure behavior of the `this` keyword, our most dangerous foe. I expect that what you will learn in this chapter will save you from unmeasurable frustration in the future.

A Quick Refresher of the JavaScript Arcana 101

In *The Basics of JavaScript Functions* we saw how **JavaScript has function scope**. That is, as opposed to C# where every block of code creates a new scope, in JavaScript it is only functions that create new scopes. Every time you declare a variable through the `var` keyword it is scoped to its containing function. You also learned the concept of hoisting and how the JavaScript runtime moves your variable declarations to the top of a function body. Finally, you discovered how **ES6 brings the `let` and `const` keywords that give you the ability to declare block-scoped variables and forget about the headaches of hoisting and function-scoped variables.**

In Function Patterns: Arbitrary Arguments you learned about the `arguments` object. It can be accessed within every function to retrieve the arguments being passed to that function at runtime. You saw how the `arguments` object, although it looks like an array, it is actually what we call an array-like object. **Array-like objects can be enumerated, indexed and have a `length` property but they lack all array methods.** You also discovered **how to convert these objects to actual arrays using `Array.prototype.slice` (or `Array.from`)** and how the new ES6 *rest operator* solves the **arguments issue completely.**

In Function Patterns: Overloading you learned how you cannot overload JavaScript functions or methods in the same way that you do in C#. Instead, you can use several patterns to achieve the same effect: Argument inspection, options objects, ES6 default arguments or functional programming with polymorphic functions.

Now that we've warmed up to JavaScript weirdest features let's take a look at the behavior of `this`.

This, Your Most Dangerous Foe

 Experiment Javascriptmancer!!
You can experiment with all examples in this chapter directly within this Jsfiddle[139] or downloading the source code from GitHub[140].

One of the most common problems when a C# developer comes to JavaScript is that it expects `this` to work exactly as it does in C#. And She or He or Zie will write this common piece of code unaware of the terrible dangers that lurk just one HTTP call away...

```
function UsersCatalog(){
  this.users = [];
  getUsers()

  function getUsers(){
    $.getJSON('https://api.github.com/users')
    .success(function updateUsers(users){
      this.users.push(users);
      // BOOOOOOOM!!!!!
      // => Uncaught TypeError:
      //    Cannot read property 'push' of undefined
    });
  }
}
var catalog = new UsersCatalog();
```

In this code example we are trying to retrieve a collection of users

---
[139] http://bit.ly/javascriptmancy-javascript-arcana
[140] https://github.com/vintharas/javascriptmancy

from the GitHub API[141]. We perform an AJAX[142] request using jQuery `getJSON` and if the request is successful the response is passed as an argument to the `updateUsers` function.

The example throws an exception `cannot read property 'push' of undefined` which is the JavaScript version of our well known nemesis: The `NullReferenceException` (*we meet again*). Essentially, when we evaluate the `updateUsers` function, the `this.users` expression takes the value of `undefined`. When we try to execute `this.users.push(users)` we're basically calling the method `push` on nothing and thus the exception being thrown.

In order to understand why this is happening we need to learn how `this` works in JavaScript. In the next sections we will do just that. By the end of the chapter, when we have demystified `this` and become this-xperts, you'll be able to understand what is the cause of the error.

JavaScript Meets This

So `this` in JavaScript is weird. Unlike in other languages, **the value of `this` in JavaScript depends on the context in which a function is invoked**. Repeat. The behavior of `this` in JavaScript is not 100% stable nor reliable at all times, **it depends on the context in which a function is invoked**.

This essentially means that depending on how you call a function, the value of `this` inside that function will vary. We can distinguish between these four scenarios:

---

[141] http://bit.ly/github-api

[142] AJAX stands for `Asynchronously JavaScript` and `XML` and is a technology that allows you to get data from a server even after a web page has already been loaded. The significance and impact of AJAX in modern web development is huge because not only does it let you create highly interactive websites but also deliver a website in chunks as they are needed. Since its inception, browsers have implemented support for AJAX via the XMLHttpRequest object. Because of its complexity, I decided to use the simpler `$.getJSON`. In the near future, you'll be able to do AJAX requests using the improved `fetch` API. Yey!

- `this` and objects
- `this` unbound
- `this` explicitly
- `this` bound

This And Objects

In the most common scenario for an OOP developer we call functions as methods. That is, we call a function that is a property within an object using the dot notation.

If we have a `hellHound` spawned in the pits of hell with the ferocious ability of breathing fire:

```
// #1. A function invoked in the context of an object (a method)
var hellHound = {
  attackWithFireBreath: function(){
    console.log(this + " jumps towards you and unleashes " +
                "his terrible breath of fire! (-3 hp, +fear)");
  },
  toString: function (){ return 'Hellhound';}
}
```

When we call its `attackWithFireBreath` method using the dot notation `this` will take the value of the object itself:

```
hellHound.attackWithFireBreath();
// => Hellhound jumps towards you and unleashes
//    his terrible breath of fire! (-3 hp, +fear)
// 'this' is the hellHound object
```

Nothing strange here. This is the version of `this` we know and love from C#. Things get a little bit trickier in the next scenario.

This Unbound

In JavaScript you can do crazy things. Things like invoking a method without the context of the object in which it was originally defined. Since functions are values we can just save the `attack-WithFireBreath` method within a variable:

```
// #2. A function invoked without the context of its object
var attackWithFireBreath = hellHound.attackWithFireBreath;
```

And invoke the function via the newly created variable:

```
attackWithFireBreath();
// => [object Window] jumps towards you and unleashes
//    his terrible breath of fire! (-3 hp, +fear)
```

Ooops! What did just happen here? `this` is no longer the hell hound but the `Window` object. You may be asking yourself: *What?* And here comes the weird part that you need to remember: **Whenever you invoke a function without an object as context the `this` automatically becomes the `Window` object.**

The Window[143] object in JavaScript represents the browser window and contains the document object model (also known as DOM) an object representation of the elements within a website.

> ## JavaScript Strict Mode
> From ES5 onwards you can use strict mode (http://bit.ly/mdn-strict-mode) to get a better experience with JavaScript. Things that cause silent or unexpected errors and can be a headache to debug prior to ES5 throw explicit errors when you enable strict mode.
>
> You can enable strict mode by writing `'strict mode'`; at the

---

[143] You can find more information about the Window object and the DOM at MDN (http://bit.ly/mdn-window-object)

> top of a JavaScript file or function.
>
> With strict mode enabled the this object in this scenario will get the value of undefined. This will likely cause an error in your code and alert you about this unwanted behavior. Fail early, fail fast and fix your code as soon as possible.
>
> You can learn more about strict mode at the end of the chapter.

As a cool exercise, you can now take that free function and add it to another object zandalf different from the original:

```
// we could add the same method to another object:
var zandalf = {
  toString: function(){return 'zandalf';}
};
zandalf.attackWithFireBreath = attackWithFireBreath;
```

Then call it as a method with the dot notation:

```
zandalf.attackWithFireBreath();
// => zandalf jumps towards you and unleashes
//    his terrible breath of fire! (-3 hp, +fear)
// => 'this' is the jaime object
```

And again, when we invoke the original function in the context of an object, **even when it is another one different from the original, this takes the value of that object**.

Let's make a summary of what you've seen up until now:

1. Call a function in the context of an object and this will take the value of the object
2. Call a function without context and this will take the value of the Window object. Unless you are in *strict mode* in which case it will take the value of undefined.

This Explicitly

All functions in JavaScript descend from the `Function` prototype[144]. This prototype provides two helpful methods that allow you to explicitly set the context in which to execute a function: `call` and `apply`.

Take the `attackWithFireBreath` function from the last example. This time, instead of calling it directly, we use its `call` method and pass the object `zandalf` as an argument:

```
attackWithFireBreath.call(zandalf);
// => zandalf...
// => 'this' is zandalf
```

The object `zandalf` becomes the context of the function and thus the value of `this`. Likewise, if we call the `apply` method on the same function and pass an object `hellHound` as argument:

```
attackWithFireBreath.apply(hellHound);
// => hell hound...
// => 'this' is hellHound
```

We can verify how the object `hellHound` becomes the context of the function and the value of `this`.

But, what happens if the original function has paremeters? Worry not! Both `call` and `apply` take additional arguments that are passed along to the original function. Take this function `attackMany-WithFireBreath` that unleashes a terrible breath of fire on many unfortunate targets:

---

[144] http://bit.ly/mdn-function-prototype

```
function attackManyWithFireBreath(){
  var targets = Array.prototype.slice.call(arguments, 0);
  console.log(this + " jumps towards " + targets.join(', ') +
    " and unleashes his terrible breath of fire! (-3 hp, +fear)");
}
```

The `call` method let's you specify a list of arguments separated by commas in addition to the value of `this`:

```
attackManyWithFireBreath.call(hellHound, 'you', 'me', 'the milkman');
// => Hellhound jumps towards you, me, the milkman and unleashes
//    his terrible breath of fire! (-3 hp, +fear)
```

Likewise, `apply` takes an array of arguments:

```
attackManyWithFireBreath.apply(hellHound, ['me', 'you', 'irene']);
// => Hellhound jumps towards me, you, irene and
//    unleashes his terrible breath of fire! (-3 hp, +fear)
```

And that's how you can set the value of `this` explicitly. Let's recapitulate what we've learned so far:

1. Call a function in the context of an object and `this` will take the value of the object
2. Call a function without context and `this` will take the value of the `Window` object. Unless you are in *strict mode* in which case it will take the value of `undefined`.
3. Call a function using `call` and `apply` passing the context explicitly as an argument and `this` will take the value of whatever you pass in.

This Bound

As of ES5, the `Function` prototype also provides a very interesting method called `bind`. `bind` lets you create new functions that **always have a fixed context**, that is, a fixed value for this [145].

---

[145] Another cool use of `bind` is *partial application*, but we'll take a look at that when we get to the tome of functional programming.

> **Bind Doesn't Cause Side Effects**
>
> It is important to note that bind will not alter the original function at all. It will return a new function that is bound to the object given as an argument.

Let's use bind to set a fixed value for this in our original attackWithFireBreath function. bind will return a new function attackBound that will have this with a value of our choosing. In this case, it will be hellHound:

```
1  // As of ES5 we can bind the context of execution of a function
2  // FOR EVER
3  attackBound = attackWithFireBreath.bind(hellHound);
```

After using bind, the value of this is bound to the hellHound object even if you are not using the dot notation:

```
1  attackBound();
2  // => Hellhound jumps towards you and unleashes
3  //    his terrible breath of fire! (-3 hp, +fear)
4  // `this` is Hellhound even though I am not using the dot notation
```

Moreover, if you assign the attackBound method to another object and call it using the dot notation, the attackBound method is executed in the context of the original object hellHound. That is, after binding a function to a context with bind, the context will remain the same even after assigning the function to another object:

```
// the function is bound even if I give the function to another obje\
ct
zandalf.attackBound = attackBound;

zandalf.attackBound();
// => Hellhound ...
// `this` is Hellhound even though I am using dot notation
// with another object
```

Once a function is bound it is not possible to un-bound it nor rebind it to another object:

```
// You cannot rebind a function that is bound
var attackReBound = attackBound.bind(zandalf);

attackReBound();
// => Hellhound ...

attackBound();
// => hellHound ...
```

But you can always use the original unbound function to create new bound versions through subsequent calls to `bind` with different contexts:

```
// But you can still bind the original
var attackRebound = attackWithFireBreath.bind(zandalf);
attackRebound();
// => zandalf ...
```

Concluding This

In summary, `this` can take different values based on how a function is invoked. It can:

- Be an object if we call a function within an object with the dot notation

Appendix B. Mysteries of the JavaScript Arcana   483

- Be the Window object or undefined (*strict mode*) if a function is invoked by itself
- Be whichever object we pass as argument to call or apply
- Be whichever object we pass as argument to bind.

If now that you are a *this-xpert* we go back to the original example you will be able to spot the problem at once. Since the updateUsers function is a callback, it is not invoked in the context of the UsersCatalog object. Callbacks are invoked as normal functions, and thus in the context of the Window object (or undefined in in *strict mode*). Because of this, the value of this within updateUsers wouldn't be catalog but undefined[146].

Because this is not the catalog object, it doesn't have a users property and thus the resulting cannot read property of undefined error:

```
function UsersCatalog(type){
  this.users = [];
  getUsers()

  function getUsers(){
    $.getJSON('https://api.github.com/users')
      .success(function(users){
        this.users.push(users);
        // BOOOOOOOM!!!!!
        // => Uncaught TypeError:
        //    Cannot read property 'push' of undefined
        // 'this' in this context is the jqXHR object
        // not our original object
      });
  }
}
var catalog = new UsersCatalog();
```

---

[146]In this particular case however, because we are using *jQuery* to perform an AJAX request, the value of this is *jQuery* jqXHR object, an object that represents the AJAX request itself (we can assume that *jQuery* calls the updateUsers callback in the context of a jqXHR object).

You can solve this issue in either of two ways. You can take advantage of JavaScript support for closures, declare a self variable that *"captures"* the value of this when it refers to the UsersCatalog object and use it within the closure function as depicted below (a very common pattern in JavaScript):

```
function UsersCatalogWithClosure(){
  "use strict";
  var self = this;

  self.users = [];
  getUsers()

  function getUsers(){
    $.getJSON('https://api.github.com/users')
     .success(function(users){
       self.users.push(users);
       console.log('success!');
     });
  }
}
var catalog = new UsersCatalogWithClosure();
```

Or you can take advantage of bind and ensure that the function that you use as callback is bound to the object that you want:

```
//#2. Using bind
function UsersCatalogWithBind(){
  "use strict";

  this.users = [];
  getUsers.bind(this)();

  function getUsers(){
    $.getJSON('https://api.github.com/users')
     .success(updateUsers.bind(this));
  }

  function updateUsers(users){
    this.users.push(users);
```

```
15      console.log('success with bind!');
16    }
17  }
18  var catalog = new UsersCatalogWithBind();
```

Later within the book, you'll see how **ES6 arrow functions** can also lend you a hand in this type of scenario.

Global Scope by Default and Namespacing in JavaScript

As you will come to appreciate by the end of the book, JavaScript has a minimalistic design. It has a limited number of primitive constructs that can be used and composed to achieve higher level abstractions and other constructs that are native to other languages. One of these constructs are **namespaces**.

> ### What about ES6 Modules?
>
> ES6 comes with modules which make this section somewhat obsolete. However, while we have now native modules there is no standard module loader yet. That is, we have a way to define modules but not a way to load them in the browser.
>
> In order to do that you'll need to setup a front-end build pipeline with one of the existing community-driven module loaders which is not a trivial thing to do at this point. Because of that, **some of you may still appreciate this simple way to define your own namespaces.**
>
> The remainder of this section will continue discussing *namespaces* in the absence of modules. Later in the series you'll learn everything about modules and how they help you manage, encapsulate and distribute your code.

Since we do not have the concept of *namespaces*, variables that are declared in a JavaScript file are part of the global scope where they are visible and accessible to every JavaScript file within your application. Yey! Party!

```
1  var dice = "d12";
2  dice;
3  // => d12
4  window.dice
5  // => d12
6  // ups... we are in the global scope/namespace
```

The problems with global variables are well known: they tightly couple different components of your application and they can cause name collisions. Imagine that you have several JavaScript files declaring variables with the same names but performing different tasks. Or imagine importing third party libraries that could overwrite your own variables. **Chaos and destruction!!** Because of these problems we want to completely avoid the use of global variables, yet we lack support for *namespaces* in JavaScript... *What to do?*

We can use objects to emulate the construct of namespaces. A commonly used pattern is depicted below where we use what we call an IIFE[147] (immediately invoked function expression) to create/augment a namespace:

---

[147] http://en.wikipedia.org/wiki/Immediately-invoked_function_expression

Appendix B. Mysteries of the JavaScript Arcana

```javascript
// IIFE - we invoke the function expression as soon as we declare it
(function(armory){
    // the armory object acts as a namespace
    // we can add properties to it
    // these would constitute the API for
    // the 'armory' module/namespace
    armory.sword = {damage: 10, speed: 15};
    armory.axe = {damage: 15, speed: 8};
    armory.mace = {damage: 16, speed: 7};
    armory.dagger = {damage: 5, speed: 20};

    // additionally you could declare private variables and
    // functions as well

// either augment or create the armory namespace
}(window.armory = window.armory || {} ));

console.log(armory.sword.damage);
// => 10
```

An immediately-invoked function expression is just that, a function expression that you invoke immediately. **By virtue of being a function it creates a new scope where you can safely have your variables and avoid name collisions with the outside world.** If you were to declare a variable with the same name of an existing variable in an outer scope, the new variable would just shadow the outer variable.

By immediately invoking the function you can extend the window.armory object with whichever properties you desire, creating a sort of public API for the armory object that becomes a namespace or module. A container where you can place properties and functions and expose them as services for the rest of your application.

We will come back to *namespacing* and higher level code organization in JavaScript within the tome on JavaScript modules.

Type Coercion Madness

In the basic ingredients of javascript-mancy you learned a little bit about type coercion in JavaScript. You learn how JavaScript provides the == and != **abstract equality operators** that let you perform loose equality between values and the === and !== operators that perform strict equality.

By using the first set of operators JavaScript will try to coerce the types being compared to a matching type before performing the comparison, whilst the second set of operators expect a matching type. You also learned how type coercion creates the concept of *falsey* and *truthy* by assigning true and false to different values and types when being converted to boolean.

I thought it would be interesting for you to learn a little bit more about this JavaScript feature and about its possible pitfalls.

JavaScript was designed to be an accessible language[148], a language that even a layman, someone with no prior programming experience could use to create interactive websites. A welcoming language that would help anyone to write their own web applications and solve their own problems. You can see this vision clearly in many of the features of JavaScript, even in some of the most controversial ones. If you think about it from this perspective, it doesn't feel so weird that the following statement evaluates to true:

```
> 42 == '42'
// => true
```

For is not 42 equal to '42'? Don't both refer to the same number? Does it really matter that they have different types? And so we have implicit conversion of types.

---

[148]Check this awesome jsJabber chapter to learn more about the origins of JavaScript from the very illustrious Brendan Eich http://bit.ly/js-origin.

Appendix B. Mysteries of the JavaScript Arcana

In my experience, taking advantage of type coercion usually results in more terse code:

```
// as opposed to (troll !== null && troll !== undefined)
> if (troll) {
    // do stuff
}
```

Taking advantage of the strict equality usually results in more correct, less bug-prone code:

```
> if (troll !== null && troll !== undefined){
// do stuff
}
```

In the first case the condition will be satisfied as long as troll has a truthy value: It could be an object, an array, a string, a number different than 0. In the second case, the condition will be satisfied whenever troll is not null nor undefined (so even it troll is equal to 0 as opposed to the previous example). **Expressiveness or correctness, choose the one that you prefer.**

The truthy and falsey values for the most common types are as follow (note how we use the !! to explicitly convert every value to booleans). Both arrays and objects are truthy, even when they are empty:

```
1  > !![1,2,3]
2  // => true
3  > !![]
4  // => true
5  > !!{message: 'hello world'}
6  // => true
7  > !!{}
8  // => true
```

A non-empty string is truthy while an empty string is falsey:

```
1  > !!"hellooooo"
2  // => true
3  > !!""
4  // => false
```

Numbers are truthy but for 0 that is falsey:

```
1  > !!42
2  // => true
3  > !!0
4  // => false
```

undefined and null are always falsey:

```
1  > !!undefined
2  // => false
3  > !!null
4  // => false
```

Using JavaScript in Strict Mode

From ES5 onwards you can use strict mode[149] to get a better experience with JavaScript. One of the main goals of strict mode

---

[149] http://bit.ly/mdn-strict-mode

Appendix B. Mysteries of the JavaScript Arcana

is to prevent you from falling into common JavaScript pitfalls by making the JavaScript runtime more proactive in throwing errors instead of causing silent ones or unwanted effects.

Take the example of the value of `this` in callbacks. Instead of setting the value of `this` to the `Window` object, when you use **strict mode** the value of `this` becomes `undefined`. This little improvement prevents you from accessing the `Window` object or extending it by mistake, and will alert you with an error as soon as you try to do it. **Short feedback loops and failing fast are sure recipes for success.**

Other improvements that come with *strict mode* are:

- trying to create a variable without declaring it (with `var`, `let` or `const`) will throw an error. Without strict mode it will add a property to the `Window` object.
- trying to assign a variable to NaN, or to a read-only or non-writable property within an object throws an exception
- trying to delete non-deletable properties within an object throws an exception
- trying to have duplicated names as arguments throws a syntax error
- and more explicit errors that will help you spot bugs faster

Additionally with strict mode enabled the JavaScript runtime is free to make certain assumptions and perform optimizations that will make your code run faster. If you want to learn more about the nitty-gritty of strict mode I recommend that you take a look at the MDN (Mozilla Developer Network)[150], the best JavaScript resource in the web.

---

[150] http://bit.ly/mdn-strict-mode

Enabling Strict Mode

You can enable strict mode by writing `'strict mode';` at the top of a JavaScript file. This will enable strict mode for the whole file:

```
'strict mode';
// my code ...
var pouch = {};
```

Alternatively, you can use the *strict mode* declaration at the top of a function. This will result in the *strict mode* only being applied within that function:

```
(function(){
  'strict mode';
  // my code ...
  var bag = {};

}());
```

Wrapping your *strict mode* declarations inside a function will prevent the *strict mode* from being applied to code that may not be prepared to handle *strict mode*. This can happen when concatenating *strict mode* scripts with *non-strict mode* scripts like external third party libraries outside of your control.

ES6 modules always use strict mode semantics.

Concluding

In this chapter you learned about the weirdest bits of JavaScript, the mysterious JavaScript Arcana. You started the chapter by reviewing parts of the JavaScript Arcana that you read about in previous chapters: function scope and variable hoisting, array-like objects and function overloading.

Appendix B. Mysteries of the JavaScript Arcana

You continued taking a look at the sneaky `this` keyword, and understood how its value depends on the context in which a function is executed:

- If you invoke a function as a method using the dot notation, the `this` value will be the object that holds that method.
- If you call a function directly the value of `this` will be the `Window` object (or `undefined` in strict mode).
- If you call a function using either `call`, `apply` or `bind`, the value of `this` will be set to the object that you pass as argument to either of these functions.
- You can use `bind` to create a new version of a function that is bound to a specific object. That is, in that new funtion `this` becomes the object for all eternity.

You saw how JavaScript assumes global scope by default and how you can achieve a similar solution to namespaces by using objects to represent them and organize your code. You examined the concept of IIFE (Immediately Invoked Function Expression) and how you can use it to create an isolated scope to declare your variables and add them to a namespace object.

After that you reviewed type coercion in JavaScript to finally wrap the chapter examining **strict mode**, a more restricted version of JavaScript that attempts to help you find bugs faster by failing more loudly.

```
/*
The small group starts walking up the mountain trail slowly.
The path becomes narrower and steeper as they gain altitude,
the air colder and crispier until it starts snowing. All of
the sudden the group is surrounded by a thick mist that removes
any sense of time or orientation.

The group continues walking for what feels like an eternity.
Suddenly Bandalf stops. This makes Zandalf crash into him,
Randalf into Zandalf and Mooleen into Randalf, Zandalf and
```

```
Bandalf. Ordinarily this wouldn't have been a problem if it
weren't for the six sand golems, the crazy monkey, the
pterodactyl and the dozen of creatures that were following
right behind.
*/

mooleen.says("That was awkward");
bandalf.says("We're here!");

/*
As it by art of magic the mist starts disolving revealing
an inmense cavern.
*/

randalf.says("Welcome to The Caves of Infinity, " +
             "headquarters of the Resistance, last remnant " +
             "of the High Order of JavaScript-mancy")
randalf.says("Now we'll start your real training");

mooleen.says("Super");
```

Exercises

 Experiment JavaScriptmancer!
You can experiment with these exercises and some possible solutions in this jsFiddle[151] or downloading the source code from GitHub[152].

---

[151] http://bit.ly/javascriptmancy-javascript-arcana-exercises
[152] https://github.com/vintharas/javascriptmancy-code-samples

Appendix B. Mysteries of the JavaScript Arcana 495

Find The Bug! Get the JavaScript-NomiCon!

The following piece of code has a bug. Fix the problem and gain access to the oh-so-powerful JavaScript-NomiCon! The most valued treaty of JavaScriptmancy known to men, elves, dwarves and gnomes alike:

```javascript
function LibraryOfTheHighOrder(){
    this.books = [];

    this.summonBooks = function(){
      $.getJSON('https://api.myjson.com/bins/3tp73')
        .then(function updateBooks(books){
            this.books.push(...books);
            // caBOOOOOOM!!!!
            // ERROOOOOORRRR!!!
            // Cannot read property push of undefined
            for(let book of books){
                console.log(book.name + ": " + book.type);
            }
        });
    };
}
var library = new LibraryOfTheHighOrder();
library.summonBooks();
```

Solution

```javascript
function LibraryOfTheHighOrder(){
    this.books = [];

    this.summonBooks = function(){
      $.getJSON('https://api.myjson.com/bins/3tp73')
        .then(function updateBooks(books){
            this.books.push(...books);
            for(let book of books){
                console.log(book.name + ": " + book.type);
            }
```

```
11          }.bind(this));
12      };
13  }
14  var library = new LibraryOfTheHighOrder();
15  library.summonBooks();
16  // => JavaScript-NomiCon: treaty of the dark and arcane arts
17  //    of JavaSCript-mancy
18  //  30 minute meals with Jamie Oliver: comfort food that
19  //     you can cook at home!
20  //  Pride and Prejudice: Novel
21
22  mooleen.says('Yes! Pride and Prejudice! I love that one!');
```

Protect The Library From Name Collisions!

Protect the library from name collisions by creating a new namespace called javascriptmacy.

If you are planning on using ES6 modules you can safely ignore this exercise.

Solution

```
1   (function(javascriptmancy){
2     javascriptmancy.LibraryOfTheHighOrder = LibraryOfTheHighOrder;
3
4     function LibraryOfTheHighOrder(){
5       this.books = [];
6       this.summonBooks = function(){
7         $.getJSON('https://api.myjson.com/bins/3tp73')
8           .then(function updateBooks(books){
9             this.books.push(...books);
10            for(let book of books){
11              console.log(book.name + ": " + book.type);
12            }
13          }.bind(this));
14      };
```

Appendix B. Mysteries of the JavaScript Arcana   497

```
15    }
16    }(window.javascriptmancy = window.javascriptmancy || {}));
17    var li = new window.javascriptmancy.LibraryOfTheHighOrder();
18    console.log(li);
19    // => LibraryOfTheHighOrder {books: Array[0]}
```

 There's a Hard To Detect Bug In This Snippet! Strict Mode To the Rescue!

Enable strict mode in this function and find out the error

```
1    (function(){
2      secretBook = 'Diary of Mooleen';
3    }());
```

Solution

```
1    (function(){
2      "use strict";
3      secretBook = 'diary of mooleen';
4      // => Uncaught ReferenceError: secretBook is not defined;
5      // We were adding a property to the window object!!! :O
6    }());
```

Appendix C. More Useful Function Patterns: Function Overloading

One same API,
to provide similar function,
that's a smart thing,
memorable, familiar, consistent

> \- Siwelluap
> Chieftain of the twisted fangs

Appendix C. More Useful Function Patterns: Function Overloading

```
randalf.sighs();
randalf.says("it didn't last long at all");
randalf.says("You know? Not everyone could tap into the power of the\
 REPL...")

/*

Only a few could harness it. And some of them, some of them were cro\
oked,
either that or they just couldn't handle the power.

Before Branden could do anything about it, they shattered the world,
enslaved the normals, herded and annihilated those of us who opposed\
 them
and that's the state of things.

We are governed by a bunch of egocentric megalomaniac mad men and wo\
men.

*/

mooleen.says("How is it that you're still here then?");
randalf.says("Well they did something worse to me. They took it");

mooleen.says("You cannot cast spells any more?");
randalf.says("I cannot. But I do remember everything");
randalf.says("Talking about knowledge. " +
             "Have you heard about the marvels of overloading?");
```

Have you Heard About The Marvels Of Overloading?

In the last couple of chapters we learned some useful patterns with functions in JavaScript that helped us achieve defaults and handling arbitrary arguments. We also saw a common thread: The fact that ES6 comes with a lot of new features that make up for past limitations of the language. Features like *native defaults* and *rest parameters* that let you solve these old problems in a more concise style.

This chapter will close this section - useful function patterns - with some tips on how you can achieve function overloading in JavaScript.

Function overloading helps you reuse a piece of functionality and provide a unified API in those situations when you have slightly different arguments yet you want to achieve the same thing. Unfortunately, there's a problem with function overloading in JavaScript.

The Problem with Function Overloading in JavaScript

 Experiment JavaScriptmancer!!
You can experiment with all examples in this chapter directly within this jsFiddle[153] or downloading the source code from GitHub[154].

There's a slight issue when you attempt to do function overloading in JavaScript like you would in C#. **You can't do it.**

Indeed, one does not simply overload functions in JavaScript willy nilly. Imagine a spell to raise a skeleton army:

```
function raiseSkeleton(){
    console.log('You raise a skeleton!!!');
}
```

And now imagine that you want to overload it to accept an argument mana that will affect how many skeletons can be raised from the dead at once:

---

[153] http://bit.ly/javascriptmancy-function-overloading
[154] https://github.com/vintharas/javascriptmancy

```
1  function raiseSkeleton(mana){
2    console.log('You raise ' + mana + ' skeletons!!!');
3  }
```

If you now try to execute the `raiseSkeleton` function with no arguments you would probably expect the first version of the function to be called (just like it would happen in C#). However, what you'll discover, to your dismay, is that `raiseSkeleton` has been completely overwritten:

```
1  raiseSkeleton();
2  // => You raise undefined skeletons!!!
```

In JavaScript, you cannot override a function by defining a new one with the same name and a different signature. If you try to do so, you'll just succeed in overwriting your original function with a new implementation.

How Do We Do Function Overloading Then?

Well, as with many things in JavaScript, you'll need to take advantage of the flexibility and freedom the language gives you to emulate function overloading yourself. In the upcoming sections you'll learn four different ways in which you can achieve it, each with their own strengths and caveats:

1. Inspecting arguments
2. Using an *options* object
3. Relying on ES6 defaults
4. Taking advantage of polymorphic functions

Function Overloading by Inspecting Arguments

One common pattern for achieving function overloading is to use the arguments object to **inspect the arguments** that are passed into a function:

```
function raiseSkeletonWithArgumentInspecting(){
  if (typeof arguments[0] === "number"){
    raiseSkeletonsInNumber(arguments[0]);
  } else if (typeof arguments[0] === "string") {
    raiseSkeletonCreature(arguments[0]);
  } else {
    console.log('raise a skeleton');
  }
}

function raiseSkeletonsInNumber(n){
  console.log('raise ' + n + ' skeletons');
}
function raiseSkeletonCreature(creature){
  console.log('raise a skeleton ' + creature);
};
```

Following this pattern you inspect each argument being passed to the overloaded function(or even the number of arguments) and determine which internal implementation to execute:

```
raiseSkeletonWithArgumentInspecting();
// => raise a skeleton
raiseSkeletonWithArgumentInspecting(4);
// => raise 4 skeletons
raiseSkeletonWithArgumentInspecting('king');
// => raise skeleton king
```

This approach can become unwieldy very quickly. As the overloaded functions and their parameters increase in number, the function becomes harder and harder to read, maintain and extend.

Appendix C. More Useful Function Patterns: Function Overloading

At this point you may be thinking: *"...checking the type of the arguments being passed? seriously?!"* and I agree with you, that's why I like to use this next approach instead.

Using an Options Object

A better way to achieve function overloading is to use an *options* object. This object acts as a container for the different parameters a function can consume:

```
function raiseSkeletonWithOptions(spellOptions){
  spellOptions = spellOptions || {};
  var armySize = spellOptions.armySize || 1,
    creatureType = spellOptions.creatureType || '';

  if (creatureType){
    console.log('raise a skeleton ' + creatureType);
  } else {
    console.log('raise ' + armySize + ' skeletons ' + creatureType);
  }
}
```

This allows you to call a function with different arguments:

```
raiseSkeletonWithOptions();
// => raise a skeleton
raiseSkeletonWithOptions({armySize: 4});
// => raise 4 skeletons
raiseSkeletonWithOptions({creatureType:'king'});
// => raise skeleton king
```

It is not strictly function overloading but it provides the same benefits: It gives you different possibilities in the form of a unified API, and additionally, named arguments and easy extensibility. That is, you can add new options without breaking any existing clients of the function.

Here is an example of both *argument inspecting* and the *options* object patterns in the wild, the jQuery ajax function[155]:

```
ajax: function( url, options ) {
  // If url is an object, simulate pre-1.5 signature
  if ( typeof url === "object" ) {
    options = url;
    url = undefined;
  }

  // Force options to be an object
  options = options || {};

  var transport,
    // URL without anti-cache param
    cacheURL,
    // Response headers
    responseHeadersString,
    responseHeaders,
    // timeout handle
    timeoutTimer,
    // etc...
}
```

Relying on ES6 Defaults

Although ES6 doesn't come with classic function overloading, it brings us default arguments which give you better support for function overloading than what we've had so far.

If you reflect about it, default arguments are a specialized version of function overloading. A subset of it, if you will, for those cases in which you can use an increasing number of predefined arguments:

---

[155] http://bit.ly/jquery-ajax-js

```js
function castIceCone(mana=5, {direction='in front of you'}={}){
  console.log(`You spend ${mana} mana and casts a ` +
    `terrible ice cone ${direction}`);
}
castIceCone();
// => You spend 5 mana and casts a terrible ice cone in front of you
castIceCone(10, {direction: 'towards Mordor'});
// => You spend 10 mana and casts a terrible ice cone towards Mordor
```

Taking Advantage of Polymorphic Functions

Yet another interesting pattern for achieving function overloading is to rely on JavaScript great support for functional programming. In the world of functional programming there is the concept of **polymorphic functions**, that is, functions which exhibit different behaviors based on their arguments.

Let's illustrate them with an example. Our starting point will be this function that we saw in the *inspecting arguments* section:

```js
function raiseSkeletonWithArgumentInspecting(){
  if (typeof arguments[0] === "number"){
    raiseSkeletonsInNumber(arguments[0]);
  } else if (typeof arguments[0] === "string") {
    raiseSkeletonCreature(arguments[0]);
  } else {
    console.log('raise a skeleton');
  }

  function raiseSkeletonsInNumber(n){
    console.log('raise ' + n + ' skeletons');
  }
  function raiseSkeletonCreature(creature){
    console.log('raise a skeleton ' + creature);
  };
}
```

We will take it and decompose it into smaller functions:

Appendix C. More Useful Function Patterns: Function Overloading   506

```js
function raiseSkeletons(number){
  if (Number.isInteger(number)){ return `raise ${number} skeletons`;}
}

function raiseSkeletonCreature(creature){
  if (creature) {return `raise a skeleton ${creature}`;}
}

function raiseSingleSkeleton(){
  return 'raise a skeleton';
}
```

And now we create an abstraction (functional programming likes abstraction) for a function that executes several other functions in sequence until one returns a valid result. Where a valid result will be any value different from undefined:

```js
// This is a higher-order function that returns a new function.
// Something like a function factory.
// We could reuse it to our heart's content.
function dispatch(...fns){

  return function(...args){
    for(let f of fns){
      let result = f.apply(null, args);
      if (exists(result)) return result;
    }
  };
}

function exists(value){
  return value !== undefined
}
```

dispatch lets us create a new function that is a combination of all the previous ones: raiseSkeletons, raiseSkeletonCreature and raiseSingleSkeleton:

Appendix C. More Useful Function Patterns: Function Overloading   507

```
let raiseSkeletonFunctionally = dispatch(
    raiseSkeletons,
    raiseSkeletonCreature,
    raiseSingleSkeleton);
```

This new function will behave in different ways based on the arguments it takes. It will delegate any call to each specific raise skeleton function until a suitable result is obtained.

```
console.log(raiseSkeletonFunctionally());
// => raise a skeleton
console.log(raiseSkeletonFunctionally(4));
// => raise 4 skeletons
console.log(raiseSkeletonFunctionally('king'));
// => raise skeleton king
```

Note how the last `raiseSingleSkeleton` is a catch-all function. It will always return a valid result regardless of the arguments being sent to the function. This will ensure that however you call `raiseSkeletonFunctionally` you'll always have a default implementation or valid result.

A super duper mega cool thing that you may or may not have noticed is the **awesome degree of composability** of this approach. If we want to extend this function later on, we can do it without modifying the original function. Take a look at this:

```
function raiseOnSteroids({number=0, type='skeleton'}={}){
  if(number) {
    return `raise ${number} ${type}s`;
  }
}

let raiseAdvanced = dispatch(raiseOnSteroids, raiseSkeletonFunctiona\
lly);
```

We now have a `raiseAdvanced` function that augments `raiseSkeletonFunctionally` with the new desired functionality represented by `raiseOnSteroids`:

```
console.log(raiseAdvanced());
// => raise a skeleton
console.log(raiseAdvanced(4));
// => raise 4 skeletons
console.log(raiseAdvanced('king'));
// => raise skeleton king
console.log(raiseAdvanced({number: 10, type: 'ghoul'}))
// => raise 10 ghouls
```

This is the OCP (Open-Closed Principle)[156] in all its glory like you've never seen it before. Functional programming is pretty awesome right? We will take a deeper dive into functional progrommming within the sacred tome of FP later in the book and you'll get the chance to experiment a lot more with both higher-order functions and function composition alike. But if you can't wait, don't let me stop you, by all means, jump on!

Concluding

Although JavaScript doesn't support function overloading you can achieve the same behavior by using different patterns: inspecting arguments, using an options object, relying on ES6 defaults or taking advantage of polymorphic functions.

You can use the arguments object and **inspect the arguments** that are being passed to a function at runtime. You should only use this solution with the simplest of implementations as it becomes unwieldly and hard to maintain as parameters and overloads are added to a function.

Or you can use an **options object** as a wrapper for parameters. This is both more readable and maintanaible than inspecting arguments, and provides two additional benefits: named arguments and a lot of flexibility to extend the function with new parameters.

---
[156] Open for extension and closed for modification. http://bit.ly/ocp-wikipedia

Appendix C. More Useful Function Patterns: Function Overloading   509

ES6 brings improved support for function overloading in some situations with native default arguments.

Finally, you can take advantage of functional programming, compose your functions from smaller ones and use a dispatching mechanism to select which function is used based on the arguments.

```
randalf.says("haha! And that's what you need to known about overload\
ing!");
mooleen.says("What am I doing here?");

randalf.says("Oh yeah that...");
randalf.says("You are the Chosen one!");

mooleen.says("Yes, yes, the chosen for what?");

randalf.says("You are going to fix everything! " +
             "Bring balance to the force and all that");

randalf.says("But first you need to learn!");
randalf.says("Right now you wouldn't stand a chance");

mooleen.says("Well I reckon that 'Great' wouldn't agree on that note\
.");

randalf.says("Oh child, that was just an avatar");
randalf.says("Do you think that this paranoid psychotic megalomaniac\
" +
             "would come to you in the flesh??");
```

Exercises

 Experiment JavaScriptmancer!

You can experiment with these exercises and some possible solutions in this jsFiddle[157] or downloading the source code from GitHub[158].

---

[157] http://bit.ly/javascriptmancy-function-overloading-exercises
[158] https://github.com/vintharas/javascriptmancy-code-samples

Create Your Own Avatar

Write a function createAvatar using function overloading by inspecting arguments. It should satisfy the following snippet:

```
1  createAvatar(/* description */ 'a blue wisp hovering around');
2  // => you create an avatar in the form of a blue wisp hovering around
3
4  createAvatar({ appearance: 'a blue wisp', stance: 'hovering around'}\
5  );
6  // => you create an avatar in the form of a blue wisp hovering around
```

Solution

```
1   mooleen.says('An avatar...');
2   mooleen.says('Let me see if I can do it myself...');
3
4   function createAvatar(){
5     if (typeof arguments[0] === "string"){
6       var description = arguments[0];
7       console.log('you create an avatar in the form of ' + description\
8   );
9     } else {
10      var attributes = arguments[0],
11          appearance = attributes.appearance,
12          stance = attributes.stance;
13      console.log('you create an avatar in the form of '
14          + appearance + " " + stance);
15    }
16  }
17
18  mooleen.weaves("createAvatar('a blue wisp hovering around')");
19  // => you create an avatar in the form of a blue wisp hovering around
20  mooleen.weaves("createAvatar(" +
21      "{ appearance: 'a blue wisp', stance: 'hovering aroun\
22  d'})");
23  // => you create an avatar in the form of a blue wisp hovering around
```

Options

Update the `createAvatar` function to use an options object that satisfies the following:

```
1  createAvatar({ description: 'a blue wisp hovering around'});
2  // => you create an avatar in the form of a blue wisp hovering around
3
4  createAvatar({ appearance: 'a blue wisp', stance: 'hovering around'}\
5  );
6  // => you create an avatar in the form of a blue wisp hovering around
```

Solution

```
1   function createAvatarOptions(options){
2     var appearance = options.appearance || 'no form',
3         stance = options.stance || 'standing',
4         description = options.description || appearance + " " + stance;
5     console.log('you create an avatar in the form of ' + description);
6   }
7
8   mooleen.weaves("createAvatarOptions("+
9                  "{ description: 'a blue wisp hovering around'})");
10  // => you create an avatar in the form of a blue wisp hovering around
11
12  mooleen.weaves("createAvatarOptions("+
13                 "{ appearance: 'a blue wisp', stance: 'hovering aroun\
14  d'})");
15  // => you create an avatar in the form of a blue wisp hovering around
```

And Now Create an Avatar Like Mooleen

Write a createAvatar function that is a polymorphic function. It should satisfy the following snippet:

```
createAvatar('a beautiful freckled young woman standing defiantly');
// => you create an avatar in the form of a beautiful freckled
      young woman standing defiantly

createAvatar({ appearance: 'a beautiful young woman',
               stance: 'standing defiantly'});
// => you create an avatar in the form of a beautiful freckled
      young woman standing defiantly

createAvatar();
// you create an avatar in shapeless form
```

Solution

```
function dispatch(...fns){
    return function(...args){
        for(let f of fns){
            let result = f.apply(null, args);
            if (exists(result)) return result;
        }
    };
}

function exists(value){
    return value !== undefined
}

function createByDescription(description){
    if (typeof description === "string"){
        return 'you create an avatar in the form of ' + description;
    }
}

function createByAttributes(attributes){
    if (typeof attributes === 'object'){
```

Appendix C. More Useful Function Patterns: Function Overloading 513

```
22      var attributes = arguments[0],
23          appearance = attributes.appearance,
24          stance = attributes.stance;
25      return 'you create an avatar in the form of ' + appearance + " "\
26   + stance;
27    }
28  }
29
30  function createDefault(){
31    return 'you create an avatar in a shapeless form';
32  }
33
34  function createAvatarFp(){
35    var createFn = dispatch(
36                    createByDescription,
37                    createByAttributes,
38                    createDefault);
39    console.log(createFn.apply(null, arguments));
40  }
41
42  createAvatarFp('a beautiful freckled young woman standing defiantly'\
43  );
44  // => you create an avatar in the form of a beautiful freckled
45  //    young woman standing defiantly
46
47  createAvatarFp({ appearance: 'a beautiful young woman',
48                   stance: 'standing defiantly'});
49  // => you create an avatar in the form of a beautiful freckled
50  //    young woman standing defiantly
51
52  createAvatarFp();
53  // => you create an avatar in a shapeless form
54
55  mooleen.says('Damn! That was creepy');
```

Appendix D. Setting Up Your Developing Environment For ES6

The best way to get started with ES6 is by using an interactive online REPL. Here is a list of some of my favorites:

- Babel REPL[159] - **bit.ly/babel-repl**. Babel is a ES6 transpiler that let's you take advantage of ES6 and ESnext features today. It is the *de facto* ES6 transpiler.
- jsBin[160] - **jsbin.com**. JsBin is a very popular web prototyping tool with a customizable set of pans to visualize HTML, CSS, JavaScript, a console and the output.
- jsFiddle[161] - **jsfiddle.net**. JsFiddle is yet another popular prototyping tool that let's you look at your HTML, CSS, JavaScript and output at a glance.
- CodePen[162] - **codepen.io** is a web prototyping tool and community.
- ES6 Katas[163] - **es6katas.org** is a collection of interactive katas to learn ES6.

Using ES6 with Node.js

In addition to using prototyping tools for the web, node.js has great support for ES6 as you can appreciate in these compatibility table[164].

---
[159] http://bit.ly/babel-repl
[160] http://www.jsbin.com
[161] http://www.jsfiddle.net
[162] http://www.codepen.io
[163] http://es6katas.org/
[164] http://kangax.github.io/compat-table/es6/

Appendix D. Setting Up Your Developing Environment For ES6   515

But it you want to be able to use all features of ES6 and ESnext you can take advatange of babel.js[165] and the babel-node REPL.

You can install it using the following command:

```
$ npm install -g babel
```

And start it using babel node:

```
$ babel-node
```

This will open a REPL that has complete support for ES6.

ES6 and Modern Browsers

Modern browsers also have an increasing support for ES6. The ES6 compability table[166] can give you a general idea as to how the efforts from the different vendors are going.

The problem with developing for the browser is that you cannot control the runtime in which your application is running like you do when developing a backend in node.js. This means that you cannot rely on your user's browser having the features that you need or want to use. Because of that, transpiling your application from ES6 to ES5 becomes crucial in these environments to make sure that it works in a myriad of devices and can reach as many users as possible.

There's a wide variety of tools that let you transpile your ES6 code to something that can work on any browser and setup a real world ES6 development environment.

---
[165] https://babeljs.io
[166] https://bit.ly/es6-compatibility

Real-World ES6 Development Environments

The *de facto* standard for transpiling ES6 is babel.js[167]. It is very extensible and can be plugged into any of the modern front-end build pipelines. It uses a plugin system that lets you easily decide which features of ES6 and ESnext you want to enable.

Depending on your build tooling of choice you'll need to follow different steps to start using Babel. You can find numerous and extensive guides for Gulp, WebPack, Grunt, Broccoli, etc at bit.ly/setup-es6[168].

---

[167] babeljs.io
[168] http://bit.ly/setup-es6

Appendix E. Fantasy Glossary

If you are not familiar with the genre of fantasy you may have a hard time understanding some of the words I use in this book. Hopefully this glossary will give you some guidance in this respect.

- **Arcane**: Something that is mysterious or secret. Known or understood by very few people.
- **Alchemy**: A science that was used in the Middle Ages with the goal of changing ordinary metals into gold. Also a power or process that changes or transforms something in a mysterious or impressive way.
- **Cimmerian barbarian**: Barbarian from the extreme confines of Cimmeria.
- **Conan**: "Hither came Conan, the Cimmerian, black-haired, sullen-eyed, sword in hand, a thief, a reaver, a slayer, with gigantic melancholies and gigantic mirth, to tread the jeweled thrones of the Earth under his sandalled feet."
- **Balefire**: Balefire is a weapon of the One Power. When a target is struck with balefire, its thread in the Pattern is destroyed, in an amount proportional to the power of the balefire strike. This translates to both the target's existence, and actions up to a certain point, being retroactively erased.
- **Gandalf**: Mighty wizard that has the magic ability to always be on time.
- **Goblin**: An ugly and sometimes evil creature that likes to cause trouble.
- **Golem**: An artificial creature being endowed with life by magic. It is often associated to different elements and materials: fire, earth, sand, etc.

- **Hobbit**: Hobbits are similar to humans, but about half their size. They're chubby, furry-footed home-bodies with a penchant for dwelling in hollowed out hillsides and a racial talent for burglary.
- **Halfling**: see Hobbit.
- **JavaScript-mancer**: Person that has mastered the art of writing awesome JavaScript and has an intimate knowledge of it.
- **JavaScript-mancy**: The arcane art of using JavaScript to alter the world around you.
- **Kender**: A race of wizened 14-year-olds that, unlike halflings, wear shoes.
- **Mana**: For those of you not familiar with magic, mana can be seen as a measure of magical stamina. As such, doing magic (like summoning minions) spends one’s mana. An empty reservoir of mana means no spellcasting just as a empty reserve of stamina means no more running.
- **Minion**: Someone who is not powerful or important and who obeys the orders of a powerful leader or boss.
- **Saruman**: Powerful wizard prone who likes white clothing and prone to evil deeds
- **Scepter**: A staff or baton borne by a sovereign as an emblem of authority. It can be imbued in magic powers.
- **Spell**: A spoken word or form of words held to have magic power.
- **Spellcasting (casting)**: Performing magic by reciting a spell.
- **Summon**: To bid a creature to come to your aid with the help of magic. It can also create a creature from nothingness.
- **Troll**: An evil giant creature than inhabitates caves, hills and bridges. Some of them show weakness to sunlight.
- **Teleport**: Transfer ones location by using magic
- **Orc**: A race of human-like creatures, characterized as ugly, warlike, and malevolent.
- **Orb**: A circular object that possess unbound magic power.

- **Wand**: A long, thin stick used by a magician to channel its powers.
- **Weave**: See spellcasting.

References

References

There's a lot of books that have inspired me while writing JavaScriptmancy. Here is a non exhaustive list of the most influential.

Specifications

- ECMAScript 6 Specification[169]
- Stamps specification[170]

Books

- JavaScript Allonge - Reginald Braithwaite
- You don't know JS - Kyle Simpson
- Functional JavaScript - Michael Fogus
- Effective JavaScript - David Herman
- Understanding ECMAScript 6 - Nicholas C. Zackas
- Secrets of the JavaScript Ninja - John Resig, Bear Bibeault
- Programming JavaScript Applications - Eric Elliott
- Principles of Object Oriented JavaScript - Nicholas C. Zackas
- Eloquent JavaScript - Adam Freeman
- JavaScript the Good Parts - Douglas Crockford

White papers

- Traits: Composable Units of Behaviour - ECOOP'2003, LNCS 2743, pp. 248–274, Springer Verlag, 2003[171]

---

[169] http://www.ecma-international.org/ecma-262/6.0
[170] https://github.com/stampit-org/stamp-specification
[171] http://scg.unibe.ch/archive/papers/Scha03aTraits.pdf

Articles

- Traits: Robust Object Composition and High-integrity Objects for ECMAScript 5[172]

---

[172] http://traitsjs.github.io/traits.js-website/files/traitsJS_PLASTIC2011_final.pdf

www.ingramcontent.com/pod-product-compliance
Lightning Source LLC
Chambersburg PA
CBHW050148230526
45470CB00001B/14